Also by Donald Spoto

Donald Spoto

SPELLBOUND

Alfred Hitchcock

BY BEAUTY

and His Leading Ladies

THREE RIVERS PRESS • NEW YORK

Published in the United States by Three Rivers Press, an imprint of the
Crown Publishing Group, a division of Random House, Inc., New York.
www.crownpublishing.com

THREE RIVERS PRESS and the Tugboat design are registered trademarks of
Random House, Inc.

Originally published in hardcover in the United States by Harmony Books,
an imprint of the Crown Publishing Group, a division of Random House, Inc.,
New York, in 2008.
www.crownpublishing.com

Library of Congress Cataloging-in-Publication Data

Spoto, Donald, 1941–
    Spellbound by beauty : Alfred Hitchcock and his leading ladies / Donald Spoto.
        p. cm.
    Includes bibliographical references.
1. Hitchcock, Alfred, 1899–1980—Relations with women.   I. Title.
    PN1998.3.H58S688 2008
    791.43023'3092—dc22
        [B]   2008008922

ISBN 978-0-307-35131-9

Design by Lauren Dong

First Paperback Edition

147468846

For Mona and Karl Malden,
with grateful love and devotion

Contents

x   Contents

Acknowledgments

My first debt is to Alfred Hitchcock, with whom I spent many hours between 1975 and 1980. He granted me a number of taped interviews in which I found him astonishingly frank on important issues. He also invited me to lunch more than once, and during those times, the talk flowed very freely indeed.

Conversations with those who appeared in his films were of critical significance in the original preparations for both of my earlier books—*The Art of Alfred Hitchcock* (1976) and *The Dark Side of Genius: The Life of Alfred Hitchcock* (1983). During the years of my research for those books (1974 through 1982), some people asked me to suppress certain material for a period of time, because of his recent death; in some cases, they asked that details not be set down during their own lifetimes. That explains some of the lacunae in my earlier work and further justifies *Spellbound by Beauty: Alfred Hitchcock and His Leading Ladies.*

I wish to acknowledge, therefore, interviews granted to me by the following actresses: Diane Baker, Anne Baxter, Ingrid Bergman, Karen Black, Doris Day, Joan Fontaine, Dolly Haas, Barbara Harris, Tippi Hedren, Grace Kelly (Princess Grace of Monaco), Janet Leigh, Margaret Lockwood, Vivien Merchant, Mildred Natwick, Claire Griswold Pollack, Elsie Randolph, Eva Marie Saint, Sylvia Sidney, Jessica Tandy, Ann Todd, Kathleen Tremaine, Alida Valli, Josephine Wilson (Lady Miles) and Teresa Wright.

A number of actors also cooperated generously: Brian Aherne, Martin Balsam, Hume Cronyn, Bruce Dern, William Devane, Jon Finch, John Forsythe, Barry Foster, John Gielgud, Farley Granger, Karl Malden, Lord Bernard Miles, Reggie Nalder, Paul Newman, Gregory Peck, Anthony Perkins, James Stewart and Rod Taylor.

Hitchcock's writers knew him in important ways others never could, for they sat with him for months and came to know how his prodigious mind worked. I was fortunate to have the confidence of Jay Presson Allen, Charles Bennett, David Freeman, John Michael Hayes, Evan Hunter, Arthur Laurents, Ernest Lehman, Brian Moore, Anthony Shaffer, Joseph Stefano and Samuel Taylor. Among Hitchcock's creative team, I also knew and interviewed Saul Bass, Henry Bumstead, Herbert Coleman, Edith Head, Peggy Robertson, Leonard South and Albert Whitlock.

The original idea for this book sprang from conversations with two of my closest friends, Gerald Pinciss and Lewis Falb. They have enthusiastically endorsed my writing for many years.

Once again, my brother-in-law, John Møller, dispatched the difficult creative task of transferring photographs onto disks. John is not only a talented designer but also a superb technician, and I am grateful for his generous allotment of time on behalf of this book.

Claus Kjær and his colleagues at the Danish Film Institute, Copenhagen, have welcomed me warmly to that prestigious archive and film library, and they have graciously invited me to be a frequent guest lecturer at the Cinematek. I am very happy in my ongoing association with the DFI.

For over thirty years, I have been represented by my friend Elaine Markson, whose name evokes respect, admiration and affection in the world of international publishing. In her New York office, I am supported by the practical help and abiding friendship of Elaine's associates Gary Johnson, Geri Thoma and Julia Kenny.

Once more, I am very fortunate to be published by Shaye Areheart at Harmony Books—a perceptive, generous, and wise friend with an unerring sense of a book's development. And my editor has again been the gifted and gracious Julia Pastore, whose creative contributions to my work I very much cherish. In her office, Kate Kennedy has cheerfully dispatched many daily tasks and has been, like Shaye and Julia, consistently helpful. No writer could ask for a better publishing team.

Ole Flemming Larsen, with whom I share my life, gives me more, every day, than I can ever deserve.

With enormous gratitude and devotion, I dedicate this book to my dear friends Mona and Karl Malden. Their presence in my life, and their loving endorsement of me and my work, mean more than I can say.

D.S.
Sjælland, Denmark
January 2008

Preface

The book you are holding is my third volume on the life and work of the great director. The first, *The Art of Alfred Hitchcock,* is an analysis and critical appreciation of each of his films; it was originally published in English in 1976, during the director's lifetime and after I had interviewed him on several occasions. I was very gratified when he celebrated and promoted the book, which is still in print, and in many languages. My second volume, *The Dark Side of Genius: The Life of Alfred Hitchcock,* appeared in 1983, three years after his death; it, too, is still available and has appeared in several dozen foreign-language editions.

Why, then, another book, with specific reference to the director and his actresses?

First, because it is remarkable how infrequently, over a period of more than fifty years, Hitchcock said anything—much less something favorable—about his players. His most repeated remark about them became a famous personal motto: "Actors are cattle," or, more puckishly, "I never said actors are cattle—I said that actors should be treated like cattle." Actors and audiences laughed together at this, but behind the sardonic statement was the undeniable fact that while he knew he needed good and attractive talent to draw audiences and so to guarantee the commercial success of his movies, he seems to have had no great opinion of actors, and he often openly resented their stardom, privileges and salaries. "Actors! I hate the sight of them!" he cried in one unusually bitter fit of pique.

Hitchcock rarely had anything to say about his male stars—estimable performers such as John Gielgud, Michael Redgrave, Laurence Olivier, Cary Grant, James Stewart, Sean Connery and Paul Newman, who were established in their careers when they came to work for him. Many of his leading ladies, on the other hand, achieved international stardom precisely because of their Hitchcock roles—Madeleine Carroll, Joan Fontaine, Grace Kelly, Janet Leigh and Tippi Hedren are good examples. That he maintained an insistent silence about the quality of their performances is a curiosity that cannot be ignored.

"Some of us actors have ideas," Ingrid Bergman said at a tribute to him, in his presence, a year before his death—"and then Hitch can become a little truculent." Princess Grace of Monaco wrote, in her foreword to my first book, that "sometimes he merely wears [actors] down until he gets what he wants." They spoke these words in the context of affectionate and laudatory remarks, and they were not nearly as taciturn about their appreciation as he was. Nor is there anything unusual or malevolent about directors making demands or seeming defiant with their actors, as Ingrid and Grace attested. Moviemaking, after all, is a collaborative craft; movie sets (even those of the punctilious Hitchcock) are usually chaotic places, laced with the strong aroma of ego and dependent on the countless variables of human temperament and technical accidents. Hitchcock had a lot to put up with, from eccentric, sometimes boorish studio moguls to mediocre workmen and moody colleagues. But his reticence, his refusal to praise or thank those who gave him their best, must be explored.

In François Truffaut's book-length series of interviews with Hitchcock—covering the production of every one of Hitchcock's films—I have counted more than 140 references to actresses. Hitchcock's remarks about them were mostly neutral but frequently hostile. Indeed, he did not have a good word to say even about the women he apparently liked, Ingrid Bergman and Grace Kelly. The best he could manage about the others was the mildly affirmative opinion that Sylvia Sidney (in *Sabotage*) "had nice understatement" and that Shirley MacLaine (in *The Trouble With Harry*) "was very good." Otherwise, one finds only Hitchcock's indifferent references to the roles actresses played; more to the point, he never once so much as uttered the names of those who contributed enormously to the success of some of his finest works—Madeleine Carroll (in *The 39 Steps* and *Secret Agent*), Nova Pilbeam (in *Young and Innocent*) and Margaret Lockwood (in *The Lady Vanishes*), for just a few examples.

In the summer of 1975, during the first of our many long interviews, I asked Hitchcock about the achievements of his actresses—just how *did* he work with them to evoke such magnificent performances? "I think it has to do with the way in which one photographs them," he replied, and that was that— not a word in favor of the women.

"As far as Hitchcock was concerned," recalled Joseph Stefano, who wrote the screenplay for *Psycho,* "if he decided to use you, that was compliment enough." John Michael Hayes, who wrote *Rear Window, To Catch a Thief, The Trouble With Harry* and *The Man Who Knew Too Much,* elaborated: "Hitch was an enigma— personally as well as professionally. He never once congratulated me or thanked me for anything I did. In his mind, if you did well, he thought it was just expected of you."

One had to learn of Hitchcock's satisfaction through others, as Hayes recalled. "Hitch's wife, Alma, came up to me once and said, 'Don't breathe a word of this to anyone, but Hitch is *immensely* pleased with you.' " Doris Day interpreted Hitchcock's stony silence during the shooting of *The Man Who Knew Too Much* in 1955 as his disapproval of her performance. It took her offer to withdraw from the film to evoke Hitchcock's lukewarm response that if he had *not* liked what she was doing, he would have said something.

These were matters I subsequently discussed in some detail with a number of his leading ladies—among them Sylvia Sidney, Margaret Lockwood, Joan Fontaine, Teresa Wright, Ingrid Bergman, Alida Valli, Anne Baxter, Grace Kelly, Janet Leigh and Tippi Hedren. His male stars seemed, for the most part, to have little to say on the matter, although Michael Redgrave, Hume Cronyn, Joseph Cotten, Gregory Peck, Farley Granger, Reggie Nalder, Rod Taylor, Paul Newman, Jon Finch and Barry Foster were singularly perceptive in their observations.

In *Spellbound by Beauty,* I detail the fine points of the significant contributions leading ladies made to Hitchcock's films—contributions often made under difficult and even painful circumstances. To a person, none of these women ever defended, praised or justified herself—that would not have done much good in any case, for Hitchcock was the powerhouse, they the mere exponents, expendable and often doomed to the merciless scythe of transient popularity.

In addition, there have been many rumors about Hitchcock's treatment of women—not only in the films themselves but also behind the scenes, during production. Stories have circulated about Hitchcock's sadistic behavior and his occasional public humiliation of actresses. The fact is that these accounts turn out to be alarmingly true in a remarkable number of cases. There is no doubt that he was enormously helpful in the advancement of some careers. But he was, equally often, unhelpful to himself when he was unkind to people—especially to women, for whom he had a strange amalgam of adoration and contempt, and whom he often tried to control in a way he dared not attempt with men.

Hitchcock was evidently attracted to women (to blondes especially), but he never spoke well of them, and most of them did not have the remotest idea of his impressions of their work. To him, they were foolish, capriciously sensual and at the mercy of wildly improbably sexual urges. This attitude of stony indifference characterized his relationships with his male players, too, but he had few emotional requirements to make of men in his work, and for the most part, he neither challenged them nor showed much interest in them. No, it was the women who preoccupied him—"Torture the women!" he said, repeating the advice of the nineteenth-century playwright Victorien Sardou about plot construction.

Hitchcock took that counsel to heart. In his first English movie, *The Lodger,* he put his star (known simply as June) in manacles, which caused her no little upset and discomfort. Madeleine Carroll was dragged around the sets of *The 39 Steps* for long periods over several days, handcuffed to her co-star Robert Donat, until she showed painful bruises. Such incidents occurred at regular intervals during his career, but nothing compared with the physical torture inflicted on Tippi Hedren during the filming of *The Birds,* or the sexual harassment she endured during the production of *Marnie.*

But a potential objection must be faced at the outset.

Why does a biographer bother to describe Hitchcock's strange psychology and even stranger conduct, however fastidiously and accurately he can document them? What does this sort of information add to our knowledge or appreciation of a great film artist and perennial entertainer?

Alfred Hitchcock died in 1980, and in the intervening years, his admirers have too often mythologized him out of all resemblance to reality. Indeed, he has become in the eyes of many a genius *tout court,* without much humanity to make him recognizable. More unrealistically, he is regarded by many as a warm and cuddly gentleman, adorably amusing, like an eccentric grandfather who tells bedtime stories—a man unworthy of what is sometimes called meretricious treatment at the hands of some writers. I have not escaped the occasional opprobrium of some Hitchcock partisans, who will not hear a syllable spoken against him and are shocked, *shocked* that such anecdotes are included in a biography.

But there can be a dangerous hypocrisy—and a fearful scholarly deficiency—at the root of such objections when they come from people who ought to know better about the links between art and life, and who ought to have a deeper appreciation of human longing and pain. In this regard, I was immensely gratified when Hitchcock's close collaborator, the playwright and screenwriter Samuel Taylor (who gave him the final script for *Vertigo*), proclaimed that *The Dark Side of Genius* was a sympathetic biography *not* of an angel or a demon, but of "a human being in all his complexity."

Writing or speaking anything other than the highest praise or failing to promote the most affectionate encomia for so august an icon as Alfred Hitchcock has become, in the eyes of many, equivalent to cultural sacrilege. But the craft of biography requires that the shadow side of subjects be set forth and comprehended—otherwise, their humanity is diminished, their pain minimized, and those they hurt are ignored. Any serious appreciation of Hitchcock's art and life must take into account the enormity of his psychological, physical and social suffering, as well as that which he (perhaps unintentionally) caused others. From his suffering came the obsessively recurring themes and the constant sense of dread with which he continues to astonish, entertain and enlighten.

History provides a very long list of the names of great artists whose characters were not always sterling and whose lives were variations on misery. No one disputes either the genius of Richard Wagner or his enduring significance in the history of great music. But Wagner was also dishonest, untruthful, unfaithful, temperamental, rude and virulently anti-Semitic. He sacrificed everything for his art, even putting up and losing his mother's pension to pay his gambling debts. He was, to put it mildly, a person to be avoided except from a distance. Similarly, Pablo Picasso was a deeply misogynistic man whose art was great but whose personality was profoundly flawed.

When I began to write *The Art of Alfred Hitchcock* in 1974, I was committed to the idea that he was history's greatest filmmaker. This I maintained because so many of his films defy the passage of time and the inevitable changes in cinematic style. I also discovered that very many of his movies continue to entertain audiences worldwide even as they deal, remarkably often, with perennially significant issues of human life and destiny. Decades later, I have no reason to alter my high estimation of his talent.

The Dark Side of Genius, which appeared in 1983, was the first of my, at last count, sixteen biographies. From it, I felt obliged to withhold some information, as several of my sources asked me to omit certain comments either for some years or until after their own deaths. I honored those requests, but now an important element of Hitchcock's life story must supplement what has preceded.

Apart from his memorable achievements, his biography remains a cautionary tale of what can go wrong in any life. It is the story of a man so unhappy, so full of self-loathing, so lonely and friendless, that his satisfactions came as much from asserting power as from spinning fantasies and acquiring wealth. The fact is that some of his conduct can only be called sexual harassment, and I do not believe there is ever any justification for that: no artistic goal justifies cruelty or exploitation. It is important to know this about Hitchcock, especially at a time when raising an artist to the pantheon leads to an injudicious minimizing or even ignoring of episodes that cast light on the strange links that can bind confident genius to a domineering cruelty. He could not have gotten away with some of his conduct today; and no one should ever be permitted to behave as he often did.

This book is not a revisionist biography, but in a sense, it is a life story with a sad motif—in the broadest sense, the motif of consuming selfishness. Sometimes he could not foresee the suffering his actions would cause; sometimes he seemed to anticipate that suffering quite clearly.

All motifs or themes in our lives have bases and backgrounds, beginnings, developments, climaxes and conclusions. Therefore, I have considered it essential to treat the subject chronologically and to provide important contextual material on the matter of some films, for Hitchcock's relationships did not occur in a professional vacuum.

In some cases, I have also considered it advisable to add some commentaries on films about which there is more to say than I had at my disposal when writing *The Art of Alfred Hitchcock*. Otherwise, readers are referred to the relevant passages of both that book and *The Dark Side of Genius*, where there are extended analyses and critical appreciations of Hitchcock's films. Mere repetition of analytical material from these earlier books, transferred wholesale to this new volume, is neither necessary nor desirable.

This book aims to explore the life of a brilliant, eccentric, tortured and essentially unhappy man who left us a legacy of great art, perhaps in spite of himself. It also attempts to offer new insights into Hitchcock the filmmaker—in particular, how he understood the element of collaboration. Finally, it is a tribute to a number of extraordinarily talented women without whose courage, grace and patience we would almost certainly not have some of the most enduring, moving, deeply rewarding motion pictures ever made.

why are we so haggard at the heart,

so care-coiled, care-killed . . . so cumbered,

when the thing we freely forfeit is kept with fonder a care,

fonder a care kept than we could have kept it . . .

GERARD MANLEY HOPKINS,
"The Leaden Echo and the Golden Echo" (1882)

Chapter One

LOVE IN
HANDCUFFS
(1920-1926)

Hitchcock's first leading lady, Virginia Valli, in *The Pleasure Garden*

For five years beginning in 1920, when he was twenty-one, Alfred Hitchcock worked in London for Famous Players—Lasky, the British production branch of Hollywood's Paramount Pictures. Most of the senior technical staff were Americans, imported to work on the two small stages, once a power station in the borough of Islington.

Hitchcock's first job, illustrating the title cards of silent movies, gave him access to various jobs on an ad hoc basis: designer for this picture, or art director, co-writer or production manager for that one. Unlike the job specialization in the American movie industry, laborers hired by English studios were encouraged to perform multiple tasks, working wherever their talents could be exploited—hence the multitalented young Hitchcock became a jack-of-all-work on at least eighteen British silent movies. "All my early training was by Americans," he said years later, "and it was far superior to the British."

In 1923, he was still putting in long hours and learning new, up-to-date production methods. That year, producer Michael Balcon took over the studio when Paramount withdrew; Balcon's goal was to sponsor entertainment for an international (especially an American) audience. Accordingly, Balcon had brought over Hollywood's Betty Compson to star in a picture called *Woman to Woman,* on which Hitchcock worked, as he said, as "general factotum. I wrote the script. I designed the sets, and I managed the production. It was the first film that I had really got my hands onto."

It was also the first of five films on which he worked for the studio's leading director, Graham Cutts, with whom he had an increasingly hostile relationship. The trouble was caused by Cutts's indiscreet extramarital liaisons, which Hitchcock considered unprofessional, as they invariably necessitated rearrangement of the production schedule. Additionally, Hitchcock may have envied Cutts his easy way with the ladies; in any case, he certainly wanted to supplant Cutts and to secure additional credits, the better to impress Balcon. "I was quite dogmatic," he said. "I would build a set and say to the director, 'Here's where it's shot from!' "

Cutts resented Hitchcock's assertive style and said so, but Balcon was impressed with the younger man's talent and drive—especially after Cutts returned to London in early 1925, after filming *The Blackguard* in Berlin. While in Germany, Hitchcock had expeditiously resolved many logistical problems caused by Cutts's ineffective balancing act of work, wife and women on the side. Soon after, Balcon asked Hitchcock to direct a motion picture.

"I had no intention of becoming a film director," Hitchcock always said of this time in his career. "I was very happy doing the scripts and the art direction. I hadn't thought of myself as a director"—which was evidently not the case. Working on productions six days weekly for almost five years, he was clearly keen for promotion: he was writing scripts, designing sets, working with editors, and was, to his chagrin, paid miserably in comparison with established directors. Eager to perform any task on a picture by dispatching quickly and effectively every challenging aspect of production, Hitchcock indeed, according to Balcon, "wanted to be a director, but it was not easy to get a young man launched in so important a job," because financiers and distributors were wary of promoting an assistant.

And so Balcon turned to his foreign partners: "I had to

arrange to have [Hitchcock direct his first two pictures] in Germany because of the resistance to his becoming a director" in London. With the screenwriter Eliot Stannard, the assistant director Alma Reville, and the cinematographer Gaetano di Ventimiglia, Hitchcock headed for exterior location shooting in northern Italy and then for studio work in Munich, where they were joined by a crew of international technicians and co-producers. Hitchcock absorbed enough rudimentary German to communicate his wishes.

His assignment was *The Pleasure Garden,* based on an unexceptional but once popular novel about two London showgirls, their shifting fidelities to the difficult men in their lives, and their dangerous sojourn in the tropics—all of it wrapped up in a dénouement of madness and murder. The principal characters were portrayed by American stars acting in Germany and Italy as if the settings were London and the Far East. Hitchcock had the task of making all this appear realistic and emotionally credible, and for the most part, he succeeded admirably.

Balcon imported a pair of Hollywood's top glamour girls, Virginia Valli and Carmelita Geraghty. Virginia had already appeared in forty-seven pictures under the direction of John Ford, King Vidor and others. She wanted to hear what Hitchcock planned and how she would look in the finished film. Carmelita had equivalent concerns.

"I was in a cold sweat," Hitchcock admitted later. "I wanted to disguise the fact that this was my first directorial effort. I dreaded to think what [Virginia Valli], an established Hollywood star, would say if she discovered that she had been brought all the way over to Europe to be directed by a beginner. I was terrified at giving her instructions. I've no idea how many times I asked my future wife [Alma Reville] if I was doing the right thing. She, sweet soul, gave me courage by swearing I was doing marvelously."

So began a historic collaboration. Alma Reville had a keen eye, she knew how stories should be structured and rendered visually, she had worked as an editor and she was not hesitant to tell Hitchcock just what she thought. Tiny and titian-haired, she gave a first impression of shy gentility, but the real Alma Reville was an acutely intelligent, self-assured woman of steely resolve, quite different from the insecure Hitchcock, who was ever self-conscious about his appearance, his tastes and his modest Cockney background. Whenever a tough decision had to be made in business or private life, Alma acted fearlessly.

Hitchcock admitted his fears, which were linked to a childhood sense of insecurity. "Fear? It has influenced my life and my career, and I've known it since my childhood. I remember when I was five or six. It was a Sunday evening, the only time my parents did not have to work. They put me to bed and went to Hyde Park for a stroll"—then a ninety-minute tram and train ride from the Hitchcock home. "They were sure I would be asleep until their return. But I woke up, called out, and no one answered. Nothing but night all around me. Shaking, I got up, wandered around the empty, dark house and, finally arriving in the kitchen, found a piece of cold meat which I ate while drying my tears."

Hitchcock was uncomfortable around his two American stars, but he knew how much he needed them. He also resented their enormous salaries, and his budget forestalled their expectations of the kind of Hollywood-style luxury they had there. "Valli was big stuff and knew it," according to Hitchcock. "She expected a brass band. She expected the red carpet. But she didn't get them. Valli was peeved, but she turned out to be sweet enough."

Filming began in June 1925 in northern Italy, before moving

to the studio interiors in Munich, which were suffocatingly hot that summer, for the ceilings were glass and air-conditioning was unknown. Everything seemed to go wrong: there were numerous delays from uncooperative extra players, and then a trained dog simply wandered off and his replacement insistently licked off the makeup applied to him to replicate his predecessor. After that, a woman hired to play a native girl arrived on the day of her swimming scene and promptly announced that her monthly period would prevent her going into the water.

This bit of news, Hitchcock claimed, was an educational experience for him. He insisted that he had never heard of the menstrual cycle because it had not been included in his schoolboy education—nor, one might add, had production design or scriptwriting. But like his assertion that he had no thought of becoming a director, this statement of ignorance simply cannot be taken at face value. He was twenty-six, had an older sister and brother, certainly must have noticed discreet advertisements for feminine hygiene products and had worked at a movie studio during the freewheeling 1920s—not generally a place and time of polite discourse. Sexually inexperienced though he claims to have been, he was not a backward, preadolescent country boy from an earlier century. Ordinary curiosity surely must have supplemented his formal education.

But word circulated that Hitchcock was an unsophisticated innocent, which (as he may have intended) evoked the benignly maternal, protective reactions of Valli and Geraghty and much improved both the tone of the production and their pliancy in his hands. Thus, he won them over not by exhibiting his sophistication, but by feigning ignorance. He employed, in other words, whatever it took to achieve the desired effect—including his demand that Virginia Valli wear a blond wig for her role.

When Balcon arrived in Munich to have a look at Hitchcock's first cut of the picture, he agreed with the director that rearrangements were called for, but for marketing purposes, he also said he liked the American look of the picture. *The Pleasure Garden* revealed, too, Hitchcock's skillful use of hallucinatory cinematic techniques (dissolves and double printing, for example)—and, for commercial appeal, the emphasis on fast-paced action alternating with scenes of violence and boudoir sex.

The final form of *The Pleasure Garden* contains several elements that would intrigue Hitchcock throughout his career: the theatrical setting (which recurs in *The Ring, Murder!, The 39 Steps, Sabotage, Young and Innocent, Saboteur, Stage Fright, North by Northwest* and *Torn Curtain*); the motif of voyeurism (especially in *Rear Window* and *Psycho*); the experience of emotional breakdown (in, for example, *Shadow of a Doubt, Spellbound, Under Capricorn, Stage Fright*, the remake of *The Man Who Knew Too Much, The Wrong Man, Vertigo, Psycho, The Birds* and *Marnie*); and the psychological torture and physical pain inflicted on women by violent men (which runs from *Blackmail* through *Family Plot*). The last element is not peculiar to Hitchcock's entertainments, of course: the damsel in distress is virtually an ancient archetype, long a staple of literature, poetry, theater, opera and movies. But Hitchcock showed the world, in stark closeup, that misogyny was part of a pandemic social pathology. He was neither moralist nor preacher, but his work consistently reveals that the fine arts of human exploitation and cruelty are symptoms of a deep fissure in the human spirit.

The Pleasure Garden opens with a close shot of women's legs, hastening down a spiral staircase toward the stage of the eponymous theater, where the women dance with wild abandon typical of the Jazz Age; the movement is so animated that this silent film suddenly becomes a kind of vivid flipbook. Hitchcock then shows the men in the audience, formally dressed and leering as they gaze at the dancers through their opera glasses. These will become mainstream themes and images for Hitchcock—

characters in the world of make-believe drawn into bizarre real-life dramas; voyeurism; the camera observing an observer; the rapid transitions from the watcher to the watched; the dizzying staircase—and mischievous humor. "What every chorus girl knows," announces a title card—and the movie then shows a woman washing her stockings in a basin. Hitchcock's bedroom scenes occur later in the movie, and there is nothing coy, bashful or boyish about them.

Life within and outside this pleasure garden, from London's Piccadilly to the tropics, is a perilous paradise—thus the ominous snake entwined around a tree on the title card designs Hitchcock devised, adding another layer of meaning to the film's title. The chase and nick-of-time rescue at the finale reveal his familiarity with filmmakers such as D. W. Griffith, and Hitchcock was certainly inspired by Charles Chaplin and Buster Keaton as much as by Germans such as F. W. Murnau and Fritz Lang, whom he had met in Berlin. One stylistic conceit particularly marked the Hitchcock style from 1925 forward: characters often gaze directly at the camera, thus making the audience a corresponding player, a participant in the drama.

Hitchcock boldly added his initials (and sometimes his full signature) to the intertitle designs. In this regard, he was again taking a page from Chaplin and Griffith, who were among the first to understand that the marketing of their own names was as critical as the selling of the properties or presenting an attractive leading lady. "Actors come and go," Hitchcock told his colleagues at London's Film Society that year, "but the name of the director should stay clearly in the mind of the audiences." That attitude led to his cameo appearances in his films: he became the artist signing his canvas, reminding viewers that this was an Alfred J. Hitchcock production.

When Balcon screened *The Pleasure Garden* in London for the press, journalists were enthusiastic—"a powerful and interesting story [that] promises well for Hitchcock's future efforts," proclaimed the trade journal *Bioscope* on March 25, 1926. But the financiers working with Balcon would not distribute the picture, claiming that its content and style would alienate British audiences accustomed to more straightforward and less visually inventive movies. Hence Balcon decided to shelve *The Pleasure Garden* for a while—but he had not lost faith in Hitchcock, to whom he gave another crack at directing. (Later, American journalists were scathing, calling the picture "sappy" and "a Wiener schnitzel," and banishing it straightaway.)

As for Virginia Valli and Carmelita Geraghty, they apparently never spoke on the record about Hitchcock, even after his international fame was secure. That was perhaps due to the dramatic changes in their lives, which led them to reject all later requests for interviews about their days as movie stars. Carmelita worked in an additional fifty-three pictures during the next decade, but then, at thirty-four, she retired and became a successful professional artist whose paintings were sold at galleries across America; she died in 1966.

Virginia turned her back on Hollywood after appearing in eighteen more movies. Real-life romance replaced the imaginary sort when she met the dashing actor Charles Farrell, whom she married in 1931, when she was thirty-three. For the next thirty-seven years, until her death in 1968, she lived more happily than any heroine she portrayed. For her as for Carmelita, glamour-girl vanity was no longer important.

On his side, Hitchcock referred to his first leading ladies only to cite the costs of their excess personal baggage and their refusal to eat the food served on European trains.

Balcon told Hitchcock to remain in Germany, where the producer had lined up another movie with another American beauty—but by now the director was unflappable, even in the face of the actress's frank and sassy sex appeal. After a spin with the Ziegfeld Follies, Brooklyn-born Anita Donna Dooley had been brought to Hollywood by John Barrymore, with whom she co-starred in *Dr. Jekyll and Mr. Hyde* in 1920. Theodosia Goodman had been renamed Theda Bara, and so a publicist changed Anita's name to Nita Naldi. With that, Nita was promoted as the daughter of a famous Italian diplomat and a descendant of Dante's Beatrice. In fact, her family background was far humbler, for she had left school to work as a model before joining Ziegfeld's chorus line. The highlight of her career had been acting opposite Rudolph Valentino in *Blood and Sand* and in DeMille's original *Ten Commandments*. Incredible though it seems decades later, audiences in the silent movie era often confused the role with the actress, and Nita's notoriety as a vamp onscreen made her unwelcome in many restaurants, on public beaches and at polite social gatherings.

When she arrived in Munich, Nita at once put Hitchcock at ease with her tough humor and lack of guile. Traveling with an older gentleman she winkingly referred to as "Daddy," she whisked Hitchcock and his assistant off for a visit to a famous brothel that was on her list of tourist attractions. Invited to participate in the customary recreations there, Hitchcock and Alma demurred, while the activities of Nita and Daddy have not been documented. It may have been at this time, or in Berlin the previous year, at some pleasure palace, that Hitchcock also rejected the advances of two young German girls who then shrugged indifferently and got into bed together. Hitchcock remained to observe at close range the lesbian encounter. "It was a very *gemütlich* [cozy] family soirée," he said.

But there was work to do with his cast that autumn of 1925. *The Mountain Eagle,* based on a tale by Balcon's story editor, concerned (of all things) scandal among Kentucky hillbillies, which was not exactly familiar territory for Hitchcock or his writer, the prolific Eliot Stannard. Very quickly the finished film, partly shot in the snowy Tyrol, vanished into oblivion, and only some still photographs survive—no loss, said Hitchcock, calling it "a very bad movie." But the trade review in London's *Kinematograph Weekly* for October 7, 1926, praised the direction as "thoroughly imaginative . . . [despite the] slow tempo and a story too full of unconvincing twists."

Nita Naldi apparently came to the production with all sorts of suggestions as to how she might make the role of a doughty schoolmarm more alluring. "She arrived on the set with finger-nails like a mandarin's," Hitchcock recalled, "and with four-inch heels and a black dog to match her black, swathed dress. She was dark, Latin, Junoesque and slinky, with slanting eyes, and her maid followed her—it was like the royalty Germany hadn't seen for years! I was thinking of a simple Kentucky Miss in a gingham gown and a cotton apron. I had to turn her into a strong woman of the mid-western mountains who handled a gun instead of a lipstick."

So occurred the first conflict between the director and an actress. First the director and his star quarreled about her fin-gernails, which she gradually trimmed. The high heels also came down, and the makeup was altered, shade by shade. After a loud altercation, Nita finally agreed to change her hair, curl by curl—always a Hitchcock fixation.

In silent films, dialogue was created only for close shots; in grand emotional scenes (as Hitchcock said), "we allowed peo-ple to say just whatever came into their heads. One day, Nita was playing a scene in which she had been run out of town by a Kentucky farmer. She had to turn on them and tell them just what she thought of them. I called out to her, 'Give them all you've got!'

"And she did! She gave it to them in English, Italian,

American, Bowery, Park Avenue and maybe double Dutch. She called them anything and everything she could lay her tongue to. She told them where they got off, where they came from, where they were going. She used words we had never heard before. When I called 'Cut!' she was shuddering and shaking with emotion, and the whole studio—none of whom had understood a word she said—burst into spontaneous applause."

That was Nita Naldi's last scheduled scene in *The Mountain Eagle*. She took no time to change her clothes, but instead called at once for her dog and her "Daddy," hurried to a waiting taxi and raced off to the train for France, "still in her gingham dress, with makeup on her face."

She made two more films in quick succession, one in Paris and one in Berlin. Her energy was prodigious, but her strong New York accent was unacceptable with the arrival of talking pictures. In the 1930s, she appeared on Broadway in a forgettable trio of plays with very short runs, and when she died alone in a Manhattan hotel room in 1961, she had been a widow for sixteen years, living on a meager stipend from The Actors Fund. "Nita turned out to be a grand person," Hitchcock said later. "For all her entourage, there was really nothing high-hat about her. She talked to everybody in her heavy New York drawl, and the Germans fell hard for this American royalty."

Like *The Pleasure Garden*, *The Mountain Eagle* left exhibitors lukewarm, and it was put on the shelf next to its predecessor until after the eventual critical and popular success of Hitchcock's third picture, *The Lodger: A Story of the London Fog*. This project was Balcon's idea, and Hitchcock and Stannard were at once enthusiastic: it was based on a superb and successful

1913 thriller by Marie Belloc Lowndes that was inspired by the ghastly crimes of Jack the Ripper in 1888. The real-life slayer was never identified, but a series of copycat murders ensued, and a general paranoia afflicted London life for years.

Eliot Stannard was the main writer on no less than eight Hitchcock silent pictures, and his contributions were significant. But as the British scholar Charles Barr observed, Hitchcock "fostered the impression that he used screenwriters like secretaries, as skilled agents for writing up his own ideas." Sidney Gilliat, who co-wrote *The Lady Vanishes* in 1937, recalled that Hitchcock routinely told the press that he alone was responsible for ninety-nine percent of the script material—an especially ironic case, for *The Lady Vanishes* was virtually complete when he came to the project.

However, the director also took enormous care in shaping whatever written material he received. As his increasing success, cameo appearances and press interviews (and later his television series) made him a celebrity, he enjoyed a power he exploited even as he affected a cool, detached and remote diffidence. Most notably, Hitchcock had a rare technical genius and floated ideas for every element in visual storytelling, from pre-production to final release. Unfortunately, he never mentioned Eliot Stannard's important participation; then, as later, Alfred Hitchcock always seemed to believe that sharing credit diminished the praise due solely to himself.

In the novel *The Lodger,* the title character, who calls himself Mr. Sleuth, appears to be a refined gentleman who comes to rent rooms in the home of a London family, Mr. and Mrs. Bunting. "It hadn't taken the landlady very long to find out that her lodger had a queer kind of fear and dislike of women. When she was doing the staircase and landings, she would often hear [him] reading aloud to himself passages in the Bible that were very uncomplimentary to her sex. But that didn't put her out. Besides, where one's lodger is concerned, a dislike of women is better than—well, than the other thing."

As it turns out, the lodger is no mere eccentric: he is the self-styled "Avenger," a mad serial killer responsible for the death of a dozen poor girls. The Buntings, unaware of their lodger's identity until very near the end, are both frightened and fascinated as they follow the Avenger's crimes in newspapers and on the wireless.

Mrs. Bunting's seventeen-year-old stepdaughter, Daisy (her husband's child by a previous marriage), does not live with them, and is very much a secondary character in the novel. She comes to visit and is courted by Joe Chandler, a detective on the Avenger case, whom she eventually marries. Daisy does not meet the lodger until very near the end, and then only briefly. Despite Mrs. Bunting's conviction that her lodger is a serial murderer, she says nothing to anyone—not even to Joe—nor does she go to the police, despite the accumulating evidence she rightly comprehends.

In the final pages of the novel, the lodger escapes and never returns to the Bunting house. The landlady "had sheltered him—kept his awful secret . . . that [he] was victim of no temporary aberration, but that he was, and had been for years, a madman, a homicidal maniac . . . [He] never came back, and at last, after many days and many nights had gone by, Mrs. Bunting left off listening for the click of the lock which she at once hoped and feared would herald her lodger's return."

At the core of this profoundly disturbing book is Mrs. Bunting's fascination for a smoothly stylish lunatic. Marie Belloc Lowndes brilliantly explored the clash of repulsion and attraction often linked to a desire to experience the darkest aspects of danger and dread—but from a distance, in art or entertainment. Very often in her novel, Mrs. Belloc Lowndes described the frank excitement of the newspaper reports, and the public's relish for the daily installments of a real-life horror thriller.

Hitchcock insisted that the central characters of the movie adaptation must be the lodger and Daisy, not the lodger and the landlady, and so the part of the girl was much enlarged, and the central conflict became the detective's jealousy of the lodger's attentions to Daisy. Mr. and Mrs. Bunting, therefore, became faintly comic characters—Cockney simpletons whom the movie treats with some class-conscious condescension.

Balcon decided that *The Lodger* would be a perfect project for the reigning matinee idol of the day, Welsh actor-author Ivor Novello, star of *The Rat,* Balcon's major hit that year. Novello also composed successful West End musicals, and his tunes were heard everywhere ("Keep the Home Fires Burning" had been the sentimental standard all during the World War). According to Hitchcock, Novello's enormous popularity would not permit him to undertake the role of a murderous madman—hence, the script could not conclude (like the novel) with a clear establishment of the lodger's guilt: "They wouldn't let Novello even be considered as a villain," Hitchcock insisted. "We had to change the [story] to show that without a doubt he was innocent."

But this statement, too, must not be accepted at face value. The novel had been freely adapted by H. A. Vachell for the London stage in 1915 (as *Who Is He?*), which Hitchcock saw before he read the novel. In this seriocomic theatrical adaptation, the lodger turns out to be an innocent young aristocrat who takes refuge in lodgings after being jilted by his lover. The darker psychological complexity of Stannard's and Hitchcock's film treatment would have been much attenuated by a straightforward tale in which a suspect turns out to be the villain after all—no final twist, no hook, no surprise, no psychological complexity.

Novello was a rather unctuous over-actor, ferociously protective of his glamorous profile to the point of applying thick lipstick and eyeliner in the style of antique theatrics. He was also clever and witty, and he enjoyed the advocacy of Noël Coward, who nevertheless preferred Ivor from a distance: "Before a camera, his face takes on a set look, his eyes become deceptively soulful, and frequently something dreadful happens to his mouth." Novello was also quite flamboyantly gay. The poet Siegfried Sassoon had been among his lovers, but Novello eventually settled down to many years of domestic bliss and professional collaboration with the actor Robert Andrews, who appeared in a number of Novello's musicals.

Unlike many of his contemporaries, Hitchcock was always comfortable working with gay men and women. "Some people might be surprised by this," said the musical star Elsie Randolph, who appeared in two Hitchcock movies over the span of forty years and often socialized with him and his family throughout the 1930s. "He was always at ease with homosexual or bisexual people. Hitch often told actors—for what mix of reasons I won't guess—that they really had to be part masculine and part feminine in order to get inside any character." Throughout his life, Hitchcock burnished his public image as a bourgeois middle-class Edwardian gentleman, but he nursed no prejudices against gays.

Ivor was an amusing colleague during the making of *The Lodger,* and Hitchcock was not hesitant to pull a practical joke, taking great care as he set up a shot with a flowerpot strategically placed on a shelf so that the actor appeared to be wearing a woman's outlandish hat. "It was just too tempting," Hitchcock told the actor-writer Rodney Ackland. "I couldn't resist it.

Anyway, with that profile, why should Ivor mind having a flower pot on his head?"

For an actress to portray Daisy Bunting, Novello suggested a former colleague, twenty-five-year-old June Howard-Tripp, a popular musical comedy star since childhood. Known professionally and credited in *The Lodger* simply as June, she had appeared in a few previous films, was quickly hired to play Daisy, and readily complied with Hitchcock's requirement that she wear a bright blond wig over her brown hair.

So we begin to see the type of woman Hitchcock preferred—Nordic, as he called them. Blondes were easier and more dramatic to photograph in monochrome, and he considered their "coolness" and elegance appropriate contrasts to the kind of passion he wanted to reveal beneath the surface. In the years to come, he obliged many actresses to color their hair a luminous, even glossily burnished blond. During his black-and-white period, for example, he took special care with the hair-dying for Anny Ondra, Joan Barry, Madeleine Carroll, Joan Fontaine and Ingrid Bergman, while Grace Kelly, Kim Novak, Eva Marie Saint and Tippi Hedren received even more obsessive attention to blond styles in his color films.

"Hitch had very strong feelings about women in his films," recalled Joseph Cotten, a leading man in two of the director's features. "To him the most feminine and most vulnerable women were usually blondes. He loved blondes and couldn't understand women not bleaching their hair for the privilege of working with him."

In addition to his personal predilection for fair-haired ladies, Hitchcock shared the popular notion that brunettes have a serious nature, while blondes are frivolous—an idea perhaps based on the assumption that comparatively few women are naturally blond, and because hair-dying was considered a characteristic of idle, shallow, often lower-class women. In ancient Rome, prostitutes were required to dye their hair yellow-gold with saffron, and literary history is full of blond women of doubtful intelligence and virtue. In George Eliot's Victorian novel *Middlemarch,* for example, the noble and self-sacrificing Dorothea is dark-haired, in contrast to the shallow, selfish, pale and blond Rosamond.

Hollywood's images of Jean Harlow, Marilyn Monroe, Jayne Mansfield and others reinforced the unwholesome and erroneous conjunction of ignorance and blondness with hypersexuality—a prejudice often imitated by the cinema worldwide, as in the cases of England's Diana Dors and Sweden's Anita Ekberg. "Gentlemen prefer blondes" perhaps because "blondes have more fun," as the twentieth-century sayings go, just as rude jokes have abounded about "dumb blondes."

June recalled that Hitchcock "spoke in a curious mixture of Cockney and North Country accents, with a laboured stress on elusive aitches [*h*'s]. His humor was salty or subtle, according to his mercurial moods, and his brilliance was patent. Hitchcock was being hailed as the Great White Hope of the lagging British motion picture industry, [and] he was so imbued with the value of unusual camera angles and lighting effects with which to create and sustain dramatic suspense, that often a [very brief] scene would take an entire morning to shoot." For one sequence, Hitchcock insisted that June repeatedly carry an iron tray of breakfast dishes up a three-story flight until he was satisfied with both "the expression of fear on my face and the atmosphere established by light and shadows. I must have made the trek twenty times, the tray seeming to grow heavier with every passing minute."

Another scene requiring multiple takes was far more unpleasant. Daisy's detective boyfriend (played by Malcolm Keen) comes to visit the Buntings with the news that he is on the case of the killer. "I'm keen on golden hair myself, same as the lodger is," run his words on an intertitle. "When I've put handcuffs on The Avenger and a noose around his neck, I'll put a ring on Daisy's finger." With that, he makes real the picture on the lodger's wall of a woman in bondage, as he playfully snaps handcuffs on Daisy—a gesture that does not amuse the girl but causes sheer panic, which was precisely what June felt when Keen snapped on the cuffs. She had not been prepared for this, and later she reasoned that Hitchcock wanted to record her shock. During many takes, she was required to run from one room on the set to another, crying out for her manacles to be removed.

Thus another Hitchcockian motif was introduced for future recurrence. "Psychologically, of course," Hitchcock said years later, "the idea of the handcuffs has deeper implications. Being tied to something—it's somewhere in the area of fetishism, isn't it? There's also a sexual connotation. When I visited the Vice Museum in Paris, I noticed there was considerable evidence of sexual aberrations through restraint." As for Novello, he, too, had an ordeal toward the end of the picture, handcuffed and suspended from an iron fence before his rescue from the fury of a vengeful mob.

Beginning with *The Lodger,* it is most often the blondes in Hitchcock's movies who are put through an ordeal, with the characters they play thrown into danger, humiliated and assaulted. As no less a venerable organization than the British Film Institute stated in a glowing tribute to Hitchcock, he seemed to have "a murderous fascination with blondes." That language sounds a bit extreme, but even a cautious film historian like Philip Kemp agrees: "Like Hitchcock himself, the serial killer in *The Lodger* seems to have it in for blondes . . . [and] Hitchcock's mischievous, semi-sadistic treatment of blondes hit its stride in Hollywood, perhaps provoked by the flawless glamour of its screen goddesses," for whom Hitchcock felt both attraction and resentment. Kemp, too, cites Hitchcock's preference for Victorien Sardou's advice to playwrights: "Torture the women!" Added Hitchcock, "The trouble today [in the 1930s] is that we don't torture women enough"—a statement he could not have made decades later without risking serious reprisals. Concluded Kemp: "Hitchcock, at least, did his best to make up for the omission."

Chapter Two

OF SOUND
AND SENSE

(1926-1934)

June, the first Hitchcock blonde, in *The Lodger*

The Lodger was June's last English movie. In 1929, she married John Alan Burns, the fourth Baron Inverclyde, and retired to take up the life of a titled socialite and hostess. But the new Lady Inverclyde's marriage failed, and she obtained a divorce, married an American businessman and relocated to New York. Her only two subsequent film appearances, both of them brief and ignored, were in Hollywood productions many years later. She died in 1985, remembered by movie historians for her anxious portrayal of a woman attracted to a fey lodger whom she neither comprehends nor resists.

"The Lodger was really my first picture," Hitchcock said. "It was the first time I really exercised my style"—or at least one kind of it, for he would modify that style markedly in the years to come. In this case, his technique and design were partly influenced by Robert Wiene's recent German film, *The Cabinet of Dr. Caligari,* a morbid horror tale about somnambulism, lunacy and murder played against deliberately artificial and angular studio sets reflecting disordered minds. This extreme example of German expressionism Hitchcock downplayed in *The Lodger,* supervising sets that were more realistic, stressing deep shadows and disorienting camera angles—and so giving *The Lodger* an acute sense of uneasy imbalance from first frame to last.

The picture opens with a closeup of a blond-haired woman screaming in terror and gazing out at us before she is discovered dead; the scene is briefly interrupted by the blinking lights of a theater marquee—"To-Night, Golden Curls." There follows a virtual documentary of the press reports about the murders—the busy teletype machine, the delivery of newspapers and the dispatchers in the news office (where Hitchcock made his first cameo appearance). We then see chorus girls backstage, as in *The Pleasure Garden,* but here they are obviously terrified. With a kind of wistful rapture, one of them hears on the wireless the latest news of a killing, while another touches her blond hair protectively ("Am I next?"). For Hitchcock, victims are as fascinated by the horror as the villains and the audience.

The narrative then moves to Daisy, glamorously outfitted and apparently wealthy—but the camera pulls back, and we see that she is a store mannequin modeling the latest fashions. At home, she lives in genteel poverty with her parents and her constant visitor, the ambitious detective Joe. In fact, his jealousy of the lodger's attentions to Daisy will soon convince him that the man is the killer. Meanwhile, the nameless lodger glides around the house, asking that all the Victorian paintings of blondes be removed ("they get on my nerves"); he paces his rooms, too, to the anxiety of the household. Soon he is Daisy's greatest admirer, watching intently as she models fashions, buying her expensive frocks and constantly staring at her. In a real sense, Novello is Hitchcock's alter ego in *The Lodger*—ever aware of the leading lady, indulging her, selecting outfits for her, observing her. In this regard, there is a straight line from *The Lodger* to *Vertigo* and beyond.

In due course, the police close in on the Bunting neighborhood as the locale of the Avenger's recent crimes, and we see Joe's mental process as he conjures the lodger's guilt—brief connective images, all passing over a footprint in the mud. The final vindication of the lodger, when the actual killer is apprehended offscreen, is not entirely convincing—nor did Hitchcock intend that it should be. The ambiguity of the situation and the character is deliberate.

Perhaps capitalizing on Novello's performance as a distracted neurasthenic, the film has a delicate poise between paranoia and security. The final macabre frisson is that Daisy's engagement to the lodger is visually associated with murder: as they embrace, the show title again flashes on a distant marquee—"To-Night, Golden Curls." Murder is thus associated with the "love night" of Daisy and the lodger, and with their future. The link between bondage and pleasure, between handcuffs and sexual teasing, has come full circle, and for the first time, Hitchcock has established an association between sex and murder, ecstasy and death. This is a key element in the disturbing psychology of his greatest works.

As the last image fades, on Daisy's tentative smile in the arms of her lodger-lover, the convention of innocence is much in doubt. After all, even if the lodger is not The Avenger, he is certainly a man who has set out to kill—to track down and murder his sister's murderer. He is a vigilante on the prowl, and so it is impossible to endorse anything like a happy union with Daisy.

The Lodger required further work after principal photography. It had atmosphere but seemed, to the distributors, to be *artistic*, which was the kiss of death in Hollywood, the ultimate commercial condemnation. In addition, very little was tidy about the picture, and Hitchcock wisely agreed to rethink, trim and reshuffle several sequences. This task was undertaken with the assistance and guidance of Ivor Montagu, a young zoologist who had given free rein to his passion for films and was much respected by Michael Balcon.

"Hitch was ungrudgingly warm," recalled Montagu many years later, "[and] eager to hear of anything that, even by chance, might make his work more acceptable. My suggestions were quickly and generously adopted," although, characteristically, Hitchcock never publicly credited Montagu, whose counsel included cutting the intertitles from several hundred down to about eighty; repeating the heroine's name alone on several intertitles, for "a menacing effect"; engaging the American designer E. McKnight Kauffer to create sinister triangle designs; and reshooting some scenes that failed in their intended effects. Montagu brought out the full potential in *The Lodger,* thus salvaging the young director's fledgling career and effectively enabling Hitchcock to become Hitchcock.

"Among the additions I made to *The Lodger,*" Hitchcock said in July 1975, "I had a flashback scene on a dance floor—it refers to the murder of the lodger's sister at her social debut. I began with a closeup of two people dancing. Then I dollied back and showed all the guests dancing, and then I went past people sitting at tables against a wall—and then I seemed to go right through a window, all without a single cut. What I actually did was to put everyone and all the furniture on a platform hooked to the camera. Then I dollied back, pulling everything along—and at a certain moment I unhooked the platform. Everything was attached to the camera! These were the kinds of little tricks I did in those days."

And these were among the moments that, as he must have foreseen, both critics and colleagues would notice and celebrate. An important element in building his career was Hitchcock's belief that movies had to be made with the press in mind—that is, they had to contain his "Hitchcock touches" that journalists and critics would recognize and publicize, mostly matters of style and technique. He wanted to make himself known as a director by being mentioned in the press *as a director;* this, he correctly reasoned, would be his ticket to creative independence.

When it was finally released, *The Lodger* was an enormous critical and popular success—"It is possible that this film is the finest British production ever made" was a typical press response—and so Balcon and Novello decided to proceed with another Hitchcock picture. The star had co-authored a play called *Down Hill,* and very quickly it was turned into Hitchcock's *Downhill*—the rather damp story of a wealthy schoolboy (improbably played by thirty-four-year-old Novello) who nobly takes the blame for his best friend's bad conduct and so is expelled from school and disowned by his family. His life degenerates into a spiral of bad fortune, poor choices, poverty and squalor, until he is restored to his rightful station—but not until he has endured a series of humiliations from an array of mean-spirited and exploitive women. The story may well reflect Novello's experience as a gay matinée idol, oppressed by unwanted female attention and ardor. That may have been the case, but the film must be assessed on its own merit, which is often considerable.

There was no single leading lady in *Downhill,* but memorably among the lot was a stylish actress named Isabel Jeans, who had already co-starred in a pair of Novello films. Established in the theater, aristocratic in deportment and projecting a kind of severe but attractive femininity, Isabel infused her role of a jaded, immoral actress with calculated carelessness and a mocking cruelty. All the female characters in *Downhill* are reprehensible cheats, liars or insatiable sensualists, but Isabel's Julia is memorable for the worst sort of chilling exploitation.

During production, she impressed Hitchcock with her inventive gestures for the silent film, and with her unerring sense of timing.* Balcon was pleased to grant Hitchcock's request that she star in his next film, also to be based on a play—Noël Coward's *Easy Virtue*.

Amid all his professional activities, Alfred Hitchcock married Alma Reville on December 2, 1926, in a Roman Catholic ceremony at the Brompton Oratory, Knightsbridge. He married her "because she asked me to," he said many years later, adding provocatively, "I could have been a poof [i.e., gay] if it were not for Alma." According to Hitchcock, the marriage remained unconsummated for more than a year, but at last there was one experience of sexual intercourse, which resulted in the conception of his only child. The girl was born on July 7, 1928, which would put her conception at some time in autumn 1927—a year after the wedding.

"Hitch and Alma were really like brother and sister," said the American playwright and screenwriter Samuel Taylor, Hitchcock's sometime collaborator. "In business matters, quiet little Alma could be a scrappy little watchdog, for she was much shrewder about people than Hitch, and a lot tougher. Their relationship was one of working partners." Elsie Randolph, among others, agreed: "Alma was his co-writer, his cook, his hausfrau—but theirs was not a grand passion, and to tell the truth, she bossed him."

As one Hitchcock scholar has observed, Hitchcock gave the

---

* In *Downhill*, as later, Hitchcock took up a pen and wrote the "Roddy letter" to be filmed and inserted. So began another type of cameo appearance, but one that has gone unnoticed in commentaries on Hitchcock. Hitchcock was having fun, but serious fun. There are dozens of examples of his handwriting in his films, and they are always significant.

impression that his marriage was (after their daughter's conception) "celibate . . . full of sublimations, foremost among which was his work, but [the sublimations included] travel, exclusive restaurants, attending both wrestling matches and symphony concerts at the Albert Hall, and collecting first editions and original works of art. One hears that the diminutive Alma more than stood up to the often grossly overweight Alfred—[she] being described as peppery and given to bossing her husband." Indeed, Hitchcock's granddaughter, Mary Stone, confirmed this: "My grandmother really had the upper hand of the relationship, as small and petite as she was. He deferred to her whether it be in personal [matters] or in his business."

At work, Hitchcock gave the women orders—although such were unnecessary during the production of *Easy Virtue*. Isabel Jeans provided a remarkably sympathetic portrait of a socially maligned woman, and her canny professionalism freed the director to explore just how publicity and the camera probe and pry into people's lives. Hitchcock insists on the potentially destructive effects on people of newspaper photos and their coyly suggestive captions, and he instructed Isabel Jeans to throw a book at a prop camera.

Very little studio production material has survived for Hitchcock's British films, and interviews with actors—like celebrity autobiographies—were not commonplace in England at the time. These factors make it difficult to document details of Hitchcock's professional relationships in the first years of his career. But the director himself provided some critical information.

Following *Easy Virtue,* Hitchcock made two more films in 1927—one based on an original idea, called *The Ring*; and *The Farmer's Wife,* based on a popular stage comedy by Eden

Phillpotts. In both, he meticulously exploited the porcelain beauty of twenty-nine-year-old Lilian Hall-Davis in two very different roles. In the first, she had a kind of edgy caprice as the fickle object of two boxers' attentions; in the second, she portrayed a widowed farmer's devoted, self-sacrificing housekeeper.

The Ring revealed Hitchcock's canny ability to combine traditional romantic melodrama—in this case, a love triangle—with a keen sense of the comic-grotesque. The chums of sideshow denizens are introduced, and Siamese twins fight over a pew in church; a giant comes to a wedding in the company of a midget; a fat lady enters with delicate tentativeness. The movie's fairground setting features later in *Stage Fright* and *Strangers on a Train,* but even in 1927 (still under the influence of *Dr. Caligari*), Hitchcock knew how to use the raucous, hallucinatory nightmare aspects of the carnival.

For sheer comic inventiveness, his film of *The Farmer's Wife* succeeded in turning a rustic stage comedy into irresistible, hilarious and even tender farce. A formal luncheon descends into madcap chaos; a maid breaks down weeping when ice cream melts; children wreak havoc everywhere; and a sturdy matriarch in an unruly wheelchair tries to negotiate her way through a crowd.

But it was the scenes with the leading lady that everyone on the production recalled—particularly when Hitchcock reduced this sensitive actress to abject weeping, proclaiming loudly that she was incompetent, that she ought to go to drama school. It is impossible to know why Lilian Hall-Davis was the object of such opprobrium, although it may have had to do with her freewheeling private life, which Hitchcock found both exciting and offensive; he may also have felt deprived of such shenanigans. "Lilian was a good actress," he said, "willing and very efficient, but rather fragile. She was married and had a child, but while we were filming *The Ring* and *The Farmer's Wife,* she had an affair with Gordon Harker [who had supporting roles in both pictures]. He was married, too, and involved with yet another young woman. Then Lilian had a nervous breakdown, and soon her career was over." Alas, so was her life: in 1933, at the age of thirty-five, Lilian Hall-Davis committed suicide.

No such intrigue attended Hitchcock's next silent picture, the 1928 comedy *Champagne.* Producers engaged the immensely popular Betty Balfour to play an irrepressible flapper who is taught a lesson by her wealthy father; her adventures take her aboard a luxury liner and then to a Parisian garret. The comedy is thin, but the picture has considerable charm and visual invention. Balfour had a strong sense of her value as the star of a motion picture, however, and this created some tension as she worked with Hitchcock, who was also intent on stardom as a director. Balfour had no hesitation in expressing her opinions of scenes as well as suggesting alternate ideas. Hitchcock, who was none too keen on this assigned project from the start, did not appreciate what he considered undesirable meddling from an actress.

There was no interference from Anny Ondra, the Polish-Czech blonde who had been directed by Graham Cutts in a pair of films and whom Hitchcock requested for *The Manxman,* produced during the summer of 1928. Her English was heavily accented, but this was irrelevant to a silent film, and she took direction to the letter. Based on a Victorian potboiler about romance and betrayal among fishermen on the Isle of Man, the movie is perhaps best remembered for its shimmeringly lovely cinematography and for the deeply felt performances by Ondra, by the Danish actor Carl Brisson (who had played in

The Ring) and by Malcolm Keen (from *The Mountain Eagle* and *The Lodger*).

Michael Powell, later a celebrated producer and director, was the on-set stills photographer for *The Manxman* and *Blackmail* (Hitchcock's next picture). "I am sure he wanted Anny as much as I did," Powell wrote frankly in his memoirs, recalling that Hitchcock (who liked to direct people in life as much as on a movie set) asked Powell for more than photos of Anny alone. He asked Powell "to get a boy with her in the hay . . . and she's pressing up against him, to feel his cock against her leg." Powell recalled how often Hitchcock "loved to talk bawdy." Such was the experience, the following year, of a young assistant whom Hitchcock asked to relay quite filthy comments to a German-speaking actress playing in the foreign-language version of one of his films.

Like the roles undertaken by June and Balfour, that of Kate in *The Manxman* was essentially a coy and fickle blonde—"that kind makes the best victim," Hitchcock said. As the same biographer added, "His women must kill or die, be humiliated, or endure a frustrating romance with an impotent hero on the run. One way or another, the beautiful women always suffered." Sometimes these beautiful women suffered as working actresses as much as their characters in the stories did. Anny Ondra was but the latest among those whom Hitchcock knew how to embarrass, to the point where she was driven to tears.

Anny tried to please her director by shrieking gaily when he played his customary rude practical jokes on colleagues and guests—in other words, she tried to be his perfect audience as well as a docile leading lady. Alma, on the other hand, grew impatient: "He never stopped playing jokes on people," she said, "and now and then I got a little apprehensive." The series of pranks contributed to the Hitchcock legend: the dinner party he gave for which all the food was dyed blue; the rude "whoopee cushions" in the Hitchcock flat in Cromwell Road; the horse he sent to the backstage dressing room of a bumptious actor; the cocktails he served laced with mysterious (even sometimes cathartic) ingredients. Later such pranks would not go over well in America, but for a time they were tolerated in Britain, where such things were not entirely unknown.

There was no time for boredom on Hitchcock's next project, based on Charles Bennett's play *Blackmail*. As historian Charles Barr has demonstrated, the film's production history is unusually complex.

> It was initially set up and shot as a silent film, but the industry's conversion to sound was gathering such momentum that, at an early stage, a decision was taken by the [studio's] management to add some dialogue, in order to make it, like many films of the period, a "part-talkie." Hitchcock, however, had been astute enough to plan ahead in such a way that it was possible, with the help of judicious reshooting and reworking, to produce a version that could be successfully marketed as a "full talkie" with dialogue scenes spread throughout the picture.

Assistant cameraman Ronald Neame (later also a director) has clarified several points about the production of *Blackmail*. "We made the film silent," he recalled in 2003,

> and then in came sound. We didn't want to reshoot the whole picture, just some scenes with important dialogue. We were using arc lights, and the sound people said we couldn't [use them for sound scenes] because they made a loud humming noise. But when we used regular incandescent lights, which were quieter, the camera department said that kind of lighting was not strong enough. There

were many such problems we had to resolve—but the greatest challenge was that we had Anny Ondra's thick accent, and she was supposed to be a Cockney girl, the daughter of a newsagent!

Maxwell was willing to dismiss Anny Ondra and reshoot her scenes with another actress, but to his credit, Hitchcock was adamant that Anny be retained—not only because he liked her and was somewhat bewitched by her, but also because she was a fine and subtle actress.

First, Hitchcock arranged a voice test for her; the sound film of it survives. In it, he stands with her, beneath a hanging microphone.

> HITCHCOCK: Now, Miss Ondra, we are going to do a sound test. Isn't that what you wanted? Now come right over here.
> ONDRA: I don't know what to say. I'm so nervous!
> HITCHCOCK: Have you been a good girl?
> ONDRA [laughing]: Oh, no!
> HITCHCOCK: No? Have you slept with men?
> ONDRA: No!
> HITCHCOCK: *No???*
> ONDRA: Oh, Hitch, you make me embarrassed. [She giggles uncontrollably.]
> HITCHCOCK: Now come right over here, Miss Ondra, and stand still in your place—or it won't come out right, as the girl said to the soldier.

Anny knew that her accent was indeed inappropriate for a London girl, but no one wanted to dismiss her, and so Hitchcock came up with a way out of the problem. The actress Joan Barry was brought in to stand just off-camera, speaking Anny's lines of dialogue into a microphone as Anny silently mouthed them. This had two drawbacks. Joan Barry's diction was too refined for a Cockney character, and there was a series of long, awkward pauses; viewers then and later sensed the off-camera cues.

For all that, *Blackmail* remains a fascinating, complex and disturbing film. The story concerns Alice White (Ondra) and her beau, detective Frank Webber (John Longden). When they quarrel one afternoon at a crowded restaurant, Alice departs on the arm of a handsome artist (Cyril Ritchard). She accepts an invitation to come to his studio, where she agrees to wear a skimpy tutu and to model for him. But he then attempts to make violent love to her, and she seizes a bread knife and stabs him to death. Webber soon suspects the truth, but then a blackmailer enters the story. He had seen Alice entering the artist's flat, and he wants hush money. But the detective implicates the blackmailer in the murder; a chase ensues; and the blackmailer falls through the dome of the British Museum. Alice tries to give herself up—but Webber prevents her. The film ends with Alice's anguish and the couple's shared, secret guilt. In *Blackmail*, as in *The Lodger*, Hitchcock thus explored the perfidy of the officials of law and order—specifically, how they permit passion to corrupt and deflect duty.

Hitchcock remains justly famous for the scene (added to the sound version) in the girl's home, after she has killed the artist. No one is yet aware of her involvement. A nosy neighbor begins to chat about the recent murder nearby. As she rambles on, the camera moves to Ondra's traumatized face, and Hitchcock imaginatively distorts the sound. The audience hears only the subjective impression of what the girl hears, as the neighbor's words blur together until only the word *knife* stabs out at her and at the audience from the sound track:

"What an awful way to kill a man—with a *knife*! Now a good stiff whack over the 'ead with a brick is one thing—

there's something *British* about *that*! But a *knife*? No, *knives* is not right! Now mind you, a *knife* is a difficult thing to handle. Not just any *knife* will do, because with a *knife* . . ."

Then Alice's father asks her to cut some bread, and she distractedly grasps a bread knife while the neighbor drones on: ". . . a *knife* . . . and if you come to Chelsea, you mustn't bring a *knife*!" And with that, the bread knife seems to leap from Alice's hands and fly to the floor. "'Ere!" says her father. "You might've *cut* someone with that!"

From the time of *Downhill*, Hitchcock had known the power of celebrity. Required to film the Underground escalator sequence of that film at night, he had come directly to the station from the theater and was formally dressed in white tie, top hat and tails, an outfit he made certain the media noticed and documented. Now, in *Blackmail*, he devised his most extended cameo appearance. As Ondra and Longden ride in the Underground, a small boy next to them leans over to Hitchcock, playing a passenger trying to read a book. The brat pokes Hitchcock's hat down over his brow, then squirms away. The director pokes him back and then cowers in fear when the boy baits him yet again.

Anny Ondra's career in the British cinema ended with *Blackmail*. She went home to Germany, divorced her husband and married the prizefighter Max Schmeling, with whom she lived happily for fifty-five years, until her death at eighty-five, in 1987. She regularly sent Christmas greetings to the Hitchcocks. "Hitchy, I'm so happy here," she added on the cards.

In 1930, producer John Maxwell at British International Pictures assigned Hitchcock the task of filming another play— Sean O'Casey's *Juno and the Paycock*—but this brought Hitchcock little satisfaction. Nor were the notices flattering:

"Hitchcock has been so faithful to his text as almost to forget the medium in which he was working—it is less a film than a play projected on the screen." And so it was.

His contract with British International, however, eased the pain, for by this time he was England's highest-paid director, with an annual income of at least £65,000 (then about $350,000). The Hitchcocks kept their modest flat in Cromwell Road, but they also purchased a country house called Winter's Grace, at Shamley Green, Guildford.

Blackmail was a huge critical success: "Under Mr. Hitchcock's guidance, the talking film has taken a very definite step forward," wrote one critic; another felt that "Hitchcock's films resemble the more intelligent and conscientious works of detective fiction." *Murder!,* the next picture, was also well received—for the first time, Hitchcock was called a "creative artist who makes films superior in intelligence and style to any from America or Germany."

With no audition and little conversation, Hitchcock chose twenty-three-year-old Norah Baring for the leading role in *Murder!.* "I asked him later if he always picked out his stars with as little ado as he did me," Norah said, "because all he seemed to do when we first met was to play silly jokes—I thought he was having a good laugh at my expense."

"Shows how little you know about it," Hitchcock told her. "You see, there you were. You had the type of face and the personality I had in mind, but you were all tied up with nerves and so tense that at first I hadn't a ghost of an idea whether you would be any use to me at all. I didn't know if you would photograph or record well enough."

"Hitchcock used to make gentle fun of me in the studio," Baring continued. "But I had to do as he wanted simply because he did not allow me to get so strung-up that I could not express the emotions the part required."

Elsie Randolph, engaged to play in *Rich and Strange* the following year, was not the object of any gentle fun. Hitchcock knew that she was allergic to smoke, and one day he summoned her for a scene in a studio telephone call box that property men filled with smoldering steam. "He was a darling," she said years later, "but a darling with a sadistic sense of humor." This was as it had been during production of Galsworthy's *The Skin Game* in late 1930, another filmed play to which Hitchcock was assigned. Playwright Rodney Ackland, a visitor to that production and subsequently a bit player in it, recalled that the director "was engrossed in thinking up wicked practical jokes to play on the more vulnerable artists or on his main butt, one of the property men."

Henry Kendall, the leading man of *Rich and Strange* in 1931, recalled his camera test for the leading role. Instead of directing the actor in a scene from the picture, "the conversation took a very Rabelaisian turn," according to Kendall, "and he kept me in fits of laughter so that I could hardly do more than stand in front of the camera and shake." Joan Barry (the off-camera voice for Anny Ondra in *Blackmail*) was the leading lady in *Rich and Strange;* she never spoke of her experience with the director.

But Jessie Matthews did. In 1933, she was England's most popular musical star, and producer Tom Arnold cast her in his independent production of Hitchcock's *Waltzes from Vienna,* about the Strauss family. Annoyed as much by her preeminence as by her salary in that picture, Hitchcock reduced her scenes whenever he could, moved the camera away from her, interrupted filming with an endless litany of needless corrections and set Matthews on the edge of nervous collapse.

"He sent me up mercilessly," she recalled, "and I was always anticipating some ghastly practical joke he was about to play on me. He was just an imperious young man who knew nothing about musicals. I felt unnerved when he tried to get me to adopt a mincing operetta style. He was out of his depth, and he showed that he knew it by ordering me around. I thought the film was perfectly dreadful." Esmond Knight, co-star to Jessie Matthews in the film, felt "continually on the *qui vive* for some elaborate leg pull at my expense, which automatically produced a feeling of nervousness."

By the end of 1933, Alfred Hitchcock was wealthy and famous—but not happy with his professional prospects. Once again, Michael Balcon came to the rescue, with a deal that gave him extraordinary freedom. His fortunes, and those of British cinema, changed dramatically when he directed *The Man Who Knew Too Much* in 1934. Collaborating with Ivor Montagu, playwright Charles Bennett and no fewer than five additional writers, Hitchcock and company prepared a shooting script about a couple on holiday whose child is kidnapped to prevent them from divulging a plan to assassinate a foreign statesman in London.

The picture opens on the bright ski runs of St. Moritz and concludes on the dark, sloping rooftops of London. In both sequences, the couple's daughter is nearly killed—first by a downhill skier, later by terrorists. Within this framework, her mother (Edna Best) is shown to be a crack shot who loses a match when her daughter (Nova Pilbeam) distracts her. "Let that be a lesson to you," she tells her opponent. "Never have children!" She then turns to her husband (Leslie Banks): "You take this brat—you *would* have this child!" The film concludes when the same challenger turns out to be an assassin—working with the villainous mastermind (Peter Lorre). Mother wins the final "match" and, by sharpshooting with a police rifle, saves the daughter she once casually dismissed.

In this first of Hitchcock's classic spy-chase thrillers, as in all those to come, the international political issue or secret is merely the pretext for exploring personal emotions. Hitchcock refuses to specify a national cause or to identify the nations involved, and so his movies never became obsolete. This plot pretext is what Hitchcock called a "MacGuffin"—what the spies are after, what gets the action going but fades into insignificance for the characters and the audience.

The odd term, Hitchcock always insisted, derived from an anecdote about two men traveling from London to Scotland by train. In the luggage rack overhead is a wrapped package.

"What have you there?"

"Oh, that's a MacGuffin."

"What's a MacGuffin?"

"It's a device for trapping lions in the Scottish Highlands."

"But there are no lions in the Scottish Highlands!"

"Well, then, that's no MacGuffin!"

The point is that a "MacGuffin" is neither relevant nor important, nor finally anyone's business: it simply gets a story going. Hitchcock's classic thrillers take from standard literary melodrama the motif of the secret or the critical documents, scientific formula or papers sought by the heroes. But this device—the thing sought—is utterly unimportant, and finally has no significance for the characters.*

---

* Examples of Hitchcock's MacGuffin: the stolen jewels in *Number Seventeen;* the planned assassination in *The Man Who Knew Too Much;* the design for a new aircraft engine in *The 39 Steps;* the espionage plots in *Secret Agent* and *Sabotage;* the tune containing a diplomatic secret in *The Lady Vanishes;* the secret clause of a treaty in *Foreign Correspondent;* the uranium ore in *Notorious;* the international politics at stake in the remake of *The Man Who Knew Too Much;* the microfilmed secrets in *North by Northwest;* and the secret formula in *Torn Curtain.*

In *The Man Who Knew Too Much,* we're never told just what country is represented by the man targeted for assassination, nor what is at stake, nor for whom the kidnappers work. Topical stories quickly become dated, but Hitchcock knew that tales with a focus on recognizable human feelings were perennials. His concern, therefore, is for the beleaguered family— thus the increasing tenderness between husband and wife.

At the time, leading lady Edna Best was married to stage actor Herbert Marshall, who had been the male lead in *Murder!* and would return even more significantly in *Foreign Correspondent.* Hitchcock was unfailingly courteous to her during production. As for fifteen-year-old Nova Pilbeam, who played the daughter with touching artlessness, Hitchcock said that she "had to be handled diplomatically [because] she lacked experience and her ideas were not always suitable. At the end of the film, when she is reunited with her parents, I made her so terrified by the ordeal that she had been through that she shrank from them," which was certainly an odd way of handling the child "diplomatically."

Once the film was completed, the Hitchcocks directed a less upsetting real-life version of the movie: they took an extended holiday—first stop, St. Moritz, as in the film—and, like the beleaguered but eventually safe family of *The Man Who Knew Too Much,* they brought along their young daughter, Pat.

Chapter Three

THE MASTERY
OF MYSTERY

(1934-1935)

Madeleine Carroll, in *Secret Agent*

From 1925 through 1933, his first nine years as a filmmaker, Alfred Hitchcock directed fifteen finished motion pictures; three of these (*The Lodger, Blackmail* and *Murder!*) could be classified as thrillers, and only one was a "whodunit." He was one of Britain's busiest, wealthiest and most famous directors, eager for the publicity he himself initiated and encouraged, and for the prestige and compensation he believed he earned.

But critics mostly rated Hitch as a formidable director of unimportant pictures—mere entertainments held in low esteem by the guardians of high culture. First for Gainsborough and then for British International, Hitchcock made what were considered skillful diversions for the masses, some of them more successful than others. This subtle condescension began to change when he went over to Balcon's Gaumont-British Studios, Shepherd's Bush, London, to direct *The Man Who Knew Too Much*, released in England at the end of 1934 and in America in early 1935.* The final script of the movie was the work of a

* Michael Balcon's Gainsborough Pictures company had produced or co-produced *The Pleasure Garden, The Mountain Eagle, The Lodger, Downhill* and *Easy Virtue*. Hitchcock then went over to producer John Maxwell at British International Pictures, where he directed *The Ring, The Farmer's Wife, Champagne, The Manxman, Blackmail, Juno and the Paycock, Murder!, The Skin Game, Number Seventeen* and *Rich and Strange*—all at Elstree; *Waltzes from Vienna* was independently produced by Tom Arnold. In 1934, Hitchcock returned to Balcon at Gaumont-British for *The Man Who Knew Too Much, The 39 Steps, Secret Agent* and *Sabotage*, all at the Shepherd's Bush studios. Balcon's Gainsborough Pictures then produced *Young and Innocent* (at Shepherd's Bush and at Pinewood) and *The Lady Vanishes* (at Islington).

committee: no less than seven writers worked on it, among them Charles Bennett.

"I am no longer concerned with cut-and-dried formulae for melodrama," Hitch said at the time. "Formulae were good enough in the old days when every hero had a heart of gold and every villain was a dyed-in-the-wool minister of the devil. A writer of melodrama merely manufactured a group of villains and a clan of heroes, dropped a plumb line between the opposing camps, cemented the action with a train wreck from which the heroine staggered forth somewhat battered, and wrote FINIS while the villain gave his mustachio a final twirl. This was genuinely touching in the age of bustles and knee breeches, but has not the slightest bearing on modern, robust melodrama, which discards highly fictionalized characters and presents instead a large-sized canvas with everyday life-like people on it."

He made these comments just after the wildly successful premiere of *The Man Who Knew Too Much,* which was "glorious melodrama," according to the *Kinematograph Weekly;* other reviews praised the picture's "great thrills, human interest, good work by a sterling cast, and excellent production qualities." An even greater triumph was to come, with *The 39 Steps,* very freely based on John Buchan's 1915 novel *The Thirty-Nine Steps.* With this film, even some serious critics began to take notice, and the Hitchcock blonde was firmly represented by one of the most accomplished, popular and strikingly beautiful women of the time—Madeleine Carroll.

"I had wanted to turn John Buchan's novel into a film for over fifteen years," Hitchcock said. "I first read the book round about 1919 or 1920, and when I read it again in late 1934, I received a shock: I found that the story as it stood was not in the least suitable" for a movie. To make it so, he turned again to Bennett for collaboration.

Eleven days older than Hitchcock, Charles Bennett had fought in the Great War as a teenager, had dabbled in espionage and had acted in plays and movies before turning to playwriting. He and Hitchcock were good partners at spinning ideas and mixing potent drinks, and they both saw the value in telling stories about ordinary people suddenly caught in extraordinary circumstances. Most of all, they wanted to avoid a tone of turgid gravity and to find the rich, ironic humor in each sequence they created. With *The 39 Steps,* they succeeded admirably, and the result was a film that survives its era and style and remains supremely entertaining.

Hitchcock and Bennett both admired the Buchan novel, but they agreed that it lacked humor, strong characters and most of all a woman for the romantic angle. There is actually a climb of thirty-nine steps in Buchan's novel, leading to a nest of spies. But as Hitchcock, Bennett, Alma and dialogue-writer Ian Hay worked on the narrative treatment for a movie, everyone agreed that the "steps" should merely refer to an organization of spies working on behalf of an unidentified country. And, they asked each other, what was at stake, what was the secret? Oh, they decided airily—merely some secret formula for the design of British fighter planes. But none of that was important: the hero's relationship to a beautiful blonde—that's what mattered. The dominant issue was to be one of trust between a man and a woman, highlighted throughout the story by contrasting sets of couples on whom the action hinges structurally: a hypocritically pious Scotsman and his benighted younger spouse; a kindly innkeeping couple; and the gentlemanly villain and his aristocratic wife.

"You owe everything to me," Hitchcock wrote to Bennett some years later—which led to Bennett's reaction:

"Everything? Hardly! By the time of *The Man Who Knew Too Much*, I had staged seven plays and directed five, written more than fifteen films and had succeeded as an actor. Arguably, Hitch owed me! My Shakespearean experience and sense of melodrama built his reputation for suspense; my play *Blackmail* was his first talkie. My story 'The Man Who Knew Too Much' launched his international reputation, and my construction of *The 39 Steps* put him out front by inventing motifs he would use in subsequent films.

"But Hitch would not acknowledge it. It always had to be Hitch! He would not acknowledge any writer. This was a very ungenerous character flaw, actually, as Hitch was totally incapable of creating or developing a story. Without me, there wouldn't have been any story. Hitchcock was never a constructionist, never a storyteller. I would take a story and turn it into something good. After that, Hitch and I would turn it into a screenplay, and then, as often as not, we'd call in certain people to write the dialogue for it. So we were a writer-director partnership, but his vanity could not credit his writers. He could give credit to no one but himself." Bennett, who collaborated on six films with Hitchcock, observed that he "had a monstrous ego that matched his appetite."

Hitch could certainly take credit for his visual inventiveness, and for his brilliance in adding to a script precisely the right images, the proper tone and atmosphere. But screenwriters from Bennett in the 1930s to Ben Hecht in the 1940s, Samuel Taylor and Ernest Lehman in the 1950s and Evan Hunter in the 1960s all quickly realized that this director's gift was not for writing dialogue but for minimizing it and allowing action and reaction, gaze and glance, to tell stories. Perhaps because he wanted to write the script entirely on his own but could not, he often resented his writers, who quickly knew not to expect gratifying compliments.

As The 39 Steps was being developed, Hitchcock required a personal assistant to read and summarize stories and to help with the many daily details in a busy production office. His choice fell on an educated, attractive twenty-eight-year-old blonde named Joan Harrison. Unmarried and a university graduate in literature, Joan quickly advanced from secretary to continuity supervisor to script consultant to dialogue writer. From 1939 to 1941, she received co-screenwriting credit on five Hitchcock films (*Jamaica Inn, Rebecca, Foreign Correspondent, Suspicion* and *Saboteur*), and she later returned as a producer of his television shows. Hitchcock and Alma valued her intelligence and, perhaps most of all, her discreet loyalty.

The 39 Steps tells of Richard Hannay (played by Robert Donat), a Canadian on holiday in London, who must establish his innocence of the stabbing murder of a mysterious brunette spy (Lucie Mannheim) and also prevent a critical national secret from passing out of the country and over to the enemy. In this, Hannay is at first hindered and betrayed, and finally helped, by a blonde (Madeleine Carroll), to whom he is handcuffed for a major portion of the action.

"He is blazingly ambitious," Hitchcock said of Donat, "a queer combination of determination and uncertainty. He is determined to do only pictures that satisfy him"—to which one might reply, "Indeed, and why not?"

As for Madeleine Carroll, Hitchcock was forthright. She had not been his first choice, she does not appear until well into the story, and there are long episodes from which she is absent. Nevertheless, the actress accepted the offer for several reasons. First, she had known Hitchcock when they were working on separate projects at British International in 1928. He was polite and respectful, and she liked his fresh ideas for storytelling. In addition, her agents negotiated a very lucrative deal with Michael Balcon for her to appear in two Hitchcock pictures that year. At the time, she was one of the highest paid performers in the world—hence valuable as a star.

Edith Madeleine Carroll was born on February 26, 1906, in West Bromwich, five miles northwest of Birmingham. Her Irish father was a language professor at the university there, and her mother was French. Raised in a bilingual household, she was encouraged to become a French teacher, took a degree with honors and then continued her studies at the Sorbonne. But Madeleine had acting ambitions, as she always confided to her closest confidante—her adored younger sister, Marguerite.

Her father, however, brooked no opposition to his professional plans for her, and when she announced that she wanted a theatrical career, he dismissed her from the house and refused to support her. At first, she took tutoring jobs while seeking work as an actress. Her film career, which began with silent films, owed a great deal to her striking glamour. She projected a rare aristocratic allure, a kind of unstuffy elegance and a restraint that attracted men and commanded the respect, if not the downright envy, of women. Directors such as Cecil B. DeMille, Lewis Milestone, Anatole Litvak, Victor Saville and John Ford adored working with her, as did actors Gary Cooper, Brian Aherne, Ronald Colman, Henry Fonda and Tyrone Power. Off-screen, her many suitors included Randolph Churchill (son of Winston).

"She is both beautiful and convincing. Her performances are full of life, sympathy and perception. She is simply radiant." So ran the typical press comments, and there was no argument. From her first appearances on stage and screen, audiences, critics and the general public who saw her photographs and the increasingly popular movies she made in England, France and

America agreed that Madeleine Carroll was one of the most exquisite women in the world.

If that was hyperbolic language, it was also difficult to counter. Journalists ransacked their vocabularies to describe her expressive, dazzling blue eyes and flawless complexion, her calmly sensual gaze and splendidly enigmatic smile. She had a rare photogenic glow, but she also had genuine talent and a lively intelligence. By 1934, when she was twenty-eight, Madeleine Carroll had appeared in a dozen plays in England and thirty-seven movies. Hollywood quickly took note, and soon she was working frequently in American studios. Her appearance in two spy melodramas inspired Hitchcock and Balcon to engage her for *The 39 Steps* and *Secret Agent,* a pair of espionage thrillers made back-to-back in 1935; both projects capitalized on her natural charm and unaffected glamour. Within two years, she was receiving more than $250,000 per picture.

"There has been a great deal of controversy over my handling of Madeleine Carroll," Hitchcock told an interviewer after he had completed two films with her. Fearful that she was going to act the spoiled celebrity when she arrived for *The 39 Steps,* he insisted that she submit herself to the uncomfortable demands of the script—especially the long sequences in which she would be painfully handcuffed to Donat.

On the first day of filming, in late January 1935, Hitchcock introduced his two stars to each other and tried to put them at ease with his usual blue humor. They should address him by his famous nickname, he said—"Hitch, without the cock." The director then set up the first sequence, in which the couple, manacled to each other, flees across the Scottish countryside. He snapped the handcuffs onto their wrists (shades of *The Lodger*), led them through a rehearsal over the dummy bridge and over fences—and then he announced that some technical problem required his attention and that they could take a tea break. Where was the key to the handcuffs? Oh, dear, he seemed to have mislaid it. "There they were," he said later, "inextricably bound—and they couldn't get away from one another until I 'found' it again." And with that, he vanished, while his crew wasted no time photographing several insert shots.

"Madeleine and I shared this enforced companionship while the hunt for the key was sustained," recalled Robert Donat. John Russell Taylor, Hitchcock's authorized biographer (writing while the director was living) states that Hitchcock took "a gleeful delight in devising indignities for Madeleine Carroll to undergo."

Eventually, Hitchcock retrieved the key, which had been deposited with a studio guard. The two actors were weary, disheveled, uncomfortable and acutely embarrassed. Donat recalled that they coped as best they could: "There was nothing else to do, so we talked of our mutual friends, of our ambitions, and of film matters generally. Gradually, our reserve thawed as we exchanged experiences. When Hitch saw that we were getting along famously, he extracted the 'missing' key from his waistcoat pocket, released us, and said with a satisfied grin, 'Now that you two know each other, we can go ahead.' "

That was not the only day of "enforced companionship" in handcuffs. "It would be hard to estimate the number of hours we were handcuffed together in the studio," Donat continued. "Shackled to me, she was dragged along roads, through ravines and across moors; humiliations were heaped upon her. Naturally, we had to play these scenes with realism: the weals and bruises which the handcuffs made on her delicate wrists were ample proofs of that—but I never heard her utter one word of complaint."

"What interests me," Hitchcock said, "is the drama of being handcuffed. There's a special terror, a sort of 'thing' about being tied up. In *The 39 Steps,* of course, it was fundamental." One Hitchcock chronicler further quotes him to the effect that handcuffs "bring out all kinds of thoughts in [the audience's] minds—for example, how do they go to the toilet was one natural, obvious question. And the linking together relates more to sex than anything else." There is something more than merely playful about this sort of thing.

"There was no better technician in the business," said Jack Whitehead, second-unit cameraman on the picture, "but when it came to personal relations, there was certainly a streak of the sadist in him." Years later, Ivor Montagu addressed the matter delicately: "It had long been my conviction, sustained by working with Hitchcock, that a good director must have something of the sadist in him. I do not necessarily mean to a pathological degree, but that his looking at things and telling characters to do this, undergo that, is necessarily akin to dominating them, ordering them about." Hitchcock himself was frank: "I sometimes wonder whether I am not—as all my friends insist—a sadist."

As for Madeleine Carroll, "she entered into the spirit of the whole thing with zest," Hitchcock said, "and I was determined not to let up at all. Dignity or self-consciousness is impossible when you're being dragged along the ground, which I made Donat do to her." When Hitchcock was ready for her, he'd call out, "Bring on the Birmingham tart!" He was "dead set on making every assault on her dignity he could—to prepare her for her on-screen indignities."

Madeleine Carroll made no noisy objection, but privately she was weary, confused and angry about the demands placed on her. (When her friend Randolph Churchill visited the set one day, he reproached Hitchcock for the rough handling of her. "I just gave him a look and then went on with the job," Hitchcock said later.) Over several days, she was dragged along in handcuffs, pushed under a waterfall, over a stream and through fences until her hair and clothes were ruined and her wrists bruised. "The roughness of the scenes was meant to strip Carroll of her poise and dignity," as one critic wrote, echoing Hitchcock's calm self-defense.

Hitch did have an ally in Ivor Montagu: "We deliberately wrote the script to include her undignified handcuff scene on the bed, and being led out from under the waterfall looking like a drowned rat. But Madeleine was a trouper and turned the tables on us by appreciating this treatment and asking for more." It must be pointed out, however, that Montagu, as associate producer, was alone in asserting her compliance: as he said, his job was to be "the defender of the director's needs [and] to act as cushion between company and creator."

To achieve his goal—to ensure that Madeleine Carroll would "enter into the spirit of the whole thing with zest"— Hitchcock actually went too far. For one scene (as she confided to her friend, the actress Googie Withers), Hitchcock wanted her to express shock. After several takes, Madeleine had still not given him what he seemed to want. "We'll do it one more time," he said, and consulted quietly with the cameraman. Hitch then went back to Carroll, who was the only one who could see that he had unbuttoned his trousers as if to expose himself to her. This produced the desired reaction. Odd though it may seem, very few actors expressed their resentment of Hitchcock's methods: his films, after all, were usually good for their careers.

"Nothing pleases me more than to knock the ladylikeness out of them," he said when filming was completed. "I don't exactly hate women, but I certainly don't think they are as good as men actors. I try to make a woman human by making her appear in awkward and comic situations and taking away her glamour." But with Donat, as with almost every one of his leading men, he plied no practical jokes or rude tactics.

Hitchcock's attitude toward and treatment of Madeleine Carroll, and of others later, must not be minimized or justified by the demands of filmmaking; indeed, one must ask the basis for these expressions of frank misogyny. Some colleagues and writers have located this kind of conduct in a deep resentment of women that sprang from Hitchcock's sexual deficiency. He "was sexually impotent," according to a recent biographer, citing Hitchcock's obesity and quoting the writer Jay Presson Allen, who wrote the final screenplay for *Marnie* in 1963. "I know that Hitch was functionally impotent because of everything he said to me," according to Allen. Hitchcock's own testimony was that he had sexual intercourse but once in his life, as he told Joseph Stefano in 1959, while they were working on the screenplay for *Psycho*: that unique occasion resulted in his daughter's conception, in 1927. "I did it with a fountain pen," the director said with a straight face.

The 39 Steps was hailed—then, as later—as a hugely enjoyable comic thriller, and even before it was released, Hitchcock, Bennett and Hay were busy on their next production for Balcon. Based on short stories by Somerset Maugham, it would be the third consecutive Hitchcock movie about spies, but more serious than its predecessors. *Secret Agent* (not *The Secret Agent*, as it is usually misidentified) is also Hitchcock's most overtly moral fable up to that time: it denounces killing as politically expedient and insists on the ethical bankruptcy of the espionage enterprise.

Thanks to her contract with Balcon, Madeleine Carroll was

ready for the early autumn filming. Her first appearance in the picture continued the deglamourization process now dear to Hitchcock's heart. In *The 39 Steps,* she is first seen wearing unflattering eyeglasses (which fall to the ground when she is kissed and are never seen again); in *Secret Agent,* she is first shown wrapped in a formless, long bath towel, cold cream splattered on her face and a makeup cap on her head. For all that, she was still luminously, irreparably beautiful.

Hitchcock had hoped to engage Robert Donat again, too, but the actor did not want to be typed as the leading man of thrillers and had gone to work for director René Clair in the comedy *The Ghost Goes West.* John Gielgud inherited the leading male role after Hitchcock said that the character was rather like a modern-day Hamlet, forced to make difficult decisions. With that, Gielgud accepted, even though this meant an exhausting schedule, for he was acting onstage every night in *Romeo and Juliet.* Alas, his role was reduced during production, and what remained was often overwhelmed by the crazy antics of Peter Lorre, whom Hitchcock brought back after *The Man Who Knew Too Much.* "Lorre was a great scene-stealer," Gielgud recalled. "He had all sort of tricks, like adding an extra line when it came to the take, or he'd move an inch and I realized I'd been upstaged by a very clever actor." To make matters worse, Lorre was a morphine addict who constantly upset the production by stepping off the set to administer his injections.

Madeleine's role was far more significant than that in *The 39 Steps.* Her character initially sees the business of spying as "something worthwhile—a thrill, excitement, a big risk, danger!" She's almost aroused by the thought of mayhem and outspoken in her anger when denied the opportunity to assist in the killing of a spy who turns out to be not a spy at all but an innocent Englishman abroad. "It's murder, and you call it fun," says Gielgud. But when she learns that they have all engineered the death of the wrong man—and that the real villain is the charming suitor played by the American actor Robert Young—she has a crisis of conscience that is at the heart of the movie.

"Madeleine Carroll was charming and we got on very well," Gielgud continued. "She was a big star, but Hitchcock was beastly to her. He was a very coarse man, fond of making dirty jokes all the time." Devoted to Carroll one moment, almost cruelly contemptuous the next, Hitchcock kept her ever on the alert. This was the first sign of a trait that marked his dealings with several actresses later: attraction and repulsion, the almost idolatrous gaze of his camera and the concomitant compulsion to tear her apart. This bifurcated attitude marked the psychological climate of his most mature films, and it was, in real life, the emotionally schizoid pattern that caused him and some of the women considerable pain during their work together.

That year, Hitchcock was at his heaviest—over three hundred pounds—and his lumbering discomfort must have augmented feelings of unattractiveness and social ineptitude, perhaps even with the concomitant envy of other people's active sexual lives, of which he felt deprived. His neatness, authority and unblinking intelligence scarcely ameliorated the sight of him as a grotesquely misshapen man, and his sudden lapses into moody silence and his inability to praise or thank anyone publicly frequently characterized him as an enigmatic and ungracious boss.

To make things even less predictable, Hitchcock was capable of surprising acts of kindness—a case of wine would arrive at a crew member's door on his birthday, or a colleague's mother would receive a lavish floral tribute on her birthday.

The train crash finale of *Secret Agent* imposed considerable discomfort on the players, but Madeleine Carroll sustained everyone's spirits during multiple retakes. According to Gielgud, she behaved magnificently, never caused a ruction, never complained; it should be added, however, that she never spoke on the record about her year's work with Alfred Hitchcock.

Seen decades later, the picture has a freshness that was much ignored at the time. Perhaps because it defied the contemporary assumptions about what constitutes patriotism and heroism, and because it condemned the nefarious nature of espionage, *Secret Agent* was unfortunately discounted as both unfashionable and insignificant.

Nowhere in his book-length interviews with Truffaut did Hitchcock mention the name of Madeleine Carroll. She was a fine and energetic actress—and a remarkable woman who gave the director two memorable performances that burnished his career and hers. She also possessed an inner strength and a depth of values of which he was perhaps not entirely aware. Because her life post-Hitchcock was not only dramatic but also heroic, it is worth summarizing, for her later years best define the woman behind the celebrated beauty.

From 1936 to 1939, Madeleine continued to work in London and Hollywood, appearing most memorably in *The General Died at Dawn* (with Gary Cooper), *Lloyd's of London* (with Tyrone Power), *The Prisoner of Zenda* (with Ronald Colman) and *Blockade* (with Henry Fonda). At Christmas 1939, her eight-year marriage to the wealthy, attractive and urbane Capt. Philip Astley was dissolved. Randolph Churchill, although married, apparently popped up again in early 1940, but his pursuit of her was futile.

That spring she was scheduled to appear in a Paramount picture called *Virginia,* delayed several times due to script and casting problems. With permission from the studio, she took a month's leave and headed for Europe in early June, intending to visit her parents in England, and the fifty war orphans to whom she had turned over her home, a chateau at Saudreville, near

Paris. She also hoped to find her fiancé, the dashing lieutenant Richard de la Rozière, who had recently gone missing in the early days of the French stand against Germany.

But in none of these aspirations was Madeleine successful, for her journey coincided with Hitler's incursion into France, and severe restrictions were put on any travel by British nationals. On June 13, 1940, she fled from Paris—there were rumors that de la Rozière was near the Spanish border—and the next morning, she arrived at the strategically significant town of Hendaye, the most southwesterly town in France, within walking distance to Spain. At that very hour, the Germans entered Paris.

There was no sign of the lieutenant in Hendaye, and Madeleine proceeded to the home of some cousins in Biarritz, fifteen miles north. There, on June 16, there was loud commotion, as all British citizens in the region were to report to Bordeaux for evacuation to England, under threat of imprisonment. One evacuation ship had already been bombed, and there were reports that many Britons were being taken for interrogation or worse. "I knew that if I went to England, I wouldn't have a chance of getting back to America," Madeleine said days later, "and I had given my word of honor [to Paramount] to take the July 10th Clipper and return to my work."

Clutching her passport and a small valise, and hoping somehow to find her way back to the United States via Spain, Madeleine drove to Madrid alone, in her family's old, cranky automobile. There, American embassy officials could discover nothing of her parents in England or of the war orphans outside Paris, but they were able to tell Madeleine that de la Rozière was safe on duty in Tunisia with a small platoon of Free French soldiers. When the diplomats undiplomatically inquired if the film star intended to marry the lieutenant when the war ended, she replied, "Who knows if any of us is going to be alive even in a month or so?" At this point, Richard de la Rozière vanishes from Madeleine Carroll's biography.

At eleven o'clock on the morning of July 11, she arrived at LaGuardia Field, New York, aboard the Pan Am Atlantic Clipper. In service only a year, this was a legendary airship whose sumptuous accommodations included a dining room where five-course meals were served on antique china, elaborate bars and lounges, private sleeping quarters and a crew of sixteen to serve the seventeen passengers who paid the equivalent of $4,000 for one-way passage. Until the Clippers were requisitioned later in wartime, they were the most luxurious means of air travel in history.

Among Madeleine's fellow travelers on the thirty-hour flight were Archduke Otto of Hapsburg, pretender to the nonexistent Austro-Hungarian throne; Ralph Paine, European managing director of the *Time-Life-Fortune* magazine corporation; and Andrew Heiskell, a writer and editor then attached to *Time*'s Paris bureau. Heiskell thought Madeleine was "the most glamorous woman I have ever met. She was wearing a blue hat, not very broad-brimmed, and a blue suit with a white blouse. She had soft blond hair, large blue eyes and classic features. She was thirty-five, ten years older than I, but there was an instantaneous flash of something between us."

Heiskell recalled that he and Madeleine "spent the entire flight talking to each other, mostly in French, which she spoke as perfectly as she did English. We ate all our meals together, had our wine and champagne together." When they landed in New York, the actress and the writer promised to stay in touch, but travelers who meet on journeys routinely say such things. Heiskell went home to his wife and children, and Madeleine proceeded to her movie assignment and her co-star, a yachtsman who was making his motion picture debut.

At six feet five with a thick crop of unruly golden hair, Sterling Hayden was touted by Paramount publicists as "The Most Beautiful Man in the Movies" and "The Beautiful Blond Viking God." He hated the hype as much as the work, which he accepted only to pay for his beloved boats and schooners. Like Heiskell, he was a full ten years younger than Madeleine, but he was unmarried. He and Madeleine were wed in 1942, but their wartime service forestalled any reasonable facsimile of a solid marriage: their time together was infrequent, and they divorced amicably in 1946.

Just as *Virginia* was completed that autumn of 1940, the Germans began massive air raid attacks on London, Southampton, Bristol, Cardiff, Liverpool and Manchester. And then Madeleine, who had been hoping for a holiday, received tragic news on October 7. Of this she gave a calm account in fluent French on the Canadian Broadcasting Corporation, hoping that her family in England would hear her statement:

I knew a young Englishwoman—like so many others, she was pretty, fond of laughter and a good comrade. When war came, she wanted to do her share. She was made to understand that she was performing a great service by remaining at her post—continuing, by her good humour and her unswerving faith in the victory of our arms, to sustain the morale of her associates.

So she remained at her work in a London store. Then came the big air raids. Ever smiling, ever confident, she went on doing her daily task. She was the first to jest after a bomb exploded close by. It was to her that her companions turned for comfort when they were in trouble. And when people congratulated her on her devotion to work and her pluck in braving the perils of this war that civilians must face just as the armed forces do, she answered, "Our airmen and sailors are doing much more, and the Germans would be delighted if they frightened us!"

She was not at all heroic, but she gave an example of the attitude to take in this struggle for our survival—a struggle in which only the courage to hold out and the will to win will assure us of victory. This girl was killed recently by a German bomb. She was my sister.

Madeleine at once decided to become directly involved in the war effort. Without detriment to her performances, she hurried through three contracted movie projects—one of them with Hayden, who volunteered for service with the Marines before Pearl Harbor and quickly rose to the rank of lieutenant. From the end of 1940 and throughout 1941, she repeatedly asked the War Department for volunteer assignments abroad, anywhere and at any peril. "In my French home at Saudreville, outside Paris, I am now sheltering two hundred homeless children," she said in her petition. "And when the war is over, it is to them and them alone that I will devote myself."

After working without compensation for the United Seamans Service Club in New York, she was permitted to train in Washington as a hospital staff aide for the Red Cross. She served in the Sixty-first Field Hospital in Bari, Italy, where she tended countless wounded men and, according to her companions, thought little of working twenty-hour days. Equally hazardous were her several return trips by ship to America, where she raised money for the Red Cross and taught schoolgirls to knit clothing for deprived European children and soldiers. At no time was she permitted to visit her family in England nor even to put through a telephone call to them.

Throughout the years of her service, Madeleine refused all

personal publicity and worked under a pseudonym. When soldiers recognized her and asked (as they often did) if she was really Madeleine Carroll, she replied, "Don't be silly. What do you think Madeleine Carroll would be doing here?"

For her outstanding humanitarian work, France awarded her the Legion of Honor in 1946; she also received the Medal of Freedom from the United States government. In 1951, still dedicated to the plight of war orphans and working full time as a volunteer for UNESCO, she received the Brotherhood Award from the National Conference of Christians and Jews. "Representatives of the three great faiths, working side by side on problems of social and civic concern," she said, accepting the award, "can and will free the world of bitterness and resentment. In the struggle for freedom, at home and abroad, our greatest weapon is our love of and faith in God."

She made her last film in 1948, when she was forty-two, and then she appeared once on Broadway (in Fay Kanin's play *Goodbye, My Fancy*). In 1950, she married the man who had been her companion a decade earlier on the Clipper flight, Andrew Heiskell, by then the publisher of *Life* magazine. She retired but for a few infrequent television and radio appearances, and she and Heiskell had a daughter, Anna Madeleine. Her marriage was dissolved in 1965, when she was fifty-nine. She never married again and devoted herself to good causes and to her daughter—who, alas, died of drug addiction at the age of thirty-three.

Madeleine Carroll then moved to Paris and finally to Marbella. She invariably refused requests for interviews and worked tirelessly for the poverty-stricken children of the world until her death, at eighty-one, in 1987. Asked how she felt about her movie career, she once said, "Let's say I got out while the going was good!" Despite the mixed memories she certainly must have sustained of her year with Hitchcock, the fact is that over a long career including forty-two movies, she is best remembered for *The 39 Steps*. Madeleine Carroll then found her fulfillment in neither fame nor wealth, but in her dedication to the needs of the wounded, the sick and the orphans of war.

Chapter Four

SHAKING
THE DUST
(1936-1938)

With Margaret Lockwood, in *The Lady Vanishes*

In 1936, Michael Balcon approved Hitchcock's request, endorsed by Ivor Montagu and Charles Bennett, that the project to follow *Secret Agent* should be a film based on Joseph Conrad's novel *The Secret Agent,* whose movie title, for obvious reasons, would have to be changed. When filming began in the spring of 1936, after three more writers contributed dialogue, they finally settled on *Sabotage;* still, the script was incomplete, and Hitchcock and his collaborators made significant decisions during production.

"I discovered while I was in Hollywood that Miss Sylvia Sidney was available for one picture in England," Balcon recalled. "I should have been a fool if I let slip the opportunity of signing up such a brilliant actress." Accomplished on the stage, the twenty-five-year-old (credited as Sylvia Sydney in *Sabotage*) had appeared in twenty films and had just co-starred with Spencer Tracy in Fritz Lang's powerful drama *Fury.* Under contract to Paramount, she was earning just under $10,000 weekly, or about $60,000 per picture. Her Hitchcock co-stars were John Loder, Oskar Homolka and seventeen-year-old Desmond Tester, who looked much younger, as the story required.

Sabotage tells the powerful story of a terrorist (Homolka) who is married to an innocent American (Sidney). He manages the Bijou movie theater, which he uses as a front for meetings with foreign spies and for the planning of violence. At the outset we see that he has sabotaged a London power plant; his next assignment is to deliver a film canister that contains a time bomb set to detonate and cause death and destruction in Piccadilly Circus. He asks his wife's brother (Tester) to deliver the package, but the boy is killed when the bomb explodes in a crowded bus. When she learns the truth, she is traumatized with shock and rage, and as she prepares dinner for her husband, he seems almost deliberately to step toward her outstretched carving knife and falls dead. Full of remorse, she longs to tell the police, but the local detective (Loder), who is in love with her, prevents her from divulging her conscience and takes her away after another terrorist bomb destroys the cinema and her husband's remains with it.

Perhaps the most brilliant and provocative change Hitchcock and his writers made from the Conrad novel was the alteration of the setting—from a corner shop to a cinema. This gave Hitchcock an opportunity to reflect on the nature of film-watching itself, since most of the action occurs in front of or behind the movie screen of the Bijou.

At the structural center of the film are two motifs. First, there is the use of Hitchcock's ubiquitous birds: "The birds will sing on Saturday at one-forty-five" refers to the time of the planned bombing, and the boy is urged to "kill two birds with one stone." In addition, the bomb maker uses his bird shop as a cover for terrorist activities. The bird imagery then comes full circle in the inspired use of the Disney cartoon *Who Killed Cock Robin?* in the Bijou cinema, which links to the second motif: things are always happening "behind the screen," as the characters say. With its economic pacing, sustained images and darkly important themes, *Sabotage* may be Hitchcock's profoundest (if not his most popular) British film.

With this movie, birds became Hitchcock's most frequently used visual marker of danger and chaos. From early medieval times, birds in art had been representations of ill luck (predatory owls devouring at night, for example), and this Hitchcock knew from his art study classes; furthermore, they became symbols of evil in late Victorian poetry. During his student days, bird-watching and the meticulous identification of various avian species were a popular British national pastime, part of the country gentleman's training he received at school.

One of the most famous late Victorian paintings studied by students synthesized the connection between birds and unpredictable eruptions of chaos. In Edward Burne-Jones's *Love and the Pilgrim* (painted 1896–1897), Love is depicted as a garlanded angel with a spear—a kind of giant "lovebird"—inviting a dark-robed pilgrim who emerges from a thicket to take the angel's hand and to follow. The country journey ahead shows thorns and brambles, and there are numerous small birds in the thicket left behind, as well as a large flock overhead, prevented from attacking only because of Love's protecting wings. This complex of ideas informs the Hitchcock catalogue from *Sabotage* through to *The Birds* (a film that completes all the bird imagery of *Psycho,* which precedes it).

"On the set [of the picture], he's a sadist," wrote C. A. Lejeune, one of the few English critics Hitchcock invited to watch him at work. "His language is fierce, and his humour rarely drawing-room. He respects nobody's feelings, but everybody respects him." Her assessment of the director was apparently based on visits during which Hitchcock was particularly hard on Sylvia Sidney and Desmond Tester (whom the director openly addressed as "Testicle").

Hitchcock had approved of Balcon's imported American star, who was well known for her portraits of suffering women: "Paramount paid me by the tear," Sylvia once joked. The false assumption that she was indeed a masochist led him to discount her questions and to reject her ideas, and he did so harshly; what better treatment to extend to a suffering servant?

"Hitch had called her and courted her for the picture," according to Bennett, "and then when she arrived, he virtually ignored her. I think she just wasn't his type. I thought she was very good. But Hitch was Hitch with her—tough to love and easy to hate." And because the director could not be bothered to explain to his star his intention in breaking up long scenes into separate closeup shots, he found her, one day, sobbing in confusion.

"Hitchcock was very strange to be with," Sylvia said years later. "He made it clear that he resented my salary, which was higher than his. I learned that he had a thing about money, and that he felt actors were all paid too much. I had to admit, when I saw the rough cut of the picture, that *Sabotage* was brilliant. What did he teach me? To be a puppet, and not to try to be creative. But at the time, I really took exception to that." Hitchcock's brief comment years later was that "she had nice understatement."

After the dark gravity of *Sabotage,* Hitchcock lightened the tone in his next picture, *Young and Innocent,* made during the spring of 1937 and freely based on Josephine Tey's novel *A Shilling for Candles.* Hitchcock and his writers completely altered the story, making a young couple the film's major characters and reducing the detective to virtual nonexistence.

The movie plot repeated Hitchcock's device of an innocent man wrongly accused, which had been so popular in *The 39 Steps* (and was later exploited in *Saboteur, Spellbound, To Catch a Thief, The Wrong Man, North by Northwest* and *Frenzy*). In this case, Derrick De Marney played the man presumed guilty of the murder of an actress who had given him money. He eludes the police with the help of the constable's daughter (Nova Pilbeam), and together they track down the real killer, a jazz drummer with a nervous twitch to his eyes.

At fifteen, Nova had done well for Hitchcock in *The Man Who Knew Too Much;* ripened now to eighteen, she had had considerable stage experience and was a much-admired actress. Her role demanded a complex of emotions, as the girl changes from feeling moral outrage against the apparent killer, to being forced to assist him, to being convinced of his innocence, to helping him clear his name.

Young and Innocent is a movie of singular mildness, benevolence, humor and charm, with the added Hitchcockian motifs of playacting and disguise. The screenwriter-hero filches identity-concealing eyeglasses to make his escape; a tramp disguises himself as a dandy to help smoke out the villain, who wears blackface to play in a band. To top it all off, Hitchcock makes a hilarious cameo appearance as a photographer, holding a tiny camera in front of his huge torso, trying vainly to get a snapshot of the commotion outside a courthouse. Everyone in *Young and Innocent* deals in illusions, and at the center of the film is the justly famous birthday party, in which children play a game of blind man's bluff—a sequence the director called an obvious symbol for the picture's theme of the quality of vision, of seeing and not seeing.

Hitchcock was enormously fond and almost paternally protective of Nova Pilbeam, but this did not short-circuit what she called his "really wicked wit." De Marney agreed: Hitchcock had a sharp tongue, much to the distress of his actors. His aim, De Marney reckoned, was to strip them of their poses, "and he finds he can do this best by infuriating them." But Hitchcock was curiously tender and patient with Nova. "He was deferential to her, both on and off the set," De Marney added; otherwise, "he spared no one"—not De Marney, and not Mary Clare (as Nova's aunt), both of whom heard Hitchcock's loudly proclaimed sarcastic comments about their performances.

One difficult and dangerous sequence stayed in Nova's memory over the years. Taking refuge from the police in an abandoned mineshaft, she and her young man are almost lost when the floor of the cave collapses. In the largest stage at Pinewood Studios, Hitchcock supervised the building of a set fifteen feet off the ground, enabling him to film a car just before its crash. Nova Pilbeam then struggled to reach Derrick De Marney's outstretched fingers (precisely the setup of the final clinging and reaching later in *Saboteur* and *North by Northwest*). The critics liked the picture and loved Nova: "She imparts sincerity to every gesture, and at the same time invests the stormy love interest with adolescent charm. This is a charming portrayal of innocent girlhood."

Hitchcock's assistant director on *Young and Innocent,* as on his previous four pictures, was young Penrose Tennyson, great-grandson of the Victorian poet. For the mineshaft scene, no doubles were used, as Nova recalled: "I did that, and it was my husband-to-be, Pen, who held me up as I dangled there. I was terrified! But Hitch had this quirky sense of humor, and he made the scene go on and on, so that I thought my arm would come out of its socket."

In 1939, Nova Pilbeam and Pen Tennyson were married. Two years later, he was flying for the admiralty's Educational Film Unit during World War II when his small plane crashed. "Had my husband not been killed, I suspect I might have stayed in the business of filming." But after a few more movies, she retired; a decade later, she married again, and in 1972, she was widowed a second time. As of 2008, she had not appeared in a film in more than sixty years and was living quietly in North London. "Her name, her beauty and her talent remain in the annals and the memory," as one film historian has rightly stated.

If Hitchcock's behavior toward Nova Pilbeam had an element of benign paternalism, his relationship with his real-life daughter, Patricia—who marked her ninth birthday in July 1937—was rather more complicated.

By this time, she was away at boarding school, where she studied and lived for two years. "It's what people did at that time," she said in 1999, but she seems not to have been very happy: "I would never send my own daughters to boarding school. I've never understood this thing with the English sending their children away. They should be absolutely shot for sending children away at that age. Well, that's the English— that's what they do."

At the Hitchcocks' country house in Shamley Green, visitors such as Elsie Randolph recalled, "There was a strange formality when Pat was home for the occasional weekend or on holiday. She had to sit alone at her own little table in the kitchen while the adults dined in grand style, and her father insisted that she curtsy and be very proper with the guests. For all that, she seemed a happy, polite child." Pat's happy memories of her childhood, however infrequently expressed, do not seem to have been unalloyed. "I never go back to England, not unless I have to," she said years later.

Did she have any happy memories of her life in England? "I don't think there's any particular thing that stands out at all," she said in 2005. There was no mention of friends, of visitors to the Hitchcock home, of travels. As she spoke to an interviewer of the early days, her life sounded thumpingly dull—nothing stands out at all. And what of her father? Only this: "He had a great sense of humor, and he said that if you couldn't look at life with a sense of humor, then you were in a lot of trouble. I inherited a sense of humor. We were a very close family." Did anything else come to mind? "My father did a lot of reading, and my parents gave me a toy kitchen set as a gift, and I served cake around to them, several friends and family." Did she ever watch her father's home movie of this, which has been preserved? "No."

After the deaths of her father and mother, Pat Hitchcock took her place among the flame-keepers. Guardian of the Hitchcock legacy and a wealthy heiress, she has celebrated her parents as if they were not creative geniuses or working artists but just an average down-home couple, with whom she had "a perfectly normal life. My parents were ordinary people. I know a lot of people insist that my father must have had a dark imagination. Well, he did not. He was a brilliant filmmaker and he knew how to tell a story. That's all." This is certainly not overstatement.

Pat adored her mother, and years later collaborated on a book celebrating Alma's contributions to Hitchcock's films. Her relationship to her father, on the other hand, was more tangled and problematic. Then, on his death, she became a very wealthy woman precisely because of movies she did not always defend, much less praise. "When my own girls were young, I wouldn't let them see *any* of his movies," she said in the autumn of 1977. "My own favorite was *Rebecca*—I thought everything went downhill after that" (although she later admitted that *Notorious* was a good picture, too). When *Vertigo* was mentioned as a great film—"Oh," she said after a pause, "was that the crazy movie with a bell tower? I never understood what was going on in that picture!" Hitchcock could not have been pleased by her estimation of what is regarded as one of his undisputed masterworks.

Hitchcock's next project came to him as a virtually completed screenplay by Frank Launder and Sidney Gilliat; ironically, it turned out to be a crowd-pleaser, and so it remains seventy years later—generally perceived as classic Hitchcock. *The Lady Vanishes* (based on a novel by Ethel Lina White) was all but ready for production in the autumn of 1937, and casting was rapidly concluded with the engagement of Margaret Lockwood, Michael Redgrave and Dame May Whitty, among a polished cast. Filming took just five weeks, on the cramped, eighty-foot-long stage of Gainsborough's Islington studio.

"I suppose what surprised me most of all about Hitchcock," recalled Lockwood, "was how little he directed us. I had done a number of films for Carol Reed, and he was quite meticulous by contrast. Hitchcock, however, didn't seem to direct us at all. He was a dozing, nodding Buddha with an enigmatic smile on his face"—the look of pleasure perhaps expressing his thoughts about the negotiations then in progress for him to conclude a deal to work in America. Redgrave agreed: "He wasn't really an actor's director. Everyone knew that his reputation was more for preparation and technique than for working closely with his cast. In fact, his own nonchalance made it rather easy for us."

Perhaps it was easy for the two leading players, but for Mary Clare (who had been razzed on the set of *Young and Innocent*), the experience was memorably uncomfortable. Swathed in black for her role as a Middle European baroness, she had had to accept the assignment under the terms of her contract with Balcon. Hitchcock, ostensibly to welcome her, had heard she did not drink alcohol, so he politely offered her a fruit drink he had prepared. The concoction was laced with strong spirits, and soon Mary Clare was hopelessly drunk.

⸺⸺

The Hitchcocks made several journeys by ship to the United States from 1936 to 1938—not primarily for holidays but for meetings with potential producers and Hollywood moguls. "He felt that he was not really respected in England," recalled Samuel Taylor, "and that British critics regarded him as the house clown. When he finally left for Hollywood, he and Alma shook the dust from their shoes, he couldn't wait to get out."

Taylor was on the mark. A number of British producers and critics expressed the widely held sentiment that Hitchcock was a great director of unimportant pictures. Such elitists believed that he was a mere technician catering to lower-class audiences—which meant that he was the most popular filmmaker in Britain, and perhaps the only one whose name alone meant success at the box office.

There were other reasons for Hitchcock's desire to quit England. British production was in decline; executives were inefficient, and not all were as committed to movies as, say, Michael Balcon had been; craftsmen and other personnel drifted from one studio to another; and budgets dropped precipitously.

"The art of filmmaking was often held in contempt by the intellectuals," Hitchcock said years later. "And that was truer of the British. No well-bred English person would be seen going into a cinema; it simply wasn't done. You see, England is strongly class-conscious, [and] the general attitude in Britain is an insular one."

For The Lady Vanishes, the New York Film Critics Circle cited Hitchcock as the best director of 1938, and this award certainly helped in his Hollywood negotiations. After tangled and protracted exchanges, a deal was concluded with David O. Selznick, for whom Hitchcock was to begin work the following year.

But there was one more promise to fulfill in London: he had agreed (without, alas, first reading the property) to direct Charles Laughton in a film of *Jamaica Inn,* the Daphne du Maurier novel. The beleaguered project, about nineteenth-century pirates on the Cornish coast, could not have been less Hitchcockian in content and style, nor could it be salvaged, even by a team of writers that included Joan Harrison (whom Hitchcock had promoted to writer status), Sidney Gilliat and the esteemed J. B. Priestley.

Produced in the autumn of 1938, *Jamaica Inn* turned out to be one of the few unadulterated failures in Hitchcock's career. Most fatally, Laughton's character (the mad squire Pengallan, mastermind of cutthroat smugglers) appears nowhere in the du Maurier novel: the role was Laughton's own invention. As co-producer, this brilliant, erratic, self-indulgent actor waved a heavy hand over every element of the picture, which (as his biographer Simon Callow accurately wrote) turned out to be "sloppy, stiff, unrhythmic [and] ugly." Daphne du Maurier succeeded in having her name removed from the opening credits.

The finished film is remarkable only as Maureen O'Hara's first major role. Then eighteen, she gamely and uncomplainingly submitted to numerous soakings with studio rain, violent wind machines, immersions in tanks designed to mimic seawater and a torturous binding and gagging by Laughton in the final sequences. As he admitted, Hitchcock was fascinated by the duality of Pengallan's Jekyll-and-Hyde mentality. Apart from those sequences, the young actress felt that "Hitchcock had little interest in the film, and he didn't make much of an impression on me. His physical appearance was very much a part of his eccentricity. He was always very neat and tidy in his appearance, but he moved very awkwardly because of his weight. He rarely socialized and usually spoke in a low Cockney whisper to keep the set quiet." Emlyn Williams, already established as both playwright and actor, was once asked what he learned from Hitchcock during the filming of *Jamaica Inn*. "I learned that it was a good time to go to Hollywood."

By the time *Jamaica Inn* was released, Alfred, Alma and Pat Hitchcock were settled in Hollywood, where Hitchcock began his seven-year contract with Selznick. The glory was now beginning, and with it, more than a few predicaments.

Chapter Five

PASSPORT TO HOLLYWOOD

(1939-1940)

With Joan Fontaine and Laurence Olivier, filming *Rebecca*

"*Rebecca* was a very pleasant experience for my father," Patricia Hitchcock said many years after the movie was made, "because [the producer] David Selznick was too busy with *Gone With the Wind* to cause any problems." *Rebecca* was, as she often said, Pat's favorite among all Alfred Hitchcock's motion pictures—but this judgment was very different from his. He always insisted that directing the film was nothing like "a very pleasant experience," precisely because Selznick interfered all the time—indeed, the producer was constantly and obsessively involved.

Eager to sign up England's most popular and successful director, Selznick was shocked to discover how independently Hitchcock was accustomed to working. Hitchcock was keen to make movies with the vast technical and financial resources of Hollywood, but he had no notion of how proprietary the American producer was, and his own creative ethos was something very different from Selznick's.

It is a well-known fact of movie history that Selznick dictated lengthy, exhaustive and exhausting memoranda by the score every day, indicating to his directors and dozens of employees just what sort of things needed attention for what he considered a Selznick production. This kind of front-office control came as a great shock to Hitchcock, who had enjoyed enormous directorial freedom in England under Michael Balcon, Edward Black and John Maxwell, and who saw a literary property as merely a starting point for a visual tale. Selznick, however, believed that

fidelity to the text of the popular novel being adapted would satisfy readers and result in good box office.

"When moving pictures are really artistic," Hitchcock had
said early in his career, "they will be created entirely by one
man." The convenient fiction that this was possible or even
desirable—that he was the sole creative force behind his
pictures—became the primary element in his self-promotion
and was essentially what he expected in Hollywood and what,
over the course of his career there, he promulgated as the truth
of his achievement. But since the release of massive American
production files and studio archives in the late 1990s, it has become clear that Hitchcock was essentially a senior supervising
collaborator. Just about the only thing he did on his own was to
create a powerful public image, and even for that he had to rely
on writers and publicists for help. Otherwise, he depended on
the talent and assistance of many.

Hitchcock routinely claimed to have planned everything in
advance—each aspect of a production, from the original ideas
to the selection of actors to the final screenplay to camera
placement to the length of a cut; from art direction and set design to wardrobe, sound effects and editing. To be sure, he had
significant experience in these areas from the beginning of his
career, but micromanagement was not realistic. Outtakes, he
said, could be rolled up and would fit in a pocket; there were
no camera angles to be used except those he had pre-chosen,
because he always "cut in the camera."

But the reality was quite different. There was no doubt that
the choice of stories and the manner of their visual telling, as
François Truffaut rightly said, made for "a coherent body of
work." But this is a valuation that could be adjudged only after
the fact. Indeed, no screenplay during Hitchcock's American
period was complete when actual filming began; major revisions occurred during shooting; scenes were excised from the

final versions; and the nature of certain key characters—far from being perfect on the page—emerged during the making of the films. Late in life (after completing what was his last picture), he seemed to acknowledge this when he discussed the subject of the recurring themes and motifs in his films. "We try to tell a good story and develop a hefty plot," he said in November 1976. "As for the themes—they *emerge* as we go along."

In his book *Hitchcock at Work,* scholar Bill Krohn devotes seven oversize pages to the so-called myths Hitchcock promulgated, to the effect that the films as we have them took their final form long before shooting began. Krohn notes that "what critics consider the key moments—the strongest moments, or the most illuminating—were often not on the map but were discovered during the long journey of making the film." In other words, themes emerged. "He thought movies," said Robert Boyle, one of Hitchcock's production designers. "He didn't have rules about movies. He was never afraid to try anything, and if it didn't work out exactly as he wished it, it didn't bother him that much, as long as he got the sense correct."

The "coherent body of work," in other words, was therefore very much a creative accident whose coherence had as much to do with the collaborators Hitchcock assembled as with any intention about what a film could *become.* His preference was to work repeatedly with writers, craftsmen, editors and artists with whom he felt comfortable; after all, they would come to know just what he wanted, and they would give it to him along with the best of their own talents.

Hence, during the sound era, writer Charles Bennett worked on six complete Hitchcock movies, John Michael Hayes and Ben Hecht on four each, and a number of writers (Ernest Lehman and Evan Hunter, for example) on two each. John J. Cox was cinematographer for ten of Hitchcock's British pictures, and Bernard Knowles for five; in America, Robert Burks filled the same position on twelve Hitchcock films. George Tomasini edited nine Hitchcock pictures, and Robert Boyle and Henry Bumstead were art directors and/or production designers on several. Louis Levy composed the music for nine English Hitchcock films, either partly or in their entirety, while Bernard Herrmann wrote the scores for eight in America.

And so it went. Whenever Hitchcock's schedule was congruent with those of men and women he admired and trusted, he saw to it that they were engaged as collaborators: he thrived on uncomplicated, polite teamwork. "He knew what he wanted" was their constant refrain about working with him. But Hitchcock's genius in visualizing a movie was not something that occurred primarily in advance, in his mind. The visual sense accumulated, as he spoke with writers about ideas and dialogue, as he made lists of shots and scenes, as he designed sequences with artists and costumers, and as he discussed mood and effects with composers. Sometimes Alma participated: she was credited on nineteen out of fifty-three Hitchcock films, although it is sometimes thought that she was involved, however tangentially, in the production of every one. At the least, her approval or disapproval of subject matter and detail was very important to her husband.

A Hitchcock movie, therefore, was a process, not something finished in advance; a movie was something for which Hitchcock needed many helpers—all of whom he guided, evoking the best they had to give. But as Charles Bennett (among others) insisted, "He could give credit to no one but himself." This was the central element in his self-promotion and in the creation of the Hitchcock myth. Few among the public guessed that it bore little relation to reality.

The inclination to engage familiar collaborators also explains Hitchcock's preference for multiple engagements with stars who were bankable and cooperative—major players such as John Longden, Malcolm Keen, Michael Wilding, Ingrid Bergman, Cary Grant, Farley Granger, James Stewart, Grace Kelly and Joseph Cotten; and supporting cast members such as Leo G. Carroll, John Williams, Percy Marmont, Jessie Royce Landis and Edmund Gwenn. Rarely but significantly, he set about creating stars—and they were women.

There were, therefore, bound to be thorny episodes in the Selznick-Hitchcock collaboration.

The Hitchcocks and Joan Harrison arrived in Los Angeles in March 1939. Principal photography on *Gone With the Wind* concluded in June, while Hitchcock and company were still at work on the screenplay of *Rebecca*. The editing of *Gone With the Wind,* the last pickup shots, the scoring, the advertising and marketing and hundreds of other details before the release of this extravaganza engaged Selznick virtually around the clock, right up to the Atlanta premiere in December. In fact, Selznick asked Hitchcock for his reactions and advice regarding several sequences of *Gone With the Wind,* and Hitchcock replied with an "analysis that . . . was cinematic and precise," as Selznick acknowledged.

But *Rebecca* occupied Selznick no less than the completion of *Gone With the Wind.* As his advertising and publicity director, Whitney Bolton, observed, "Hitchcock was not always the most consistently amiable of human creatures. He delighted in needling those around him. He needled stars, staff, and press agents, any and all. He had a way of speaking that commands attention, and if he didn't get it, he tended to fret a little."

The Hitchcock picture was, remarkably, Selznick's sixty-ninth production in sixteen years. At the age of thirty-seven, his prodigious energies had many sources and supports: his wife, Irene, the daughter of MGM studio mogul Louis B. Mayer;

Selznick's meticulous attention to detail and his ability to engage the best directors, designers, artists and actors (not to say wealthy investors); his keen intelligence and considerable charm; and a daily diet of dangerously addictive amphetamines and barbiturates.* He spent money imprudently, presuming that good luck at gambling would provide what he needed; it never did, and his monthly losses cost him enormously: in the first nine months of 1940, for example, he lost $56,378 at card games.

"It's not a Hitchcock picture," the director said flatly of *Rebecca;* it was, on the contrary, very much a Selznick picture—a project to which Hitchcock was once attracted, but for which he had lost all interest even before it was definitively assigned to him. The first Selznick-Hitchcock project, wisely abandoned even before there was a draft screenplay, was to have been about the sinking of the historic ship *Titanic.* But a movie of Daphne du Maurier's bestselling novel, Selznick reasoned, was sure to be a hit. Hundreds of thousands of copies had been sold in England and America since its publication in 1938, and there were dozens of translations.

Rebecca is very much a modern Gothic romance in the tradition of Charlotte Brontë's 1847 novel *Jane Eyre.* Both stories feature shy young women tormented by self-doubt; obsessed, gloomy older men harboring dreadful secrets; stately, immense and isolated manor houses; the influence of the past and the dead; catastrophic fires; and happy endings that are not entirely so. Perhaps neither *Jane Eyre* nor *Rebecca* is wholly satisfactory for some twenty-first-century readers, but they both retain considerable popular appeal.

---

* Among Selznick's credits after he began producing at the age of twenty-one, in 1923: *King Kong, Dinner at Eight, Anna Karenina, The Prisoner of Zenda* and *Intermezzo.* Katharine Hepburn's first film and Ingrid Bergman's American debut were both Selznick productions.

"Screen Play by Robert E. Sherwood and Joan Harrison"—so it is noted among the opening credits of *Rebecca;* and below those words, "Adaptation by Philip MacDonald and Michael Hogan." After all the script versions are compared and contrasted, it is clear that fully ninety percent of the finished work was done by Michael Hogan, with some rewrites by Joan Harrison; MacDonald, a writer of thrillers, worked on the early treatment. Very little, at the end, was contributed by the one who is most famous and most prominently credited: Sherwood.

Alma had worked with Michael Hogan on a non-Hitchcock screenplay in England, in 1935. She liked and admired him, and persuaded her husband to put him on the project even before they left London. Hitchcock simultaneously promoted Harrison, who was becoming ever more important to him. As for Alma, she received credit and compensation on four subsequent Hitchcock pictures, and her encouragement and persuasion in private were apparently considerable throughout his career. But the production records show that her direct, daily presence and detailed involvement on his pictures diminished during the American period; in addition, she was lovingly and attentively raising their daughter.

Pat Hitchcock made somewhat larger claims for Alma, most notably in her authorized book *Alma Hitchcock: The Woman Behind the Man* (one fourth of which is devoted to Alma's culinary recipes). She wrote, for example, that her father "made all the important decisions with Alma as his closest collaborator" and that "Alma's participation was constant." This was certainly evidence of a daughter's affection, but it does not confirm her inference that Alfred Hitchcock would not have been successful without the habitual, regular collaboration of Alma Reville. The idea may provide a tender revisionist history in praise of a supposedly underrated wife, but it does not stand up to scrutiny, and Alma herself would have swiftly deflected such hyperbolic praise (indeed, she did when it was implied over the years). That Alma's mind and voice were respected and often heeded by her husband is beyond dispute, and it is reasonable to suppose that she and Hitchcock discussed the work in private at home. But to go further—to imply that we would not have his masterworks without her—seems an unwarranted thesis.

As for Joan Harrison, "she was widely assumed to be Hitch's mistress," as his authorized biographer, John Russell Taylor, wrote twenty-five years after the director's death. Harrison was never asked about the matter, and Hitchcock vehemently denied it. When the subject came up with producer and actor John Houseman (who worked with Hitchcock in 1941), he said, "I would put my hand in the fire to swear that [Harrison] was never his mistress. I ought to know, because for some time she was mine"—and, as Taylor adds, she was also Clark Gable's mistress at about the same time.

Joan and Alma remained on friendly terms and, from 1939 to 1942, they occasionally discussed script problems for Hitchcock's films. "There are only two women I ever could have married," Hitchcock told Charles Bennett, "Alma, whom I did, and Joan, whom I didn't." As Hitchcock said of his wife, "She puts up with a lot from me." (In the 1950s, Joan Harrison returned to the Hitchcock industry as sometime producer of his television series; in 1958, she married the writer Eric Ambler.)

Rebecca's casting problems, nothing less than an exercise in frustration, have been exhaustively documented, and the results were fascinating. To portray the handsome and enigmatic hero Maxim de Winter, Selznick signed Laurence Olivier, who had just come to major stardom in the film of *Wuthering Heights*. At once, Olivier began an intense campaign for his inamorata, Vivien Leigh, to play the nameless second Mrs. de Winter, the title character's successor and the novel's narrator, identified as "I" in the screenplay. Leigh was just completing her historic performance in *Gone With the Wind,* but there was unanimous feeling that she would have been very wrong in *Rebecca* (as her surviving screen tests confirm). Dozens of actresses were considered for the role all during June, July and August, but Selznick could not make a final decision on the matter until four days prior to principal photography, which began on September 8, 1939.

His favor had come down to a choice among Margaret Sullavan, Anne Baxter and Joan Fontaine. Sullavan, whom many of Selznick's colleagues preferred, finally seemed too quirkily autonomous for the part of a shy, anxious ingénue. Baxter had admirable stage experience and appeared eminently sincere, and she also had the enthusiastic support of many others at the studio. But she was only sixteen, and it was hard for the producer to see her opposite Olivier, who was thirty-two and would be presented as even older. Alma Reville and Joan Harrison supported Baxter, insisting (along with others) that Joan Fontaine was "too coy and simpering to a degree that is intolerable." Hitchcock took their point but waited for Selznick's deciding vote. Notwithstanding others' judgments, Fontaine's screen tests for *Rebecca* (which have also survived) revealed a touching simplicity and a muted disquiet. Many thought that those qualities simply reflected her insecurities and lack of experience during the tests.

In addition, David O. Selznick had been (as his authorized biographer wrote) "much in love with Joan Fontaine from the summer of 1938." His passion may have been blunted by her marriage, on August 20, 1939, to the actor Brian Aherne—but Selznick's ardor was not forthwith extinguished, and he still believed Joan was right for the role. When informed that she had won it, she interrupted her honeymoon and went immediately to work, the last and most important player to sign on for *Rebecca*.

Born in 1917 to English parents and raised from childhood in California, Joan Fontaine had acted to no great effect in more than a dozen movies, and in 1938 RKO had dropped her from its roster of players. Pretty, slim and photogenic, she was like very many other young Hollywood hopefuls, and nothing like a bankable star. Contrariwise, the career of her sister, Olivia de Havilland, was already impressive and would become more so after the release of *Gone With the Wind,* in which she had the major supporting role of Melanie.

About to turn twenty-two that autumn, Fontaine was polished and literate, and what she lacked in professional self-confidence she handily offset with a certain wry hauteur that later increased with her relatively short-lived stardom. Selznick found her charming; Hitchcock, who did not, "knew ways of pressuring her insecurities, and making her his" instead of Selznick's, as the latter's authorized biographer wrote.

In the two pages Fontaine dedicates to *Rebecca* in her autobiography, she tells readers virtually nothing about the film that made her career or the people involved in it—except that she was badly treated by just about everyone on the picture. Of Hitchcock, she wrote, "We liked each other and I knew he was rooting for me. He had a strange way of going about it, as actors who have worked with him have verified. His technique was 'Divide and conquer.' He wanted total loyalty, but only to him."

To establish that loyalty and to evoke from Fontaine the anxiety and sense of isolation necessary for the character of the second Mrs. de Winter, Hitchcock told her that Olivier had wanted Vivien in the role; that Olivier disliked her intensely; and that

Olivier thought she should be replaced. Olivier himself told her that he disapproved of Aherne, her new husband—whereupon the bride went home and "gazed upon my Prince Charming with new eyes. Try as I would to forget his remark, Larry [Olivier] had rudely awakened me from my pillow dream." She was, it seems, certainly impressionable, love and/or passion to the contrary notwithstanding. In any case, her husband was sanguine during the six years of their marriage. "Joan is young, pretty, gay and utterly charming—and no actress, thank God," Brian Aherne wrote in his memoirs.

Hitchcock's apparent segregation of Fontaine from the rest of the cast was unrelenting. Claiming that she was cold-shouldered on and off the set by Gladys Cooper, Judith Anderson, Nigel Bruce, George Sanders and others, she added, "The British brigade couldn't be bothered to attend" a little birthday celebration in her honor at the studio on October 22. Was this collective snub an example of what Joan termed Hitchcock's "Divide and conquer" conspiracy, devilishly devised to make her feel as unwanted and unloved as her character? That is extremely unlikely: no matter how much her co-stars were "a cliquey lot" (Fontaine's phrase), the entire cast would surely never have been so rude, nor is it probable that Hitchcock would have effectively diminished himself in everyone's eyes by arranging such a callous tactic. More to the point, to presume otherwise is to take for granted that Hitchcock's order to any and every actor, even regarding off-the-set behavior, was taken as an imperial command never to be contravened.

There are other explanations. Had Hitchcock believed that his leading lady was doing a fine job from day one, she might have become too relaxed, and her performance as a frightened little doe would have suffered. To avoid that, he pursued a scheme to ensure her utter dependence on him and to prevent her from approaching the other players. "He seemed to want total possession of me," she said years later.

> He was a Svengali. He controlled me totally. He took me aside and whispered, "Now, kid, you go in there and you do this and you do that." And then he said, "Do you know what So-and-so said about you today? Well, never you mind. You just listen to me." Now some of what he told me might have been true, but of course it also made me feel absolutely miserable all the time. To be honest, he was divisive with us. He wanted total control over me, and he seemed to relish the cast not liking one another, actor for actor, by the end of the film. This helped my performance, since I was supposed to be terrified of everyone, and it gave a lot of tension to my scenes. It kept him in command, and it was part of the upheaval he wanted. He kept me off balance, much to his own delight . . . But he didn't give me what I needed most, which was confidence.

Poor Fontaine did not help her cause when, perhaps desperately, she boasted to a member of the cast, "My grandmother was the Honorable Lady de Havilland, the first lady of Guernsey!" Hitchcock's whispered response: "That's like being the first lady of Catalina"—the rocky, sparsely inhabited island off the coast of Los Angeles. As a Hitchcock biographer succinctly wrote of Fontaine, "She was not, it must be said, all that popular." Nor could she have much appreciated being paid $166 per day when Olivier's rate was $695 and Judith Anderson's $291; but they, of course, had far more experience.

Still, the entire emotional weight of the movie depended on Fontaine's performance, which Hitchcock had to entice, cajole and coax from her with painstaking direction. "She was not a good enough actress to play in *Rebecca*—she really was not," recalled Selznick's executive assistant, the perceptive, discreet and efficient Marcella Rabwin. This realization even dawned on the once-smitten Selznick: "I am aware that it takes time to get a performance out of Joan Fontaine, but every picture I have ever worked on had some such difficulty . . . Miss Fontaine requires work."

"I think Joan has been handled with great restraint," Selznick added as filming concluded, "but I think we've got to be careful not to lose what little variety there is in the role by underplaying her in her emotional moments . . . [We must not] make it seem as though Joan is simply not capable of the big moments." But in fact she was not capable of the big moments, and Hitchcock had to confer with cameraman George Barnes to cover some thorny shots when Fontaine could not provide what was required.

Recalling these incidents with the star, script supervisor Lydia Schiller said, "She was practically a puppet," and Leonard Leff, who devoted an entire book to the Selznick-Hitchcock years, put it tersely when he wrote, "A well-trained actress would have used her reserves to counter such obstacles as long hours and inhospitable colleagues; young and inexperienced, Joan Fontaine immediately drew on her capital, and, at its rapid depletion, became vulnerable to fatigue and even self-destruction." At one point, Selznick was so fearful of her "weakness" that he asked his wife to look at the footage shot thus far—should the film be scrapped? No, said Irene Selznick, it will be a fine picture.

But the journey to success was tortuous. Much of Fontaine's speech had to be rerecorded—"dozens of isolated lines," according to Leonard Leff. And when principal photography was concluded, Selznick himself had to sit with editor

Hal Kern and fine-tune Fontaine's portrayal. "He often grafted improved line readings onto weak visuals," Leff continued, "and he revised scenes to highlight Fontaine's best moments. When he had no suitable take of the actress from which to choose, he neutralized her performance on especially marginal readings by using (where possible) master shots or closeups of other actors." The finished film and Fontaine's performance, in other words, was remarkably enhanced in the editing and dubbing rooms.

"Although Hitchcock is full of kind impulses," one reporter wrote after visiting the studio, "he is never happier than when seeing someone writhe. The sadistic cruelty which Mrs. Danvers [played by Judith Anderson] manifests toward the second Mrs. de Winter is precisely the sort of thing which brings the roses to Mr. Hitchcock's rather extensive cheeks." Leff put it well: "Many of the actors with whom Hitchcock worked found him endearing, but his humor had a darker side, sometimes abusive and inescapably deliberate . . . Hitchcock's épée was his wit, wielded with grace, speed, and a sometimes unexpected fatality."

Judith Anderson summarized the atmosphere of the production with polite reticence: "There were very unpleasant things I prefer not to discuss," she said years later. Anderson may well have meant the day described by Joan Fontaine as "unforgettable"—when Hitchcock (at her own request) slapped her so that she could bring forth the tears required for an emotional scene. Or perhaps Anderson was thinking of another day, when Fontaine, alone with Hitchcock and ready for a closeup shot, saw him in his director's chair, facing her. "Then I saw that he had put the cork of a champagne bottle in his crotch,"

Fontaine remembered, "so that it looked like something else sticking out. He could be very naughty."

As Marcella Rabwin recalled, Hitchcock did not hesitate to tell anyone at the studio "the dirtiest joke in the world, and he never cracked a smile." Florence Bates, then fifty-one, was receiving her first movie credit for her role as the aggressively vulgar matron Edythe Van Hopper in the Monte Carlo sequences. Of keen humor and intelligence, Bates was the first woman to receive a law degree in her home state of Texas, and Hitchcock (who had seen her onstage at the Pasadena Playhouse) recommended her to Selznick. One morning at the studio, just before one of her scenes with Fontaine, Bates stood silently in a corner, facing an off-camera mirror and trying out a gesture. She was not someone easily embarrassed by salty language or manly crudeness, but she was astonished to hear Hitchcock's voice suddenly booming over the studio loudspeaker system: "Well, Miss Bates—when did you start playing with yourself?" Such coarse double entendres were par for the Hitchcock course.

Lydia Schiller's ordeal as script supervisor lasted longer. Ordered by Selznick to report to him whenever Hitchcock deviated in any significant way from what the producer had approved, Schiller had of course to follow instructions. This she had done only once when the director learned of what he considered an ambush. "You're supposed to be working with me, for me," he told her angrily. "Instead, you've been spying on me, reporting on me." With that, Schiller said, her "baptism of fire" began,

and I had no peace from then on. In his very quiet way, as we sat and worked over the script, he said these things to me—they were obscenities. I didn't even know what they meant. It was just shattering to me. Two or three times, I just had to leave. Finally, I was able to overcome that feeling of revulsion and continue with my work.

Rebecca was completed before the end of November 1939 and released in the spring of 1940, just after *Gone With the Wind* was awarded ten Academy Awards, including Best Picture—for which the statuette was handed to the producer, David O. Selznick. The following year, Selznick again won, for *Rebecca,* and George Barnes won an Oscar for the film's black-and-white cinematography. Hitchcock was nominated in the directing category but lost (to John Ford, for *The Grapes of Wrath*)—a situation that would be repeated four times in his career and that understandably infuriated him.

During production, Laurence Olivier was uncomfortable with his co-star, his role and his director's apparent diffidence, and in the finished film, he can be seen rubbing his temples, passing his hand over his forehead and sighing deeply, as if confusing emotional anguish with a sinus headache. "His pauses are the most ungodly slow and deliberate reactions I have ever seen," Selznick noted—"as though he were deciding whether or not to run for president, instead of whether or not to give a ball."

As for Fontaine, she, like Olivier and Anderson, was nominated by the Academy for her performance. American critics generally, if not passionately, liked her acting, but the British were unsympathetic: "Joan Fontaine at moments even succeeds in coming, however artificially, alive." Charmingly awkward in the first half hour, she then gave what might be called a successful example of a one-note performance—rather like Judith Anderson's, but pleasanter to watch. To be fair, it is difficult to tell if the fault is in the actress or the script, which makes her a Gothic heroine who is just too "coy and simpering"—precisely what Alma Reville and Joan Harrison found so repugnant in her tests.

Rebecca offers dashing Laurence Olivier in one of his rare indifferent performances and attractive Joan Fontaine in one of her few good ones. The film remains entertaining hokum, leavened with occasional (but not enough) humor—a Selznick picture more than a Hitchcock one, as the director himself said. Together, producer and director enlivened a prolix and complicated story that seemed to end two or three times, and they created a palpable sense of horror in the notion that someone dead may be witnessing and even controlling one's destiny. To this latter premise, Hitchcock would return in *Vertigo* and *Psycho*.

For a $54,000 profit, Selznick then loaned out Hitchcock to producer Walter Wanger for an independent picture made at the Goldwyn Studios on Santa Monica Boulevard. *Foreign Correspondent* was one of the director's warmest and wittiest thrillers—a story short on politics and long on human interest and astounding special effects that are still impressive decades later. Charles Bennett wrote the snappy screenplay; Joan Harrison did some editing and polishing; humorist Robert Benchley wrote his own comic scenes as a tippling journalist; and James Hilton and Ben Hecht contributed to this or that scene—in other words, it was a collaborative effort, as usual with Hitchcock and Hollywood.

Foreign Correspondent was a massive project, both financially and technically, and its enormous sets and set pieces (central Amsterdam, Waterloo Station, the Dutch countryside, Westminster and the middle of the Atlantic Ocean) required the most creative artists and technicians then working in movies. For his leading players, Hitchcock could not have his first choices (Gary Cooper and Barbara Stanwyck), and he thought he was settling for B-list talent when the leading roles went to Joel McCrea and Laraine Day.

In neither of these estimable actors did he demonstrate any interest; that was reserved for the participation of Herbert Marshall (from *Murder!* a decade earlier); for the venerable German immigrant actor, Albert Bassermann; and for the film's extraordinary special effects, which required six hundred carpenters, electricians, plumbers, property men and engineers. For the famous rain sequence on the steps of the Amsterdam Town Hall—built on a back lot—the Colorado River was diverted, an elaborate sewer system was constructed, and water splashed down on hundreds of extras for long hours over three days.*

Laraine Day, a lively twenty-year-old brunette with superb comic timing, was borrowed from Metro-Goldwyn-Mayer to be the leading lady opposite McCrea, an appealing, competent and altogether effective player. "Hitchcock had a habit of drinking a pint of champagne at lunch," McCrea recalled. "One afternoon, there was a long scene with me just standing and talking. When the scene was over, I expected to hear 'Cut!' but I looked over and there was Hitchcock, snoring! So I said 'Cut!' and he woke up and asked, 'Was it any good?' I replied, 'The best in the picture!' and he said, 'Print it!'"

"Hitch was always playing practical jokes on people during production," added Laraine Day, who had played a nurse seven times in the *Dr. Kildare* movies. "Once, he nailed shut my exit door in a scene—and another time, there was a false wall sud-

---

* *Foreign Correspondent* was nominated in six Oscar categories but won none: Supporting Actor (Albert Bassermann), Black-and-White Art Direction (Alexander Golitzen), Black-and-White Cinematography (Rudolph Maté), Special Effects and Sound (Paul Eagler and Thomas T. Moulton), Original Screenplay (Bennett and Harrison) and Best Picture (Wanger). Hitchcock was again denied the Oscar.

denly put up on the other side of another exit door. This kind of thing threw me off, of course, but Hitch loved to play his gags on actors." But the actors in *Foreign Correspondent* were apparently spared the cruder and more uncomfortable sort of Hitchcock pranks: neither Laraine nor McCrea could recall foul language, and there was no sign of handcuffs or ill-placed champagne corks. Hitchcock may have begun to realize that Hollywood was not as phlegmatic as London about such shenanigans.

But coarse words, spoken merrily and prodigally, were heard at the RKO Studios in the autumn of 1940, when Hitchcock arrived there to film—of all things—a screwball comedy starring the popular blond comedienne Carole Lombard, best known for her raucously amusing movies and liberal use of language that could make sailors blush. She had married Clark Gable the year before, and the Hitchcocks were renting her former Bel Air home while they sought a permanent residence.

The two families socialized from time to time, and Hitchcock later claimed that as a personal favor to Lombard, he agreed to direct *Mr. and Mrs. Smith,* a droll tale of marital mishap. He added that he did not really understand the squabbling American couple of Norman Krasna's screenplay, which concerned a devoted but high-strung married couple (to be played by Lombard and Robert Montgomery) who learn that because of a geographical technicality, their marriage has not been legal. The ultra-thin narrative takes them through a series of jokey sequences until they realize they were meant for each other all along. To direct this and a second film for RKO, executives at that studio borrowed Hitchcock, in the autumn of 1940, from Selznick—who, as usual, pocketed an enormous weekly profit from loaning out people he had under contract, while continuing to pay them only their stipulated salaries.

Interestingly, the RKO archives tell a story that veers from Hitchcock's stated indifference to the project and his mere acquiescence to Lombard's request that he find an idea. The studio had already bought the script for her, and when Hitchcock learned this, he at once expressed an enthusiastic desire to direct it—not only for the chance to work with Lombard but also because he was more eager to go to RKO than to return to servitude under Selznick. The highly paid Lombard made it happen.

After the English story and characters of *Rebecca* and the European settings of *Foreign Correspondent*, Hitchcock wanted to direct an American comedy about typical Americans, presumably for a typical American audience. The result, *Mr. and Mrs. Smith*, was one of the great hits at the Radio City Music Hall, New York, beginning in January 1941. The public loved it, although reviews were lukewarm—it seemed so anomalous a Hitchcock work—and the critics were soon almost unanimous in proclaiming it a minor and tedious work. Seen almost seventy years later, it is a harmless, faintly amusing bit of moviemaking—verbose, sweet-minded, perhaps too traditionally moral for its own good, but superbly acted by everyone, including the bit players.

"I liked [Carole] very much," Hitchcock said later. "She had a bawdy sense of humor and used the language men use with each other. I'd never heard a woman speak that way. She was a forceful personality—stronger, I felt, than Gable." And Hitchcock simply could not make her uncomfortable with any vivid language or dirty story. After he saw the rough cut of a scene one day, he encountered Lombard. "Oh, you've looked at the rushes without me," she cried. He assured her that everything looked just fine. "I don't give a fuck about that," she said. "How did my new tits look?"

Aware of Hitchcock's reputation for practical jokes, Carole then prepared a few of her own. He had agreed to let her direct his cameo appearance—a long shot as he strolls past an apartment building. Straight-faced and utterly serious, she put him through several hours of exercise, requesting that he walk repeatedly, eight, ten, fifteen times until, she said, he had it just right. A week later, she had another prank ready when Hitchcock arrived on the set. Were actors really cattle? Carole had set up a pen with three heifers, which stomped and mooed, bearing the names of the movie's three stars on neck tags. Hitchcock was not inclined to handcuff or insult her, and as for obscenities, she outdid him every day in that department.

Chapter Six

CHILLING
ELEGANCE

(1941-1942)

Directing Cary Grant and Joan Fontaine, in *Suspicion*

The next project was to have been the first under the RKO deal, but it was delayed by a chain of thorny script problems and so was temporarily replaced with the less challenging story about the cranky Mr. and Mrs. Smith. For the second picture it took the writers four months to complete their first draft of a script, and revisions almost past counting continued even during filming, which lasted from February through July 1941. The production, eventually titled *Suspicion* (a title Hitchcock disliked but had to accept from studio executives), was based on a 1935 British novel by Anthony Berkeley Cox, writing as Francis Iles.

Published as *Before the Fact,* this was an experimental psychological tale told from the viewpoint of a wealthy woman who gradually learns not only that her adored husband is a cad, a liar and an embezzler but also that he plans to kill her for her money. She does not wish to live without him, but also does not wish him to live on through their (yet unborn) child, and so she plans to accept death by poisoning at his hands. Before the fact, however, she writes a letter to her mother, explaining everything and implicating her husband in all his crimes as well as in her murder. She then asks her husband to post the sealed letter, and she downs the fatal drink and dies. The novel thus explores the psychological extremes of one woman's passionate, obsessive and finally self-destructive love.

However odd this property, Hitchcock always claimed this was precisely the story he wanted to film, starring Cary Grant against type.

> He brings his wife a fatal glass of milk. She knows that she is going to be killed, so she writes a letter to her mother: "I'm in love with him, I don't want to live anymore, he's going to kill me, but society should be protected." Folds the letter up, leaves it by the bed, says, "Would you mind mailing that for me?" She drinks the milk, he watches her die. Last shot of the picture is Cary Grant whistling very cheerfully, going to the mailbox and popping in the letter. But that was heresy, to do that to Cary Grant in those days . . . I wasn't in charge at that time. I had to be more or less compromising. I was loaned out to RKO by Selznick and they had the whole thing set up.

And so, according to Hitchcock, the studio would not allow the role of a killer to be played by the actor chosen for the role—Cary Grant, who had specialized in romantic comedies and whose fans would not accept him in so unsympathetic a role.* This admixture of the sinister with Grant's familiar appeal was, of course, precisely what Hitchcock had wanted to exploit. RKO's refusal to allow this (so Hitchcock said) was just like the earlier situation with Ivor Novello in *The Lodger*: in both cases, front-office interference based on audience expectations supposedly ruined a good movie.

---

* During the course of his forty-five-year career in seventy-three movies, Cary Grant appeared with (among others) Jean Arthur, Tallulah Bankhead, Ethel Barrymore, Constance Bennett, Joan Bennett, Ingrid Bergman, Leslie Caron, Doris Day, Marlene Dietrich, Irene Dunne, Joan Fontaine, Kay Francis, Jean Harlow, Audrey Hepburn, Katharine Hepburn, Grace Kelly, Deborah Kerr, Carole Lombard, Sophia Loren, Myrna Loy, Marilyn Monroe, Ginger Rogers, Rosalind Russell, Ann Sheridan, Eva Marie Saint, Sylvia Sidney, Shirley Temple, Mae West and Loretta Young. But not Greta Garbo.

Of course, well might we ask why should Cary Grant *not* have appeared in such a role? After all, Robert Montgomery, also best known for romantic comedies such as *Mr. and Mrs. Smith,* had recently played a lunatic killer in *Night Must Fall.* In that case, MGM did not insist on altering the play and substituting a happy ending; in fact, in the bargain, Montgomery received a Best Actor Oscar nomination. Could RKO not be persuaded to risk Grant in the unsympathetic role of Johnnie Aysgarth?

For the leading lady, Hitchcock was eager to have the French star Michèle Morgan, in her American debut, as Lina. But *Rebecca* had made Joan Fontaine a major Hollywood presence, and RKO borrowed her, too, from Selznick, for the role of the wife. This was to be a variation on her role of the beleaguered young lady of *Rebecca,* except that she is a far more disturbed little rosebud in *Suspicion.* She is also photographed even more beautifully, which is part of the movie's problem: as the shy wife is transformed by love, she becomes more splendidly coiffed and dressed as the picture progresses. This makes it difficult for viewers to accept an important part of the film—her unbalanced emotional life, an extreme of love that is ultimately fatal.

Typically, Hitchcock's marker of this transformation was his subtle but unmistakable insistence on eyeglasses for his leading lady. In the opening train compartment scene, Lina's repression is signified not only by her body language but also by her unattractive spectacles. Like Madeleine Carroll in the first scene of *The 39 Steps,* Ingrid Bergman wears eyeglasses during her first scenes of *Spellbound,* but once she develops an interest in Gregory Peck—no more of them. Hitchcock fitted Kay Walsh for eyeglasses in *Stage Fright;* Laura Elliott and Pat Hitchcock have them in *Strangers on a Train;* and Barbara Bel Geddes wears eyeglasses in *Vertigo.* Hitchcock even insisted that Carol

Stevens, his Hollywood secretary and business manager, choose four or five pairs of eyeglasses specially designed for her by a studio optician. "If I came on the set without my glasses on," she recalled, "it irritated the devil out of Hitch. He had a fetish about glasses." But then he also often ordered her to remove them.

What seems to be behind all this? For Hitchcock, the removal of eyeglasses disclosed a partially concealed beauty, but the gesture also rendered the wearer vulnerable and somewhat isolated, removed from a situation. The glasses, in other words, became Hitchcock's modern version of the Venetian mask—a kind of prop that both concealed and revealed.

The screenplay for *Suspicion* had a knotty history. Various scenes were written, sometimes filmed, then removed, then reinserted elsewhere, and different endings were discussed, occasionally filmed and then reedited. All this has been painstakingly researched more than the texts of any other Hitchcock picture. The project was in a state of chaos even when filming began in February 1941, and all during production no one was quite sure how the picture would end. This is not a rare dilemma in moviemaking: *Casablanca* was bedeviled by precisely the same situation a year later.

What is clear is that the first draft of the screenplay, and most of what ultimately remained, was written by Samson Raphaelson, author of *The Jazz Singer,* a playwright and screenwriter who had written (among other highly regarded projects) several brilliant scripts for Ernst Lubitsch. Hitchcock apparently asked Raphaelson's approval to give on-screen writing credit to Alma, who was also being paid by RKO; generously, Raphaelson acquiesced. Hitchcock pressed on, asking if Joan Harrison could also have screenplay credit, which she needed to get other jobs, as she was planning to leave Hitch-cock and strike out on her own. Raphaelson agreed to that, too. Hence the final credits for *Suspicion:*

SCREEN PLAY BY
Samson Raphaelson
Joan Harrison
Alma Reville

"Hitchcock's material was never very close to mine," Raphaelson reflected years later. "I was more comfortable with Lubitsch's style and tone. After I was off the project, Hitch had Alma and Joan work on it, and perhaps this [joint effort] as much as studio interference explains why the picture has less of the Hitchcock insignia than any of his pictures—there's no dis-tinguishing scene of the kind for which he's famous." And given the changes in studio management that season, the vigilance of the censors, the pressure of Cary Grant's fans and the endless rewrites, it was perhaps inevitable that *Suspicion,* in its final form and as we have it, is not an entirely satisfying picture. Nevertheless (whether by design or accident may never be known), it is, in the last analysis, a movie with a fascinating, distorted treatment of romantic love that was unusual for Hol-lywood in 1941—but just the sort of thing that also intrigued the director.

The story was made more complex than the novel, if not more credible. Lina McLaidlaw (Fontaine) is the shy daughter of proper and wealthy country gentlefolk (Sir Cedric Hard-wicke and Dame May Whitty), who presume Lina is destined for spinsterhood. But she precipitously elopes with the reckless playboy Johnnie Aysgrath (Grant). Aware of his immaturity, his spendthrift habits, his laziness and his irresponsibility—and eventually convinced that he is guilty of more serious crimes of theft—she nevertheless readily forgives him every time she is confronted with his felonies and lies, for she fears, most of all, that she will lose his love. From this obsession she is not deterred, even when she believes he plans to kill her. But she is wrong about his murderous instincts, and at the end it seems as if the couple may rebuild a better relationship.

Hitchcock always claimed that his intention even toward the end of filming was that the glass of milk (highlighted by a light bulb inside the glass) contained poison that Lina would drink—hence the letter she had written (as in the novel) implicating her husband, which he unwittingly posts as she dies. The changed ending, as we have it—with the couple surviving and Lina's suspicions revealed as a chain of neurotic imaginings—was not what Hitchcock said he wanted but was what audiences wanted and RKO gave them.

Yet sometimes, in important interviews, Hitchcock gave the impression that he knew from the beginning that he would be denied his intention and so concocted alternatives. When, for example, François Truffaut asked him in 1962 if Cary Grant would have refused the role of a murderer, Hitchcock replied, "No, not necessarily. But the producers *would surely have refused* [emphasis mine]." As late as 1972, he said, "The whole subject of the film is the woman's mind—'Is my husband a murderer?' " His remarks suggest that Hitchcock knew from day one that he would have to provide an ending different from his preference.

Yet there was evidently another ending screened for a preview audience in Hollywood, one the viewers had rejected—the woman's acceptance of death for love was hooted, and the audience resented the overturning of Cary Grant's amiable public image. And so was inserted the last-minute ending in which it is revealed that Johnnie was planning to kill himself, not his wife, but he knew that this was too cowardly a way out of his troubles. He was, therefore, going to deliver her to the care of her mother and then return alone to face the consequences of his crimes. But the final image—a rear viewpoint of Johnnie and Lina driving home in their open roadster—is highly ambiguous, as they seem to return to life as it was. By the time this last shot was filmed, the leading actors were off the picture, and the stand-ins used are very obviously not Joan Fontaine and Cary Grant.

Nothing seemed to go right during production. Cinematographer Harry Stradling (who had photographed *Jamaica Inn* and *Mrs. and Mrs. Smith*) had been assigned by RKO to work simultaneously on another project. Informed of this, Hitchcock stormed into the office of RKO's executive producer Harry Edington and threatened to stop directing unless he could be guaranteed Stradling's undivided collaboration. "I have a raving maniac on my hands with Hitchcock!" Edington wrote to a colleague. A week later, Stradling was removed from the second picture and turned over to a still-pouting Hitchcock.

The problems multiplied. The lack of an ending threw the actors into confusion, for no scene had a sure purpose. For the first time in years, Hitchcock fell ill, and shooting was suspended for a week. He returned exhausted and depressed, and Fontaine felt that he was disinterested in her as well as in the picture. "Hitchcock does not appear to be giving as close attention to this picture as he should be," one of Edington's staff reported, "and we have good cause to worry. As a matter of fact, Joan Fontaine has indicated that Hitchcock has not been so exacting on his requirements for her as he was on *Rebecca*."

In addition, Fontaine and Grant were not friendly. "The scenario," Fontaine wrote in her autobiography, "was one Cary felt would give him a serious acting role—unlike the comedies he'd been making, such as *The Awful Truth* and *Bringing Up Baby*." She praised his professionalism, his timing, his technical expertise.

"The only mistake he made on *Suspicion* was not realizing that the part of Lina was the major role. It was through her eyes that the story unfolded. She had all the sympathy. He was the villain. Cary found this out halfway through the shooting schedule. That, plus Hitchcock's 'divide and conquer' technique created . . . tension on the set." Fontaine also recalled Hitchcock's "habit of saying 'this silly old actor over there,' or 'that idiot,' or whatever it was, and [he] probably did the same about me."

Much of the tension certainly derived from Grant's unpleasant insistence that Fontaine was "stepping in [his] lights," which would obscure or overshadow him—an objection that rightly puzzled her, for Stradling and Hitchcock knew what they were doing, and the actress was unable to do such a thing even had she so desired. But Grant could not be dissuaded from his unjustified apprehension: as his authorized memoirist has written, he "did not feel the rapport with his costar, Joan Fontaine, that he had with Rosalind Russell or Irene Dunne" on earlier pictures. To muddy the waters further, it was understandable that Fontaine was anxious: although her stock had risen after *Rebecca,* she had not worked on another movie from the autumn of 1939 until she began *Suspicion* in 1941.

Typically, Grant frequently contradicted himself (and Hitchcock) about *Suspicion* in later years. Sometimes he seemed to have been in favor of Hitchcock's original intention; sometimes he was convinced that it would have been impossible. "I thought the original was marvelous. It was a perfect Hitchcock ending. But the studio insisted that they didn't want to have me play a murderer." And contrariwise: "But I'm sure I didn't do it [i.e., the killing]. My character wasn't that sort of chap at all. He couldn't possibly have murdered her. My character was a rogue, not a rat."

There is no accounting for public taste, nor can predictions ever indicate the final reception of any entertainment. By early autumn 1941, the movie was complete, a November release date was set, everyone was nervous and Hitchcock was ready to disclaim the picture. But one major New York critic wrote that *Suspicion* was "far finer than *Rebecca* . . . Hitchcock has made another brilliant film." Others were not completely enthusiastic: "The ending is not up to Mr. Hitchcock's usual style," ran the review in *The New York Times*. "Still, he has managed to bring through a tense and exciting tale, a psychological thriller which is packed with lively suspense." That was not generally the sort of encomium later lavished on *Suspicion*: even among Hitchcock's most ardent fans, a large proportion have always agreed with Cary Grant that it is the "least satisfying" of his four films with Hitchcock—and less than first-rate Hitchcock.

Yet *Suspicion* was nominated for an Oscar as Best Picture of the year, and Franz Waxman for his musical score. Those awards went to others, but Joan Fontaine won the statuette for Best Actress—an honor judged by many to be compensation for her loss in *Rebecca*. When she turned ninety, in 2007, she was living quietly in northern California, four marriages and her career long since over. Her abilities as an actress were perhaps never as refined or richly nuanced as those of her sister, Olivia de Havilland, who was nominated five times for Academy Awards and won twice. Still, Joan Fontaine was the only performer in a Hitchcock movie ever to take home an Oscar.

No honors or nominations came to Hitchcock's next picture, *Saboteur*. This was a disappointing film whose occasionally inventive sequences cannot make up for its cluttered story about fascists destroying American defense plants and generally planning countrywide havoc. The first of two pictures for which Selznick loaned Hitchcock to Universal Studios, *Saboteur* was an obvious but futile attempt to repeat the picaresque structure of *The 39 Steps,* but Hitchcock and his writers (Peter Viertel, Dorothy Parker and Joan Harrison) somehow could not make things work. John Houseman, by now associated with Selznick, went over to Universal with Hitchcock as a de facto but transient producer.

"I had heard that [Hitch] was an unappealing man who told filthy stories and cultivated his image as a gourmet and wine connoisseur," according to Houseman. "But there was more to Hitch than that. He was also unusually sensitive, and everyone who worked with him found him amusing as well as a brilliant moviemaker. Some of his sarcasm may have owed to the fact that Hitch was still in revolt against the British class system. He was certainly one of the most gifted directors, and I can think of no other filmmaker who was so exquisitely prepared for the day's work."

For his leading actors, Hitchcock had hoped to have Gary Cooper and Barbara Stanwyck, who had been a successful team in Frank Capra's *Meet John Doe.* "But I had to take [Universal's contract player] Priscilla Lane, a blonde who wasn't the right type for a Hitchcock picture. And I was also handed Robert Cummings, who has a comedy face, and so you don't believe the situations." *Saboteur* was completed in February 1942, and the memory of it always evoked Hitchcock's criticism. With a weak script and scant interest in his actors, he simply accumulated scenes, took refuge in a series of jokes, and devised cinematic tricks, such as the villain's fall from the Statue of Liberty.

But by the time the movie was released that spring, Alfred Hitchcock had been told a story that would provide him with the basis of his first American masterwork—and, in the bargain, he would cast a leading lady he much admired.

Gordon McDonell, the husband of one of Selznick's story editors, told Hitchcock about a 1939 news story concerning a serial killer of rich widows. "Uncle Charlie," as McDonell called his fictionalized version of the idea, was just an outline for what he planned as a novel about a homicidal maniac who hides from the police with his sister's family, only to be found out by his beloved niece. Hitchcock asked the producers at Universal to hire dramatist Thornton Wilder as screenwriter, reasoning that the author of *Our Town* would provide the necessary sense of modest American life. Together, playwright and director scouted locations in Northern California and expeditiously concocted a masterful first-draft script; when Wilder went off to military service after a six-week collaboration, writer Sally Benson, actress Patricia Collinge and Alma Hitchcock made additional contributions.

Casting was completed in July 1942 for what became *Shadow of a Doubt*. Hitchcock assigned the role of the chillingly elegant, apparently kindly but sociopathic Uncle Charlie to tall, courtly Joseph Cotten, who had recently appeared in *Citizen Kane* and *The Magnificent Ambersons*. On advice from Thornton Wilder, the director asked Universal to borrow Teresa Wright, then under contract to Samuel Goldwyn.

Muriel Teresa Wright was born in New York City in 1918 and raised in Manhattan and suburban New Jersey. Her parents separated when she was a child, and she was shuttled from one relative to another. As a high school student, she occasionally attended the theater, and at Christmastime 1935 she went with a school group to see Helen Hayes on Broadway in *Victoria Regina*. "I was seventeen, and although I had seen plays and even acted in a few at school, the idea of being an actress had never occurred to me until that Saturday matinée. From that day, I knew—I felt that my life was being shaped, even while I was on the train going home that evening." Informed that there

was already a working actress named Muriel Wright, she abandoned her first name professionally.

In early 1938, when Teresa was nineteen, Thornton Wilder
and producer-director Jed Harris selected her to understudy
the leading role of Emily Webb in *Our Town*—a part she ultimately assumed when the play toured. She was back in New
York in the autumn of 1939, appearing in the historic comedy
Life With Father, which eventually ran for 3,224 performances
and eight years. The senior drama critic of *The New York Times*
praised her uncommon charm and delicate skill.

Things then happened quickly. Lillian Hellman, on the
lookout to recommend players for important roles in the up-
coming screen version of her hit play *The Little Foxes,* saw *Life
With Father* and contacted producer Samuel Goldwyn. Before
the end of 1940, Teresa had left Broadway and was preparing
for her movie debut as Alexandra Giddens, on-screen daughter
of Bette Davis. At the same time, Goldwyn signed Teresa to a
contract. But she was wary of certain movie-star traditions
and, politely but firmly, stipulated what she would and would
not do as a player in the Goldwyn Studios game.

Her requirements gently ridiculed the absurdities of the
Hollywood publicity machine:

> I will not pose for publicity photographs in a bathing
> suit—unless I'm doing a water scene in a picture. I will
> not be photographed on the beach with my hair flying in
> the wind, holding aloft a beach ball. I will not pose in
> shorts, playing with a cute cocker spaniel. I will not be
> shown happily whipping up a meal for a huge family. I will
> not be dressed in firecrackers for the Fourth of July. I
> will not look insinuatingly at a turkey on Thanksgiving. I
> will not wear a bunny cap with long ears for Easter. I will
> not twinkle for the camera on prop snow, in a skiing outfit,

while a fan blows my scarf. And I will not assume an athletic stance while pretending to hit something or other with a bow and arrow.

Perhaps to everyone's astonishment, Goldwyn acceded to her demands.

Those who worked with Teresa in the theater, movies and television over the course of her long career were unanimous: her warm and unassuming manner, her humor and gift for mimicry, her unassailable professionalism and enormous kindness were accompanied by an admirable toughness when that was required. Nor was her career impeded by her pellucid beauty, flawless alabaster skin, expressive blue eyes and a radiant, unaffected smile. When *The Little Foxes* was released in the summer of 1941, director William Wyler (not a man for hyperbole) described Teresa as the most gifted and promising young actress he had ever met; he directed her twice more, always insisting he would have liked to multiply those collaborations.

But Teresa did not want to abandon her stage career, and during the summer of 1941 she starred in Molnár's *The King's Maid* at the Bass Rocks Theatre in Gloucester, Massachusetts. Her co-star was Karl Malden, who was also commencing a long and distinguished career; Teresa counted him and his wife, Mona, among her lifelong friends.

Wyler's judgment had been on the mark. The Academy nominated Teresa as Best Supporting Actress for her debut in *The Little Foxes,* and the following year, she was nominated in two categories—as Best Actress in Sam Wood's *The Pride of the Yankees* and again as Best Supporting Actress in Wyler's *Mrs. Miniver,* for which she won. After less than a year in Hollywood, Teresa was receiving more than ten thousand fan letters a week and was (according to the Associated Press) "the best actress Hollywood has stolen from Broadway in a good many years."

Precisely because she projected a rare, unsentimental sincerity and suggested a credible core of strength and purpose, Hitchcock considered for *Shadow of a Doubt* no other actress for the role of Charlotte "Charlie" Newton. "When he invited me in to talk about *Shadow,*" Teresa recalled, speaking of their first meeting in June 1942, "it was as if he had finished the picture—he had it completely in his mind even before we began. And every sound effect had a reason. If a character was strumming his fingers on a table, for example, it wasn't just an idle gesture—Hitch put a beat to it, like a musical pattern, a sound refrain. If someone was walking or rustling a paper, tearing an envelope or whistling, or if there was a flutter of birds or some outdoor sound—Hitch orchestrated everything carefully."

She recalled, too, his endless word games and puns for the entertainment of the cast and crew. His ideal production company, he said, would consist of a leading lady named Dolly Shot; a leading man called Ward Robe; a villain, Mike Shadow; a German spy known as Herr Dresser; a character designated as Mae Kupp; a cameraman, Otto Focus; a child actress named Fay Doubt; the cutter, Eddie Tor; the designer named Art Director. This was not sophisticated humor, but he loved it.

"I got on very well with Teresa," Hitchcock said in July 1975. "She was easy to work with, and she made no demands. She seemed very happy." In fact, that May (just before she met Hitchcock, and two months before the start of filming *Shadow*), Teresa had married the writer Niven Busch. She was twenty-three, a seasoned professional and neither naïve nor prudish; nevertheless, sometimes she did not know how to react when Hitchcock—just before he called "Action!"—whispered something utterly obscene to her, "usually," as she recalled, "having to do with a young bride on a honeymoon." Hitchcock also could not resist muttering inappropriate comments about her husband, who was fifteen years her senior. But she coped by simply smiling, as if she did not understand, or as if the remarks were the politest kinds of compliments.

This was not, of course, the first time Hitchcock indulged in verbal mischief with a leading lady. Perhaps most of all, he wanted a reaction, a sudden expression of dismay before a certain difficult, emotional scene; such tactics are not unusual among those in charge of actors, singers or dancers. But he was also on a lifelong mission to shock, in person as in art. In this regard, Hitchcock's professional garb, invariably a suit, white shirt and tie; his calmness during the work day; his refusal to shout or cause a fracas; his deliberate air of bourgeois respectability—all these contrasted with unexpected explosions of the crudest kind of language.

Shadow of a Doubt offers a virtual textbook in extraordinary acting. The picture was, of course, shot out of sequence—all the location exteriors were filmed in Santa Rosa; then followed the interior studio work in Hollywood. This made special demands on Teresa, who appeared in almost the entire picture and created a portrait of a girl in her late teens who goes through a kind of moral education. She demonstrated in every sequence a natural suppleness of understanding, so that the character's ordeal seems both shocking and inevitable. Her appeal, her credulity and her authentic sweetness are never cloying, her charm never artificial.

In her scenes with veteran performers Henry Travers and Patricia Collinge (as her parents), she was such an acute listener that one listens with her—hence our identification with young Charlie deepens. Opposite the pliant lure of Joseph Cotten, with whom another ingénue might have seemed diminished because his role is so strongly idiosyncratic, Teresa allowed the maturing young woman to emerge without forcing the issue. This is a lesson in nuanced, exquisitely rendered characterization, and she gives *Shadow of a Doubt* much of its coherence, force and complexity.

Appearing later in almost one hundred films and television dramas, Teresa Wright worked with directors Fred Zinnemann, George Cukor, Richard Brooks, Francis Ford Coppola and others, and she was chosen to be the leading lady in Marlon Brando's first movie. Her stage work encompassed classic plays by Shakespeare and Ibsen and modern works by William Inge, Arthur Miller, Eugene O'Neill, Tennessee Williams, Clifford Odets and her second husband, Robert Anderson.

"She had a genius for decency," as one critic wrote, "and a gentleness of spirit that has gone out of style. Hitchcock often ravished his actresses with horrified open-mouthed reaction shots, but here [in *Shadow of a Doubt*], he was satisfied to let Wright play almost the entire progression of niece Charlie's tragedy in her eyes and face."

In her fifties and sixties and beyond, Teresa was remarkable for the assistance, encouragement and support she gave to young actors, writers, students and scholars, and she was never too busy for her legion of friends and fans. In 1997, at seventy-eight, she appeared in what turned out to be her last movie (Coppola's *The Rainmaker*), whose young stars—Matt Damon and Claire Danes—very quickly came to love and admire her. Shooting on location in Memphis, Teresa said how thrilled she was to be working with Coppola, and with such a serious and gifted cast. "Matt and Claire are so dear and so full of energy!" she said. "They give us hope for the future of the movies. And Francis has us all together as if this were a family reunion."

Teresa Wright died of a heart attack on March 6, 2005, at the age of eighty-six. The previous evening, she was in high spirits during a telephone call from her home in Connecticut, her voice warm, youthful and enthusiastic, as always. "It has been chilly," she said, "but I think the first spring flowers are about to bloom in our garden. There are robins here, and daffodils peeping!"

Chapter Seven

FROM RAW STUFF TO POETRY

(1943-1944)

Directing Ingrid Bergman in *Spellbound*

After a year of script preparation and preproduction, Hitchcock's next picture was finally ready to roll
at Twentieth Century-Fox in late August 1943. He set
himself a daunting challenge, for which this movie is something of a curiosity: all the action occurs in the eponymous
Lifeboat. Based on an idea by John Steinbeck and developed by
several writers, the narrative presents a motley crew of wartime survivors cramped into a small space in the middle of the
Atlantic Ocean. A studio tank was constructed into which the
cast had to climb by ladders, and there was generous use of
rear-projection films of sea, sky and storms.

"We were always falling in and out of the water," recalled
actor Hume Cronyn. "We were covered with crude oil, and
when we finished a scene there might be an hour or so of waiting time for a new camera setup. We were soaking wet, there
were wind fans and water-spraying machines, and then we
waited under hot lights, were soaked again—and as a result,
all of us in the cast came down with colds and sore throats, and
some got even sicker." In her memoirs, Tallulah Bankhead, the
star of the picture, recalled that she was "black and blue from
the downpours and the lurchings. Thanks to the heat, the
lights, the fake fog and submersions followed by rapid dryings-
out, I came up with pneumonia early in November."

Tallulah, then forty-one, was talented, audacious, brash
and eventually self-destructive, a casualty of almost manic

promiscuity, alcoholism and drug addiction. After a childhood spent with her southern family (which boasted several members of the United States Congress), she achieved great success on the London stage in the 1920s. Subsequently she played the leading roles in the Broadway productions of *Dark Victory, Rain, The Little Foxes* and—just before she began work on *Lifeboat*—the new play by Thornton Wilder, *The Skin of Our Teeth*. She had also appeared in a dozen unremarkable films. Hitchcock, and Fox's Darryl F. Zanuck, planned to capitalize on her bravado and make her a major wartime movie star.

Difficult, eccentric and unpredictable, Tallulah also had an indefinable star quality, and her baritone voice, raw sensuality and quick humor made her a unique personality in both her career and her social life. "Have you ever been mistaken for a man on the telephone?" columnist Earl Wilson once asked her. Her immediate reply: "No—have you?" Her lovers, according to her and her biographers, were a legion of men and women. One day in New York she spotted an ex-boyfriend she had not seen in eight years. Rushing up to him, she cried, "I thought I told you to wait in the car!"

Of all her peculiarities, the most frequently documented was her exhibitionism: Bankhead thought nothing of completely disrobing at a party—her own or another's—and she routinely continued a conversation from the toilet, leaving the door wide open. Trouper though she was during the rigors of filming *Lifeboat*, Bankhead raised eyebrows in Hollywood as elsewhere. "She had no inhibitions at all," Hitchcock said. "Now some people can take this, others can't." He could, and he relished her bawdiness and swapped filthy stories with her on the set, as he had with Carole Lombard. But things reached critical mass when Tallulah, drenched like all the players, grew tired of changing her underwear so often.

"We all had to climb ladders to get up into this boat," Hume Cronyn recalled,

and to avoid getting her dress wet, she cinched it up above her waist—and there she was, stark naked, no underwear, and exposed for everyone to see. This got to be her regular procedure! One day, a lady journalist from *Good Housekeeping* [magazine] visited the set, and she was outraged. She went off to the front office and raised absolute hell—this was a disgrace, everything she had heard about Hollywood was true, and so forth and so on. Well, the head of publicity at Fox came down to the set and told the unit manager, "Look, this has got to stop. You get Miss Bankhead to wear some underclothes or else we close the set. And if we close the set, it's a damn nuisance, because we lose major publicity for the picture." The unit manager wouldn't risk going near Tallulah with this objection, so he went to Hitch and asked him to speak to her. But Hitch said, "I always try to avoid getting involved in departmental disputes, and in a case like this it's hard to say where the responsibility lies. You might consider this is a matter for the wardrobe department, or perhaps for the makeup people—or maybe it's for hairdressing." I don't think anyone ever got pants on Tallulah.

In every way, *Lifeboat* was a difficult and awkward production, and the troubles persisted when it was released in 1944. Some critics openly condemned it as anti-American, misperceiving the picture as an elevation of the Nazi ideal of the Superman because the German, played by Walter Slezak, was inventive and intelligent—but he was also cruel, murderous and deceptive. There was wide astonishment when the film was nominated for three Oscars, including one for Best Director. No awards were handed out for *Lifeboat* at the Academy's rites of spring, but the nominations helped at the box office.

"I was under contract to Selznick, and so was Hitchcock— and one day at the studio, I just happened to be walking by, and Hitch said to someone, 'Well, she could play in my next picture.'" It was typical of Ingrid Bergman not to exaggerate the circumstances, or to describe just how important she and Hitchcock were to Selznick's fortunes; in fact, their meeting and eventual collaboration were not so dependent on mere accident during an afternoon stroll. Ingrid was Selznick's most valuable contract player, as Hitchcock was his most prestigious director. For significant profits accruing to Selznick, they had both been loaned out to other studios; now Selznick was actively searching for a project for them to do together, which he could produce.

After his enormous successes with *Gone With the Wind* and *Rebecca,* Selznick had fallen into a clinical depression that was aggravated by both his manic work habits and dependence on various pills. By early 1944, he was regularly consulting a psychiatrist; so was the prolific screenwriter Ben Hecht.

Hitchcock happened to have the film rights to a 1927 novel he thought might become the basis for a picture to be written by Hecht and starring Ingrid; he sold those rights to Selznick for a tidy sum, and the necessary deals were made with uncommon speed. But it took more than a year from the first work on the project to the premiere of what was ultimately called *Spellbound,* a title suggested by studio secretary Ruth Rickman.

The book was *The House of Dr. Edwardes,* by John Leslie Palmer and Hilary Aidan St. George Saunders (writing under the joint pseudonym Francis Beeding). It was a bizarre and complicated tale of witchcraft, satanic cults and murder, all of it set in a European lunatic asylum, and it certainly did not seem suitable material for either Hitchcock or Selznick. But it could be substantially reworked to become a thriller about a psychoanalyst who solves a mystery and so saves the life of her patient, an innocent man wrongly suspected of murder. Selznick wasted no time in telling Ingrid that this was her next assignment.

Ingrid Bergman's life was very much a study in courage and consistently high achievement. She had lost both parents before adolescence, was raised by relatives who either died or abandoned her, attended drama school in Stockholm and after a successful career on stage and screen in Sweden, had come to America and to a Selznick contract in 1939. She had then appeared to great success in major films—*Intermezzo, Dr. Jekyll and Mr. Hyde, Casablanca, For Whom the Bell Tolls* and *Gaslight* (for which she won the first of her three Oscars). In early 1944, she was twenty-eight, highly esteemed by colleagues, admired by the press and idolized by an adoring public. Married to the dentist Petter Lindstrom, who was training to be a neurologist, Ingrid was supporting him and their six-year-old daughter, Pia. "Lindstrom was terribly tough on Ingrid," said their friend the Swedish artist W. H. Dietrich. "She returned from a day's work at the studio tired but happy, and Lindstrom said, 'Well, are you going to do something worthwhile now?' Whatever she replied, he would say, 'No, you should do such-and-such instead.' I wondered how he could be that way with her—after all, he was not yet set up in practice, and she was bringing in all the money." Then, as throughout her life, Ingrid was committed to doing good work more than she was to amassing wealth, possessions and all the trappings and entrapments of celebrity.

Hitchcock and Hecht outlined their ideas to Selznick, who became, as he said, "almost desperately anxious to do this psychological or psychiatric story." Director and writer then visited various mental hospitals in and around New York (convenient to Hecht's suburban home, where they preferred to work), and then they sat down to compose the script—with Hitchcock, as Hecht observed, "beaming amid his nightmares." Hecht, with his experience of psychoanalysis, and Hitchcock, with his experience of social isolation, created a new kind of psychological thriller about guilt and tortured romance—all of it interlaced with the images and atmosphere of dreams.

As the first day of production approached in July 1944, Ingrid met her co-star, another contract player at the Selznick Studios, Gregory Peck, whose first movie had been released in June. He was, as the saying went, being intensely groomed for stardom. But the script for *Spellbound* troubled Ingrid, who found incredible the mingling of professional psychiatric duty with romance. "I won't do this movie because I don't believe the love story," she announced. "The heroine is an intellectual woman, a doctor, and an intellectual woman simply does not fall in love so deeply, so quickly."

Selznick could simply have forced Ingrid into the role of Dr. Constance Peterson without further ado, but he preferred her to warm to the idea, and so, to dispel her misgivings, he called a meeting with the director, writer and leading lady. Everyone likes a good love story, Hitchcock said at the outset, and if they wanted to commit to stern realism above all else, they ought to make documentaries. This argument did not carry nearly as much weight for Ingrid as did Hitchcock's ability to charm her even as he spun the complexities of the plot. As he did, Ingrid sensed the flow of the entire picture. She had admired the bold darkness of *Shadow of a Doubt;* now she understood that the unusual love story and the technical innovations would provide much of the uniqueness of *Spellbound.* In addition, she was fascinated with the plans to have brilliantly disturbing dream sequences designed by Salvador Dalì.

At this point in the meeting, Selznick was called away. "Don't worry about the psychiatric jargon," Hitchcock then whispered conspiratorially to Ingrid. "Just remember, audiences don't know much about that." He was on the mark: Freud had died only five years earlier, and talk of guilt complexes, father fixations and dream symbolism was not in common currency, however much it had been fancied by some writers. Hence, what had initially appeared to Ingrid as a simplistic conclusion to the thriller aspect of *Spellbound* could be made fresh and fascinating. It was to be a story with unexpected twists and turns and (as she later said) "that touch of art."

"Before we began to shoot the picture, he invited me and my husband to dinner at his home," Ingrid recalled.

> He had just bought the house [in Bel Air] and they were still putting up pictures and selecting fabrics for furniture. There were good food and wine, and after dinner, we rolled back the carpet and danced. I had the impression that Hitch was very exclusive and chose his friends very carefully. Cary Grant was there, and Teresa Wright and her husband . . . Hitch didn't mingle with a lot of people—he was polite, but I think there was a little bit of the snob in him, and a fear of social rejection, too. He sat and told jokes and all that, but he wanted to be in control of things. If people got noisy, he would lower his voice—lower and lower until he was pretending he was talking but he wasn't. That's how he [commanded] silence, that's how he got people to pay attention to him.

Hitchcock's tactic for control of the situation was the same on the set of *Spellbound,* which began filming at the Selznick

Studios in Culver City on July 10—Ingrid's seventh wedding anniversary, which he honored with a huge cake for the cast and crew at the end of the day's work. Everyone was in good spirits.

As usual, script problems arose during production—some from Selznick's interference, some from the effort to integrate Dalì's angular, allusive designs, some from the unexpected accidents of filmmaking itself. Hitchcock may have been a bit surprised that Bergman and Peck took everything with absolute gravity, to the point of requesting discussions with him about scene and dialogue changes. "Selznick believed in treating his actors like little tin gods," Peck said years later, "but he was a little hard on directors. On the other hand, Hitchcock could be hard on actors, but he learned to take a tin-god producer in stride."

Ingrid recalled just how the stride was achieved. "When Selznick came down to the set to inspect progress, the camera suddenly stopped, and Hitch told him the cameraman couldn't get it going again—'I don't know what's wrong with it,' he would say. 'They're working on it, they're working on it.' Finally, Selznick would leave, and miraculously the camera would start rolling again. After this happened a few times, David of course guessed what was going on. They were two strong men, but I think they really had great respect for each other."

Selznick's respect for Ingrid was another critical element in the success of *Spellbound*. When he learned that she was sitting for still photos on her picture *Saratoga Trunk* during May 1943, for example, he wrote to Joe Steele, his publicity director. The letter is important for details of Ingrid's professionalism:

> Ingrid is so extraordinarily cooperative that I think we must lean over backwards not to take advantage of her good nature or someday even her wonderful character will

rear up and react against us, just as happened with Garbo at Metro as the result of early lack of consideration of her by their publicity department.

In all the years I have been in the picture business, I have never heard of a girl going through so tough a schedule as Ingrid has had in recent months, and even though this has been entirely by her own wish, I think it behooves us to be very sure that she at least gets her Sundays for rest and her child. *For Whom the Bell Tolls,* with its terribly difficult location trip, would have been enough to knock out any average person, and to cause them to absolutely require a rest. And it must be borne in mind that, by Ingrid's wish, she started *Bell Tolls* with literally not even a single day off following the completion of *Casablanca.* On top of this, she started *Saratoga Trunk* without any rest . . . and has worked for over ten weeks without one single day free—something I have never heard of before. I tried very hard to force rest days on Ingrid, but she wouldn't take them, and the very least we can do is to be certain that her Sundays are not cut into. It must also be borne in mind that Ingrid doesn't even take the one day off monthly that is the habit of feminine stars, once they achieve stardom— and as you know, some of them insist on two or three days.

This was the first of a trio of films in which Hitchcock directed Ingrid; it was also the beginning of a friendship that endured until his death thirty-six years later. But however mutually rewarding professionally, it was deeply problematic personally, for Hitchcock fell passionately in love with her and nursed feelings she could not and did not reciprocate. Ingrid respected his genius and had enormous filial affection for him—but there her sentiments ceased. This made their collaboration a great joy and a painful trial for them both.

Throughout her personal and professional life, Ingrid Bergman was attracted to intelligent, artistic, dynamic men with good humor and a zest for life—these were qualities she found more appealing than mere good looks. Later, for example, she had romances with musician Larry Adler and photographer Robert Capa, who could hardly be described in terms of movie-star glamour. From the first meeting with Hitchcock, she found him irresistible as mentor and father figure, for he put her at ease, explained things clearly but without condescension and appreciated her European sensibility. She laughed easily, was charmingly flirtatious and liked a good martini at the end of the day. Hitchcock, alas, mistook her buoyant camaraderie as amorous and her response as identical with his: hence, he was quickly smitten like a schoolboy. That summer of 1944, *Spellbound* began, as did a complex, disturbing and finally touching relationship.

"It was sometimes not easy for me," she said quietly many years after Hitchcock's death,

> because I had to keep things light and not [allow him] to get too serious. This led to some disagreements during *Spellbound*. One day, I said, "Oh, Hitch, I don't think I can give you that kind of emotion in this scene." He took me aside for a few moments and told me a story of a man who worked behind the scenes in Hollywood studios. He knew that everything is fake—the beauty is fake, the hair is fake, the teeth are fake, even the food is not what it looks like. So one day, he goes to the studio restaurant and asks for a cup of coffee and a piece of pie, and the server says to him, "I'm sorry, sir, but we're out of pie." And the man answers, "Well, then, fake it!" And that was his answer to me when I told him I couldn't do such and such a scene, or I couldn't give him that emotion or walk this way, or whatever was

my objection. He sat and listened patiently, and just when I thought I'd won him over to my viewpoint, he said very sweetly, "Ingrid, fake it." And that's how he got what he wanted. Usually, of course, he was right.

When they first met for story conferences, Hitchcock had been fascinated by Ingrid's agile mind and willingness to learn, but by the time they were filming, he was like a helpless romantic. He directed her with wit and tenderness, he provided explanations for her, and he told amusing stories; more to the point, he promised that she would star in his next picture, a promise that of course was not within his power to grant.

To Gregory Peck, Hitchcock was markedly different. "He really didn't give me very much help," Peck recalled, "although I was so inexperienced that I felt I needed a good deal of direction. In answer to my questions about mood or reaction, he would simply say that I was to drain my face of all expression and he would then photograph me. But I wanted more than that—the business was so new to me. He didn't give me direction, but he did give me a case of wine when he found out I was a novice about wine—he was more than willing to improve my education in that regard."

As Leonard Leff rightly noted, "Although Hitchcock meticulously sculpted the performances of many youthful or untrained actresses, he could neglect actors. His superior pose and his preference for medium and close shots over the master shots that gave performers their bearings in a scene could strain relations between director and actor. And if Hitchcock did not like an actor, he could prove alternately sarcastic and distant," which he certainly was, on occasion, with Peck.

Regarding Ingrid, Peck was puzzled: "She was marvelous to work with, but whenever he was with her, I had the feeling there was something ailing him, and it was difficult to know exactly the cause of his suffering, although some of us had our suspicions."

"Sometimes, to irritate us," Ingrid added, "Hitch said, 'Well, all my fun is over now that you actors are here.' He insisted that most of his enjoyment was in the preparation, the writing, the planning of camera setups—the fantasy of seeing the picture in his mind—and he regarded us actors as intruders into his fantasy. But he was always very controlled. He never lost his temper or screamed at anyone—yet he always got what he wanted."

As for the actual direction: "He watches what you're doing, he tells you what to do, and then he rearranges what he wants for information and stress and speed. Sometimes he acted something out—I have so many photographs of him doing that. He doesn't want you to imitate him; he wants to hear what the intonation is."

A great part of his fantasy concerned his selection of leading ladies like Ingrid. "He doesn't talk much about acting," according to Ingrid. "I think he later chose Grace Kelly and Tippi Hedren because of what they looked like, the same with me."

"I have to consider," Hitchcock had said, "whether she is the kind of girl I can mold into the heroine of my imagination," and his imagination was amazingly and sometimes alarmingly fertile. About the time of *Spellbound*'s release, for example, Hitchcock began to tell an elaborate tale, forged in the workshop of his capacious imagination—a fantastic account of what he said happened one evening. After a dinner party at the Hitchcock residence, Ingrid supposedly refused to leave his bedroom until he made love to her. If this fiction were not so sad and pathetic, it would be amusing, but Hitchcock insisted it was the truth. He and Ingrid, so he believed with all his heart, would be the perfect couple, if only . . . if only they were not, as he wrote for her to say in *Spellbound,* "just bundles of inhibitions."

Quite apart from the fact that their spouses were in the adjoining room, it would have been entirely out of character for Ingrid to behave this way with a man for whom her feelings were never erotic. "Some people really believed his story," she said years later, with compassion, and with a gentle, dismissive laugh. "I never got angry when it came back to me. People will believe what they want to believe—Hitch, just like anyone else. I loved him, but not his way. Well, I wanted to keep his friendship, and I did."

Indeed, Ingrid did nothing to foster Hitchcock's amorous inclinations, but, as so often happens, her restraint had the opposite effect on him. He was courtly and attentive on the set but never effusive in the presence of others. Disallowing the emergence of his deepest feelings, he added—at the last moment— a telling bit of dialogue (hastily written in his own hand) for Ingrid and actor John Emery, who was playing a colleague whose infatuation, like Hitchcock's, she does not reciprocate:

DR. FLEUROT (EMERY): You're a sweet, pulsing, adorable woman underneath. I sense it every time I come near you.

CONSTANCE (INGRID): You sense only your own desires and pulsations. I assure you, mine in no way resemble them.

Hitchcock took her caution for diplomacy, and so he redoubled his efforts to attach her permanently to his life. To that end, he spun the outlines of this and that story for them to make as films together; more than once, word of this got back to Selznick, who politely and diplomatically had to remind them that he was in charge of their future projects.

Just as Ingrid had to live within a world of vivid imagination in order to create credible feelings for her characters, so the power of Hitchcock's films owed to his unassailable genius as a visual storyteller who worked with the raw material of his own fantasies. All objections notwithstanding, he had no other material with which to work than his daydreams and imagination—and that, after all, must be said of every storyteller and artist; to maintain otherwise is to exhibit a profound ignorance of the creative process.

Hitchcock could not leave himself at home when he went to a studio; had he been able to do so—and if those fantasies had not been more or less recognizable as universal human possibilities—then we would certainly not have the universally popular Hitchcock movies we have. His pictures are part of him and us: our response to them must be, "Yes, some of life is like this—and all of life is in danger of becoming like this."

During his long creative life, he existed within a kind of prison. His frustrated passion for several of his leading ladies brought him great pain. He allowed the constant struggle with morbid obesity to isolate him, making any kind of physical intimacy impossible; indeed, Hitchcock created the ultimate physical prison for himself. During a year, beginning in late 1942, he had lost almost one hundred pounds, but that loss did not make him a slender man: at less than 5 feet, 8 inches, 225 pounds was still a hefty number. By 1945, the weight was slowly going back on, and by 1951, he was again well over 300 pounds. He then went on another reducing plan, and by 1953 was back down to 200—and then the reverse cycle continued, a sine curve of gain, loss and gain.

Yet it was precisely Hitchcock's emotional separation from

others that gave the world a legacy of great films. His art was realized in the kiln of a lifelong pattern of discontent, from which he often sought refuge at the dining table and the bar. Much of his despondency had to do with the fact that he seemed to long for romance and for true friendship but had the gift for neither—except in his fantasy life, and in this regard, he left a profound spiritual autobiography in his work.

Perhaps when his daughter, Pat, denied this aspect of her father's character, as she regularly did after his death, she really (and rather poignantly) believed that there was no connection between Hitchcock's life and his art. Insisting that his movies had nothing to do with his life, his own feelings, his own emotions—that they were merely stories—could she have been so acutely unaware of the constant connection that invariably must exist between the storyteller and the story, however transmuted the story becomes?

"Hitch couldn't stand the interference from Selznick," Ingrid said.

> David would come down to the set, saying "Hurry up!" or "There are too many mistakes!" or "Don't the actors know their lines?" And he arrived with friends, which made it seem as if Hitch was incompetent. But dear Hitch had a way of dealing with this: he went into perfect double-talk. There were words, you could hear them, but none of it made any sense—it was his way of getting rid of Selznick. He'd say to me, so the producer could hear him, "Now, my dear, you see those lights . . ." and then he'd talk about a closeup or a long shot or a focus problem, and in between, there were words that made no sense at all—and you would just die laughing, because you knew what he was

doing—driving them off the set, so he could get back to work!

As the making of *Spellbound* proceeded, Ingrid told her family and friends how much she enjoyed working with her director: "I have started my new movie," she wrote in Swedish to her father-in-law on August 3, "and all is well. I'm playing a doctor, and this is different from the films I have acted in before. I like it that I can play different roles—and that is seldom done by actors in Hollywood. They usually play the same types over and over again until they die!" On October 10, she wrote to him again: "I finished my film, 'Spellbound,' and I believe it will be an interesting one. I really enjoyed working with Alfred Hitchcock, and I am so happy—it looks as if his next film will also be with me. It is a spy story."

The enduring appeal of *Spellbound* does not derive from its complicated and incredible plot, but rather from the natural and understated performance by Ingrid Bergman and the vulnerable characterization by Gregory Peck. In the delicacy of Ingrid's portrayal of Constance Peterson, in the way she turns her head, folds her hands or stifles an inchoate sob, there is a long lesson in screen acting—much of it already part of Ingrid's equipment, and all of it endorsed by Hitchcock. Of all that she learned from him, the most valuable lesson was the significance of her closeup—a simple glance downward, or to the left or the right, could reveal anxiety, a thought or a sudden reflection. Underplaying, what Hitchcock bluntly referred to as "not acting," was something Ingrid instinctively comprehended. She did not require systematic guidance through a scene: she understood from the first reading what was called for, and any modification was readily effected in a matter of moments, with few words.

Perhaps the most moving example of this occurs when the character of her teacher, Dr. Brulov (impeccably played by Michael Chekhov) bids Constance (Ingrid) farewell, and it seems that she has forever lost her beloved (Peck). "It is very sad to love and lose somebody," the teacher says, just before the dénouement saves the day. "But in a while you will forget and you will take up the threads of your life where you left off not long ago. And you will work hard. There is lots of happiness in working hard—maybe the most." There is enormous kindness here, and the scene became the perfect representation for the delicate relationship between Ingrid and her director.

Once released, *Spellbound* never lost its popularity, even after its specifically psychiatric elements were parsed as flawed and simplistic. But Hitchcock correctly made a distinction between *psychological* films and *psychoanalytical* films. The latter, stories about illness, doctors, patients and treatment, he dismissed as "a passing phase." But the assertion that he had no interest in *psychological* films can be made only by someone unfamiliar with Hitchcock's career, for human psychology fascinated him; indeed, his pictures are about little else.

"The psychological film is quite a different thing from the psychoanalytical," he said as early as 1946. "If, by psychological film, you mean a particular way of telling a story, by trying to get at the characters, then I think it is inevitable that the psychological approach to story will be employed more and more frequently as the screen comes of age." (The screen came of age at least partly because of Hitchcock films such as *Suspicion, Shadow of a Doubt, Notorious, Strangers on a Train, The Wrong Man, Vertigo, Psycho* and *Marnie*.)

Spellbound was a far greater success than anyone could have predicted: it cost $1.7 million to produce and grossed more than $7.0 million in its first release, thus making it one of the two or three most lucrative movies of the 1940s. It also received six Oscar nominations—for Best Picture, Director, Supporting Actor, Cinematography, Special Effects and Musical Score; only Miklós Rózsa won, in the last category. This was also the first American film in which Ingrid Bergman received star billing, and Selznick—perhaps to everyone's astonishment—officially called the picture "Alfred Hitchcock's *Spellbound*." So it appears in the opening credits, "because [Selznick said] I think he is entitled to it . . . and due to the fact that Hitchcock secured such remarkable quality with such prompt efficiency and without the slightest set supervision on my part, either."

Chapter Eight

DESIRES AND PULSATIONS

(1945-1946)

Shooting the closeup of the key in Ingrid Bergman's hand,
in *Notorious*

ven before *Spellbound* was completed in October 1944, Selznick had passed along to Hitchcock and Hecht the basis of a story he wished to turn into a film. One of Selznick's story editors had found the germ of an idea in a piece of short fiction published in *The Saturday Evening Post* in 1921, but as usual, the finished film became something far different, richer, more complex and disturbing, and infinitely more appealing.

According to the earliest studio memoranda about the production, Ingrid was to portray a hard-drinking woman of easy virtue carefully trained for an espionage assignment in which she is forced to marry a spy in order to smoke out a dangerous Nazi plot. The man she really loves, who gets her into this unattractive game of sexual blackmail, is afraid of her romantically even while he needs her professionally. This premise went through several development stages and was continually altered even during filming (from October 1945 until early February 1946) before it became (in the final editing) a taut masterwork of motion picture entertainment.

Notorious, as it was titled, is a testament to Ingrid's enormous, subtle, wide-ranging and deeply affecting talent: never for a moment do viewers doubt they are watching the complicated character named Alicia Huberman. Ingrid gloried in playing a variety of women, and she was fortunate to have opportunities to do so even as Selznick loaned her out for most of her pictures. Before her role as a psychiatrist in *Spellbound,* her

American films had featured her as a dedicated teacher (in *Intermezzo*); a companion (in *Adam Had Four Sons*); a wife (in *Rage in Heaven*); a bewildered lover (in *Casablanca*); a brutalized girl who finds love amid political terrorism (in *For Whom the Bell Tolls*); an implacable adventuress (in *Saratoga Trunk*); the intended victim of a murderous thief (in *Gaslight*); and an unconventional, flesh-and-blood nun (in *The Bells of St. Mary's*). Her role in *Notorious* added still another very different jewel to her crown. In addition, her leading man was to be Cary Grant, back for his second Hitchcock movie and, playing an emotionally repressed intelligence agent, in a role once again contrary to his image.

Notorious is the story of the wounded, cynical, but lovesick Alicia Huberman and the emotionally withdrawn T. R. Devlin, a man wondering how to become a man—and of his rival, Alexander Sebastian (Claude Rains), who is betrayed by his devotion to Alicia. The element of espionage and its details are Hitchcock's MacGuffin—his excuse to spin a romance, a profound exploration of adult confusions. In retrospect, it is astonishing that this movie could have been produced and released in 1946: it has blunt dialogue about government-sponsored prostitution and it offers up supposedly heroic American intelligence agents advancing the expediency of sexual blackmail. The moral murkiness and the implicit denunciation of American officials were unprecedented storylines in Hollywood circa late 1945, when the Allied victory in war had just inaugurated an era of perhaps understandable but ultimately dangerous chauvinism. The conventional wisdom was that the United States government could never be tainted with scandal or corruption, but *Notorious* is not so sure of that.

Hitchcock did something behind the scenes that was atypical in his career thus far: he made Ingrid his closest collaborator on the picture. "But Hitch," she said one day, "the girl's look is wrong in this shot. You have her registering surprise too soon. I think she would do it this way"—and with that, Ingrid did the scene again, her way.

There was not a sound on the set, for Hitchcock did not suffer actors' ideas gladly—he knew what he wanted, and what he did not want was interference from mere performers. But Ingrid often came up with good ideas, and that day—to everyone's surprise—Hitchcock said, "I think you're right."

Hitchcock, doubtless aware by this time that his own chances with her were impossible, agreed to Ingrid's request that Robert Capa, with whom she was having an affair, be the publicity photographer on the set of *Notorious*. Capa took historic still photos of the party sequence in which Ingrid furtively clasps the wine cellar key—a scene justly famous for its crane shot, in which the camera descends without a cut from a vast overview of a grand foyer to a tight closeup of the key clutched in Ingrid's hand. This extraordinary moment was not simply technical wizardry devised by a clever director; it was, on the other hand, crucial for him to emphasize two levels of reality within a single sweeping image. The literal key to something dangerous lies within an impressive setting—one spatial continuum, in other words, contains a double reality, just as the expensive bottles of wine contain uranium ore, and just as (elsewhere in the film) affectionate gestures camouflage multiple realities.

Yet Hitchcock's engagement of Capa may not be so difficult to comprehend. Many unrequited lovers try to please the object of their affection—and if they are going to suffer, they are often intent on real suffering. This, after all, is the core of the romantic fallacy, as the unrequited lover nurtures his anguish. History is rich with the names of those whose personal pain nourished their public art in music, on canvas, in words and on film.

Seeing Ingrid and Capa together must have been a kind

of agony for Hitchcock, even though the photographer's contributions to the movie's publicity were invaluable. This triangular complex of emotions was itself a kind of scenario, alternately ruthless and touching. And to make the situation even more byzantine, Ingrid's marriage to Lindstrom was effectively over. But the American movie-going public, who followed such things with religious intensity, read only the devotional articles served up in magazines and newspapers, and so they believed that Ingrid's brilliant career was complemented by an ideal home life; in reality, she was miserably lonely in her marriage, from which she had sought refuge in a few intense affairs. A rueful smile may have crossed her face when she read in an interview that year, "Miss Bergman just can't help being a good girl on the screen because that's the way she is."

In August 1945, Ingrid turned thirty, but there was still a girlish, callow aspect to her personality; in some ways, she was not the worldly, contented woman the public regarded so highly. Her early life had been spent on unstable ground, and by the time she married (at twenty-two), she was willing to rely on her husband for life's practical decisions, so that she would be free to pursue work she loved. Uninterested in financial matters throughout her life, she readily left the management of them to others, presuming that her husbands, especially, would act reasonably with studio executives, producers and agents.

Ingrid's refusal to prevaricate or to affect airs and graces endeared her to colleagues as much as to the press and public. If people placed her on a pedestal and adored her, the cult was of their own invention—to evoke their loyalty and support, she only worked (brilliantly) as an actress. Admirers prized her beauty more than Ingrid herself did: she was never hesitant to

appear plain for the truth of a role, and as she aged, she refused
to cling to an unrealistic attitude about eternal youth. "It's hard
for me to find good roles," she said when she was fifty-seven,
"because I'm too old to play a young lover and too young to
play one of those haggard old grandmothers. You might say I'm
at that awkward, in-between stage." In fact, she undertook the
right roles for her age as long as she could work.

At first, marriage had brought her great consolation. Always
attracted to intelligent, mature men rather than merely attractive and sporting types, she had found those qualities along
with a kind of protective paternalism in Lindstrom, eight years
her senior and an honorable man. But they were two people of
their time and culture, when the husband's supremacy was presumed and unquestioned—a situation Ingrid very soon resented. Once the Lindstroms had settled in America, she
worked constantly to support herself and her family, but soon
the marriage was troubled by Lindstrom's overbearing domination and his excessive and unreasonable interference in the
business details of her career. At the same time, Ingrid's eventual extramarital romances were not the cause of her failed
marriage but the result of a union that had already turned sour.

Seeking guidance from one she always regarded as a mentor, Ingrid confided in Hitchcock, who loved to hear (and from
others' more embellished versions) about her brief but intense
affairs with Capa, Adler and the director Victor Fleming. Her
relations with these men blazed and cooled during the time
Hitchcock and Ingrid collaborated on a trio of films.

Ingrid's liaisons ought perhaps to be regarded as those of a
woman of significant inner resources who mimicked love in art
but who felt deprived of it in life. It was not merely sexual attraction that drew her to lovers; it was their strong dispositions,
their creative lives, their unique outlooks and their lack of any
desire to control her (as her husband did). Capa, for example,

with his keen eye and Gothic philosophical disposition, swept her away with his energy and his sheer desire for life. "You have become an industry," he told Ingrid. "Your husband is driving you; the film companies are driving you; you let everybody drive you." In a way, he was correct—but none of this "driving" could have occurred without her cooperation. Capa did not want a life with her in Hollywood, but on the road, in places exotic and distant (especially wherever there was the high drama of war). He desired the woman, not the film star—but not for a wife, and this, along with his heavy drinking and a certain recklessness, put the brakes on the velocity of their affair.

Ingrid met the married Larry Adler when she went abroad to entertain troops during the war. "I fell in love with her immediately," he revealed years later. He thought she was the least affected person he had ever met, and the most generous performer who came to the front. He also felt that she was not exactly right for the task: "The boys wanted comic book humor, burlesque, raw stuff—and there was Ingrid, reading mostly from plays and poems."

It was her seriousness and her respect for his musicianship that changed Adler's life: "If it wasn't for Ingrid, I would never have become a composer. She encouraged me to learn to read and write music, not just improvise." Later, after studies with Ernst Toch, Adler became famous as a virtuoso of the harmonica, which he elevated to concert status. Darius Milhaud and Ralph Vaughan Williams wrote works especially for him, and Maurice Ravel was so impressed with Adler's arrangement of the *Boléro* for harmonica that he asked to keep the holograph as a souvenir. Adler also wrote film scores and played with many of the world's symphony orchestras. Ingrid and Larry's brief liaison very quickly became a platonic friendship, and this endured until her death.

Victor Fleming had directed many films (and completed *The*

Wizard of Oz and *Gone With the Wind*) before Ingrid's heartbreaking performance for him in *Dr. Jekyll and Mr. Hyde*. "By the time that film was over," Ingrid recalled, "I was deeply in love with Victor Fleming. But he wasn't in love with me. I was just part of another picture he directed."

Fleming was a rough-and-tumble racing car addict with a limited education but infinite arrogance, a craggy-handsome face and a reputation to rival that of Casanova. He was also short-tempered. If a neighbor's whining cat or barking dog disturbed his sleep, he simply reached for a rifle and with one clean shot stopped the noise. Twenty-six years older than Ingrid, he was married and a father, but was evidently emotionally accessible only to drinking buddies such as Clark Gable and Spencer Tracy. He ordered the word *love* excised from his marriage ceremony and then, as further witness to his spirit of blithe convenience, refused to bring his wife into his home until she became pregnant a year later. After that, the hapless Mrs. Fleming was alarmingly often the butt of sadistic manipulations: toward her he behaved (according to their daughter, Victoria) "like a cat with a mouse." Of all this Ingrid was unaware at the time.

Notorious, which Selznick sold as a package to RKO when he became obsessed with his production of *Duel in the Sun,* reestablished Cary Grant as a serious actor with hitherto unexplored depths.* His career was foundering when he was chosen for the part, a man almost pathologically afraid of women—a man who can kiss but not commit, who very nearly

---

* Selznick received $25,000 a week from RKO for Hitchcock's services and $20,000 a week for Ingrid's; they, of course, received their usual salary from Selznick, which was slightly more than 10 percent of those sums.

sends the heroine to her death. Unlike his experience with
Joan Fontaine, Cary worked harmoniously with Ingrid, and
they formed a lifelong friendship; wild rumors to the contrary,
there was no romance or affair.

In his quiet, proprietary manner, Hitchcock gave Ingrid and
Grant the impression that he virtually owned them—or at
least had rented them for the time of his production. As with
Fontaine, one way of establishing his primacy was (as Leonard
Leff wrote) by "dominating." One day at RKO, Hitchcock saw
his secretary Carol Stevens chatting with several studio employees. Later he told her, "You think everyone likes you—
well, Cary Grant *hates* you!" Stevens was astonished, and
privately she approached Grant. "Good heavens!" he replied.
"*You* ought to know how possessive Hitch is!"

Hitchcock took special, whimsical pleasure in writing the
three-minute balcony kissing scene in which Grant and Ingrid
nibble at each other's lips, ears and neck while talking about
their plans to cook a chicken dinner. (When Ben Hecht saw
the pages of dialogue, he said, "I don't get all this talk about
a chicken.") Devised by Hitchcock in an attempt to circum-
vent the Hollywood restrictions against prolonged kissing, the
scene, he said, gave the public

> the great privilege of embracing Cary Grant and Ingrid
> Bergman together. It was a kind of temporary ménage à
> trois. I felt that they should remain in an embrace and that
> we should join them. So when they got to the phone, the
> camera followed them, never leaving the closeup all the
> way, right over to the door—all in one continuous shot.
> The idea came to me many, many years ago when I was on
> a train going from Boulogne to Paris. There's a big, old red-
> brick factory, and at one end of the factory was this huge,
> high brick wall. There were two little figures at the bottom

of the wall—a boy and a girl. The boy was urinating against the wall, but the girl had hold of his arm and she never let go. She'd look down at what he was doing, and then look around at the scenery, and down again to see how far he'd got on. And that was what gave me the idea. She couldn't let go. Romance must not be interrupted, even by urinating. [Grant and Bergman] told me they felt very awkward in that scene in *Notorious*. But I told them not to worry, it would look great on film, and that's all that mattered. It's one of my most famous scenes.

While filming *Notorious,* as Ingrid recalled, "Hitch could be a little shocking sometimes. It wasn't so much what he said as how he said it and the moment he chose to say it—it was sometimes inappropriate, and people could feel embarrassed. But he was absolutely a genius." The inappropriate remarks were generally of the schoolboy type, a little British toilet humor or a sexual limerick.

Hitchcock was justifiably proud of the scene in which Ingrid goes to the office of the American intelligence agents in Rio to tell them that Claude Rains has proposed marriage and wants an answer before lunch. "You might think," Hitchcock said in July 1975, "that I would concentrate on the reactions of the men in the room—what they thought of the idea, what their expressions would be, and so forth. But I didn't do that. I kept the camera on Grant and Bergman, because it was their glances and expressions that carried the emotional weight of the scene. The other people in the room were incidental—what the audience needed to feel was the tension between Grant and Bergman. Would he break his silence? What did he feel about her? Here she was, wondering if he would let her do this—so I concentrated on closeups of them and ignored the rest."

Throughout, Ingrid was brilliant, and Hitchcock, who

had few criticisms for her, routinely kept her a few moments at the end of the day's work. Never given to praise any actor, he offered her a drink, smiled and said, "It was very good today, Ingrid—very good." In fact, every day was good, and they both knew it, as would the critics. "Ingrid Bergman's performance here is the best that I have ever seen," wrote James Agee, who was not easily pleased, and the *Film Bulletin* summarized the critical consensus, praising "Ingrid Bergman's brilliant portrayal, [which] again makes her a candidate for an Academy Award" (for which, amazingly, she was not even nominated—nor was anyone connected with this master-work).

In any case, Ingrid was more concerned with the quality of her acting than with the accumulation of awards. "I really don't know much about acting," she said. "As for my one year of [drama] school [in Stockholm], I'm sure I learned about using the voice, using the body, listening to others. But instinct is what I go on. The only thing I go for is simplicity and honesty, because if something isn't simple and honest, then it doesn't reach people. It's lost." Regarding the role of Alicia in *Notorious,* she added, "I like to portray characters whose lives have been irregular, or sometimes even a little abnormal—people who have been affected by unusual circumstances, or who have been reared in unusual environments."

As for the undercurrent of tension between actress and director, she ensured that their friendship would remain intact, and she encouraged Hitchcock to think of future projects for them to share. "He was very exclusive with me all during production," she said. "All of us were like his pieces of chess on a board. As long as we held to our assigned place on the board, we had a lot of range—with our expression, for example. But if he thought we were getting something wrong, or going away from our place on the board, he said so at once. Hitch and I were good friends and worked very closely together. He was very controlled—he knew that he had to be, and that I had to be. The most awful things were going on for both of us in our lives, but he kept his temper. I never heard him raise his voice or yell or scream—even when I was stubborn and demanding!"

The basic concern of *Notorious* is a twofold redemption— a woman's need to be trusted and loved, which will enable her to transcend a life that has become empty of affection and riddled with guilt; and a man's need to open himself to love, which will enable him to overcome a life of severe emotional repression. Aptly, Hitchcock and Hecht chose to locate this romance about trust and its betrayal within the plot of an espionage thriller, for spies are characterized by their exploitation of trust. Going one step further, the motif was represented in the image of drinking. Instead of standing for unity, toasting health or celebrating prosperity, all the drinking in *Notorious* is either socially empty or downright poisonous—thus the opening whiskey-soaked party; Alicia's pattern of camouflaging emotional rejection by pouring herself a drink; the ingredient for the bomb hidden within a wine bottle; and the poisoned coffee.

There is an actress in *Notorious* about whom little has been written in recent decades but whose role is central to the picture and whose performance is unforgettably, deliciously villainous. The mother of Claude Rains was to have been played by Ethel Barrymore, but she turned down the part. RKO then suggested Mildred Natwick. But the role of the spidery, tyrannical matron demanded a stronger, older presence. To the rescue came Reinhold Schünzel, who portrays a surprisingly benevolent Nazi scientist of whom Alicia becomes genuinely fond. Schünzel, an actor and director perhaps best known for the original *Viktor Viktoria,* proposed one of the great actresses of prewar Germany, Leopoldine Konstantin. Tall and aristocratic, she spoke English with a clearly enunciated Teutonic accent. She was at the time fifty-nine years old, but audiences had no trouble accepting her as the mother of Claude Rains, who was fifty-six.

Leopoldine Konstantin came from a wealthy Austro-Hungarian family who were horrified when she expressed a yearning to go on the stage; in fact, they all but disowned her until she had triumphantly acted with Max Reinhardt's respected Deutsches Theater. Her specialty was, of all things, light drawing-room comedy, in which she excelled. Eventually, she formed her own touring repertory company and continued acting in films (which she had done since 1910, when she was twenty-four). In 1937, Konstantin fled Hitler and settled in Hollywood, where she believed she was destined for permanent retirement. When her only son died in a London air raid early in the war, she lost all interest in acting.

But then Hitchcock, frustrated in his search for the perfect "Madame Sebastian," heard from Schünzel that Konstantin was living quietly in Hollywood. He remembered seeing her onstage in Munich twenty years earlier, and he sought her out. Encouraged by friends and reassured by Hitchcock, she accepted the role. "I almost frightened myself," she recalled after completing the picture. "Never before have I attempted such a role. When I saw it, I thought, 'My God, I'm a female Boris Karloff! What will my friends ever think of me?' " In person, she was a woman of quick wit and enormous warmth, nothing at all like Madame Sebastian. *Notorious* was her only American film. In the early 1950s, she returned to Europe, settled in Vienna and died there in 1965, aged seventy-nine. Leopoldine Konstantin's singular performance in the picture won for her a richly deserved American legacy.

The final moments of *Notorious* are remarkable for Hitchcock's ability to evoke power from camera movement, lighting and performances. Perhaps rarely in the history of the movies has an actress been so delicately, adoringly photographed as Ingrid in the final bedroom scene. As a woman sick unto death, she was rendered in shadow and half-light, enveloped in a radiant tenderness. Hitchcock disallowed any accompanying music for the scene, whose whispers and muted gestures lead to Devlin's final admission to Alicia that he loves her. "Oh, you love me!" she whispers. "Why didn't you tell me before?" As the camera encircles them both, he replies, "I was a fat-headed guy, full of pain. It tore me up not having you."

It is usually easy, watching movies, to recognize the difference between, on the one hand, a director's aesthetic distance and, on the other hand, a deeply personal emotional involvement. The former attitude characterized, for example, the appreciative detachment of D. W. Griffith's approach to Lillian Gish and F. W. Murnau's to Janet Gaynor. But the sentimental attachment was obvious in Josef von Sternberg's rendering of Marlene Dietrich, and Hitchcock's presentation of Madeleine Carroll, Ingrid Bergman, Grace Kelly and Tippi Hedren. In this regard, all the motifs of *Notorious,* and all the tangle of emotions that comprised the relationship between Alfred Hitchcock and Ingrid Bergman, coalesce in the final sequence, wherein he created perhaps the most deeply felt love scene of his career.

Straight from the pages of a fairy tale—the Prince saves

Sleeping Beauty—it remains every romantic's ultimate fantasy: to save the beloved from the jaws of death. That it remains so compelling many decades later is a tribute to the talents and sentiments of its director, his writer, his leading man— and perhaps most of all to Ingrid Bergman, the closest actor-collaborator in Hitchcock's career.

Chapter Nine

BREAKING AND ENTERING

(1947-1948)

Ann Todd, in *The Paradine Case*

David O. Selznick liked to think of himself as a star-maker. He brought Vivien Leigh to America and assured her international celebrity when he cast her in *Gone With the Wind*. He enabled Joan Fontaine to graduate to A status in Hollywood when he gave her the leading role in *Rebecca*. He believed that Phylis Isley, a deeply insecure and not hugely talented girl with a slight speech impediment, could be turned into a star. He made her over as Jennifer Jones; saw to it that Twentieth Century-Fox engaged her for the title role in *The Song of Bernadette,* for which she won an Oscar as Best Actress; and eventually married her. In 1946, Selznick decided to create another new star.

Since its publication in 1933, he had been intrigued by the Robert Hichens novel *The Paradine Case*. That year, Selznick went to work at MGM, and at his urging, the studio bought the film rights and hoped to interest Garbo for the leading role. But she had no liking for it, and there the project lay, undeveloped and unscripted. At one point, MGM announced that John and Lionel Barrymore would co-star with Diana Wynyard. Finally, in 1946, the now-independent Selznick bought the rights from MGM and showed the novel to Hitchcock, who took it on with considerable enthusiasm. Everyone knew that the book would require wholesale cutting, reshaping and simplification, and that its transformation into a movie was an enormous challenge. Still, Selznick and Hitchcock warmed to the task. At more than 525 pages, *The Paradine Case* was essentially a novel of interlocking character studies.

The story seemed straightforward. In England, Ingrid Paradine murders her husband, Colonel Paradine, a military hero. Her defending lawyer jeopardizes his marriage when he falls in love with her. Acquitted of the crime, the guilty woman then takes her own life. Other lawyers figure in the case, and there are a judge and his wife and ancillary characters who illuminate the plot and one another.

Hitchcock liked the English setting, the courtroom drama, the sense of romantic obsession and the murky psychology of just about everyone in the book. He was also at the end of his contract with Selznick and was planning to produce his own films, alternately in London and Hollywood. This he would do through Transatlantic Pictures, his newly formed partnership with his old acquaintance Sidney Bernstein, a founding member of the British Film Society and the head of Granada (the film, television and publishing combine).* Travel costs for preparatory meetings with Bernstein in London, Hitchcock reasoned, could be borne by Selznick when Hitchcock went over for some background shooting for *The Paradine Case.*

The success of the new picture depended, first, on casting an appealing British leading man in the role of the married but obsessed lawyer, Anthony Keane. Hitchcock voted for Laurence Olivier or Ronald Colman; Selznick gave the part to Gregory Peck, who was under contract, and from day one Hitchcock made no secret of his displeasure with the choice. Of even greater importance was the casting of Mrs. Paradine. Garbo again passed, and Selznick hoped for Ingrid Bergman, but her contract with him, too, was expiring, and she had her

---

*Transatlantic Pictures had no connection to Transatlantic Productions (1934–1954), a company formed by Noël Coward to present his plays in the UK and the United States.

own plans for the future. Dozens of other actresses were considered, including Ginger Rogers, which would have been a dramatic example of casting against type.

Among the last players to be cast in the film, the Italian star Alida Valli signed a Selznick contract and was given the role of Mrs. Paradine after the producer saw one of her recent European pictures: that, in any case, was his version of what happened. But his account was mere Hollywood hype, and it conveniently ignored the far more interesting truth of how this fine actress got the part and began a short but memorable American period in her long international career.

As early as June 1945—eighteen months before shooting for *The Paradine Case* began, without Alida Valli—an executive of Selznick's production company saw one of Valli's Italian pictures in Paris and arranged an introduction to her in Rome. "Whatever Miss Valli thought of us at that first meeting," recalled a journalist who acted as interpreter, "we doubted that she was a film star. She was good-looking, all right, and her eyes had that photogenic something, but she was dressed simply, almost plainly, and she had none of the gaudy, glamorizing patina that an American comes to associate with a movie star." As they were instructed by another Selznick rep in Paris, the Roman contingent told Valli that the producer might be interested in employing her if his European team could send good photos and one of her films. To this, she was politely noncommittal. In the meantime, would she like to come to the local American officers' club to see a Hollywood movie?

The screening for which she showed up consisted of a newsreel of the 1944 Army-Navy football game, along with a dreadful musical. "Miss Valli thanked us as though she had seen the ten best pictures of the year," according to the journalist, and then she and her husband, the composer Oscar De Mejo, departed. Soon after, the Selznick staff—still quite vague about

Valli's European career—sent for a few of her movies, of which there were more than twenty from which to choose. They watched . . . and they watched some more . . . and by September 1945, they excitedly contacted Selznick with the news that Miss Valli could be another Greta Garbo, or another Ingrid Bergman. Negotiations to sign Valli to a Selznick contract took a year—not because she was difficult but because Selznick was occupied with other projects, and then he temporized, simultaneously wishing and fearing to create a new star. When he finally decided to do so, he stipulated that she be known only by her surname, as Valli—like Garbo.

It took a while before anyone in Hollywood did some homework and appreciated the significance of the actress Selznick was getting.

Alida von Altenburger, Baroness of Marckenstein and Freuenberg, was born on May 31, 1921, in northern Italy's Istria region (now part of Croatia). Her father, the baron, was a professor and music critic; her mother, a culturally sophisticated aristocrat. From the age of eight, Alida took part in amateur and charity performances, and at nine she appeared in a seventeen-minute musical called *Gypsy Land*—produced by, of all people, Michael Balcon. After her father's death, the teenage Alida and her mother moved to Rome, where the girl enrolled at the Centro Sperimentale di Cinematografia. She appeared in a dozen Italian film comedies in the 1930s, abandoning her German surname and presenting herself as Alida Valli (taking the new name from the telephone book, she said). Turning to serious film dramas, she had great success, and in 1941 was hailed as best actress at the Venice Film Festival for her performance in Mario Soldati's *Piccolo Mondo Antico*. In her next picture, her co-star was Rossano Brazzi, and with him, she began

Alma Reville and Alfred Hitchcock,
about the time of their marriage

The Hitchcocks, 1964

Hitchcock's first leading lady, Virginia Valli, in *The Pleasure Garden*

June, the first Hitchcock blonde, in *The Lodger*

Isabel Jeans, in *Easy Virtue*

Lilian Hall-Davis,
in *The Ring*

Anny Ondra,
in *Blackmail*

Joan Barry,
in *Rich and
Strange*

Jessie Matthews, in
Waltzes from Vienna

Directing Madeleine Carroll and
Robert Donat in *The 39 Steps*

Madeleine Carroll in
Secret Agent

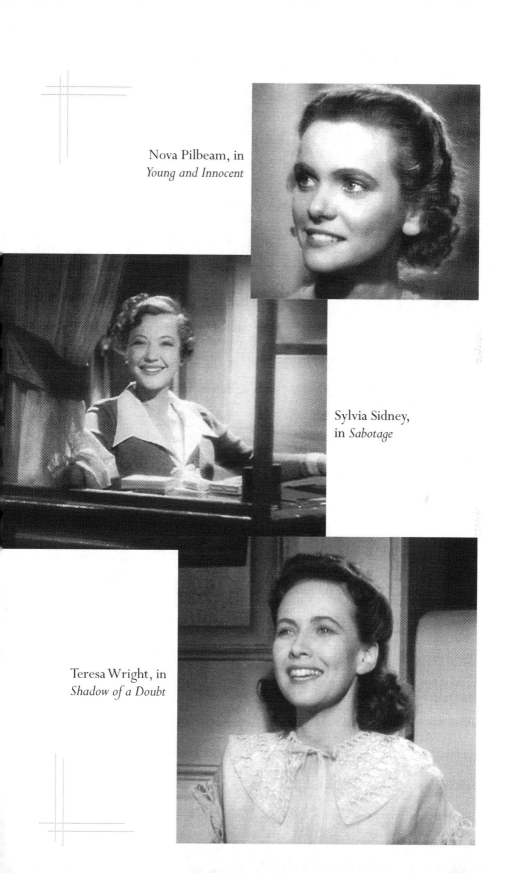

Nova Pilbeam, in
Young and Innocent

Sylvia Sidney,
in *Sabotage*

Teresa Wright, in
Shadow of a Doubt

Directing Cary Grant
and Joan Fontaine,
in *Suspicion*

Directing *Shadow of a Doubt*,
in Santa Rosa, California

With Tallulah Bankhead,
during production of *Lifeboat*

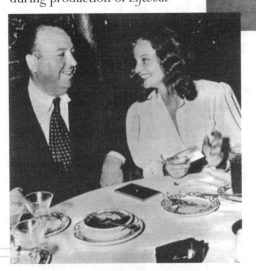

Opposite page, above:
With Margaret
Lockwood, in *The
Lady Vanishes*

Opposite page, below:
Directing Ingrid
Bergman in
Spellbound

Alida Valli, in *The Paradine Case*

Ann Todd, in *The Paradine Case*

Ingrid Bergman, in *Under Capricorn*

Jane Wyman, in *Stage Fright*

Anne Baxter, in *I Confess*

Marlene Dietrich, in *Stage Fright*

Vera Miles

Directing Vera Miles,
in *The Wrong Man*

Directing Grace Kelly, in
Dial "M" for Murder

Directing Doris Day, in
The Man Who Knew Too Much

With Grace Kelly, on the
set of *Rear Window*

Directing Kim Novak,
in *Vertigo*

Directing Eva Marie Saint,
in *North by Northwest*

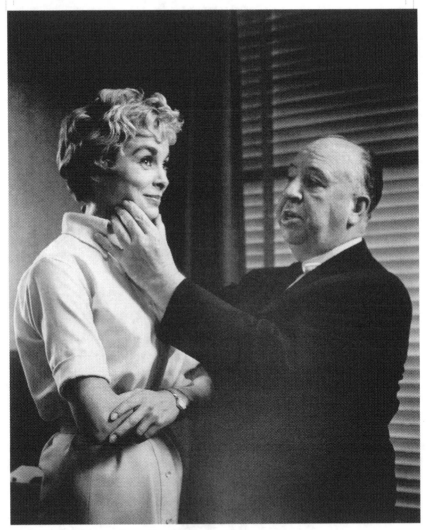

Directing Janet Leigh, in *Psycho*

Directing Janet Leigh, in *Psycho*

Tippi Hedren, during the final ordeal of *The Birds*

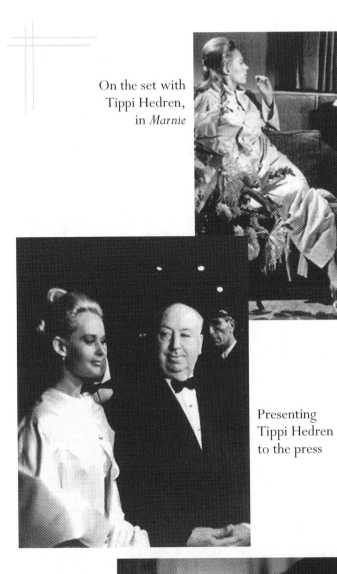

On the set with
Tippi Hedren,
in *Marnie*

Presenting
Tippi Hedren
to the press

Diane Baker,
in *Marnie*

to work with antifascist resistance groups against the Mussolini regime.

But in 1943 the government ordered her to appear in fascist propaganda films, and to avoid this, she bravely went into hiding. In a tragic accident, her beloved mother was shot and wounded by Alida's antifascist colleagues, who mistook her for a collaborator. While in virtual seclusion, Valli continued her fight against fascism and married the painter and composer Oscar De Mejo, with whom she eventually had two sons. At five feet, five inches, with luxuriant dark hair, high cheekbones, fine skin and intense, widely spaced green eyes, Valli in her twenties had an austere, patrician beauty and was photogenic in virtually any light and from any angle. At the end of the war, when she met Selznick's scouts, she was one of Italy's most popular and respected actresses, equally successful in light comedies and serious dramas.

As an Italian national, she was officially designated an enemy alien by the U.S. Department of State when her agents applied for her to travel to Hollywood for Selznick. Falsely and outrageously called the mistress of Joseph Goebbels, she had a grueling time clearing her name of the charge, which was singularly repellent in light of her antifascist activities. Finally, in January 1947, with *The Paradine Case* already in production, Alida, her husband and one son arrived in America. "On the train ride from New York to Los Angeles, I read the script they had sent me—and when I arrived at the studio, I found that it had very little to do with the film they were making!" That was easily explained: after discarding the scenario prepared by Hitchcock, Alma, Ben Hecht and a team of writers, Selznick was drafting the screenplay himself—page after page, day by day, while filming progressed.

This was Valli's first English-language picture, and in addition to that challenge, she was subjected to a typical Hollywood makeover. Selznick thought she was overweight, so she quickly slenderized; Selznick thought her teeth were uneven, so they were capped; Selznick thought her hair needed colorizing, and so it was done. With all this and the daily memorizing of new script pages, Alida felt overwhelmed, but she was a willing learner. "I never heard a whisper of complaint from her," said Gregory Peck.

New to the vast and complex conditions of American moviemaking, Alida was, as she recalled, "shaking all over at first—I just couldn't stand still, I was so nervous. But really, everyone was very kind and helped me out." In fact, Hitchcock was enormously gentle and patient with her and spent extra hours explaining and preparing her for her long and difficult scenes.

Hitchcock had to cope with the new pages of script rushed down to him and his actors each morning. "This, of course, drove him to distraction," recalled Gregory Peck.

> Selznick was totally disorganized but essentially a lovable man, while Hitchcock, whose manner was not quite so lovable, was totally organized. This created an unavoidable tension between them, and it clearly affected Hitchcock's attitude during production. He seemed bored with the whole thing, and often we looked over and he would be— or pretended to be—asleep. Something was troubling him even more than during *Spellbound*. He was never sadistic or cruel or openly unkind to anyone on the film, but he was obviously suffering terribly over something during the shooting of *The Paradine Case*.

Indeed, this was an anxious time in Hitchcock's life. He was directing a difficult project; was uncertain of his future, as the security of his Selznick era was ending; was unsure he could make a success of his own inchoate production company, which had to deal with risky postwar economies; and was sorely disappointed that *The Paradine Case* was being torn to shreds, diluted and turned into an enamelized Selznick vehicle.

Any studio would have signed him to a lucrative contract, but Hitchcock was, as always, terrified of poverty. He was one of the most highly paid and secure directors—but money was an obsession for him, and obsessions know no logic. As colleagues such as John Houseman noted, "Hitchcock [had a] lifelong and highly neurotic preoccupation with money." He was a collector of modern art, he purchased oil stock and cattle ranches, he grew richer by the year—and yet "he drove us crazy," as his secretary said, recalling his demands for frequent accountings of his net worth.

Despite all his worries, Hitchcock was unfailingly polite with Alida, who was both respectful and willing to learn. He genuinely liked her; he sympathized with her uneasiness in English and her occasional awkwardness amid the oddities of Hollywood—and he consistently put her at ease. Years later, recalling his courtesies to her, she still felt that on *The Paradine Case* "he was not a director of actors. He dealt more with the technical aspect of things. He left actors to themselves, but he had precise instructions for the camera." Decades later, Alida Valli's performance in *The Paradine Case* seems richer, subtler and more complex than it did for audiences in 1948, just as the picture itself is arguably a far finer one than even Hitchcock's partisans have allowed.

Also playing a major role in *The Paradine Case* was the British actress Ann Todd, who was making her American movie debut, too. In 1930, Hitchcock had seen her onstage in London, in *Honour's Easy,* and had told a journalist, "In the right part, she would do extremely well." He now thought that the role of Gay Keane, the lawyer's wife, was the right part. At thirty-nine, Ann was a strikingly elegant, cool blonde with expressive eyes and a restrained technique; she had been in films since 1931, and had made a huge success most recently as a troubled pianist in *The Seventh Veil*.

"He took the trouble to study his actors quite apart from what we were playing," Ann recalled years later, "and so he was able to bring out hidden things. But he was also very puckish— he waited for silence on the set before he called 'Action!' and then he whispered the naughtiest things to me, just before he took a closeup shot. Later, I learned that he did this with many of his leading ladies, in England and in America. I think he wanted to pull us down, in a way—it gave him a feeling of domination." (This was not something Hitchcock tried with Alida, perhaps because he thought she wouldn't understand the language, and perhaps because her husband was never far away; Ann's husband, on the other hand, was at home in London.)

Hitchcock was also, Ann realized,

a very complex man—an overgrown schoolboy, really, who never grew up and lived in his own special fantasy world. He had a schoolboy's obsession with sex that went on and on in a very peculiar way. He had an endless supply of very nasty, vulgar and naughty stories and jokes. These amused him more than they amused anyone else, but I think he was really a very sad person. I feel that he wanted to be what he was not—a good-looking man, like Cary Grant—and he never came to terms with what he himself was.

While filming *The Paradine Case*, Hitchcock's way with Ann, on one occasion at least, was more physical than verbal. "There was a scene with Greg [Peck], and I was reclining on a bed,

wearing an elegant dressing gown. Suddenly, Hitch took a flying leap, ran across the set, jumped on me and shouted,
'Relax!' For a moment, I thought he might have broken my
bones."

Peck and Ann may have been the players who most clearly
understood the conflict between Selznick and Hitchcock. "I
think power was very important to Hitch," Ann said years later.

> That was perhaps the most basic thing, beneath all the
> masks and veils he wore—power over his cast, power over
> his leading ladies, power with studio executives. Perhaps
> this compensated for his feeling that he was ugly and un-
> presentable in polite society. But his desire for power
> clashed with David's. For example, Hitch prepared an
> elaborate five-minute take early in the picture. Greg was
> to come in the door of the house, climb a staircase, meet
> me in the upstairs hallway and go into a room, with both
> of us talking all the while. We rehearsed it with all its com-
> plications, then shot it perhaps thirty times to get it ex-
> actly right. But when Selznick heard about it, he came
> down to the set and demanded that the whole thing be
> done in the ordinary way, in short takes and with cuts.
> "We're not doing a theater piece!" he cried. Of course,
> Hitch had to give in—he knew whom he could bully, but
> he also knew whom he had to obey.

After the conclusion of *The Paradine Case* in the spring of
1947, Ann Todd returned to England. Two years later, she became the third of David Lean's six wives, and he directed her in
three pictures before they divorced in 1957. Her career continued virtually without interruption, and in the 1960s and
1970s, she directed impressive travel documentaries in Egypt,
Nepal, Greece, Iran, Australia and Jordan. She published her

autobiography *(The Eighth Veil)* in 1980 and, in her late seventies and into her eighties, was a handsome, spry and intellectually curious woman. In person, Ann Todd had none of the aloof chilliness many of her roles required. "I have written 200 pages of my novel," she wrote in a letter late in her life, "and it seems to be turning out as a story for a TV series—it's much harder work than writing about myself!" Declining health prevented her from finishing the task, but not from welcoming friends to her cozy flat in Kensington. She died of a stroke in 1993, at the age of eighty-four.

After four more English-language films, Alida Valli returned to Europe—without her husband, who had found a career as an artist in America. At the age of thirty, she resumed a busy career in Italy, France and Germany, but unfortunately, she was tangentially involved in a scandal in the spring of 1953. Divorced from De Mejo, she was visiting the producer Carlo Ponti at his Amalfi villa with the composer Piero Piccioni when Piccioni was charged with involvement in a notorious drug murder. Alida never wavered in providing details of his alibi, but the ugly media exposure severely hindered her career for several years. A second marriage, to director Giancarlo Zagni, ended after less than a decade.

When she finally resumed working after the Piccioni affair, Alida was triumphantly in demand for another fifty years. In addition to movie thrillers and romances, she excelled onstage in the works of Shakespeare, Ibsen, Pirandello, Williams, O'Neill and Miller. As she aged, she accepted supporting and even minor roles and often worked in television melodramas.

According to many journalists, Alida was a shy, rather distant woman who refused to talk about the past. But in her senior years, she seemed a warm Italian *mamma* with a ready smile and bright eyes, speaking respectfully but realistically of her limited time in Hollywood. "Hitchcock was very kind to me—everyone in *Il Caso Paradine* was kind to me when I was a newcomer in America," she recalled, "but maybe I was not right for movies here. Anyway, I was happy to go home."

In the 1970s Valli seemed pleased when some Hitchcock partisans revaluated the generally negative criticism of *The Paradine Case,* and she was glad to be remembered after so long an absence from Hollywood—pleased and glad, but not to the point of excitement or rapture. Alida Valli's niche was always in Europe. She knew that and made the most of it; she could count many awards from Italian and French cultural institutions and universities, and later she was especially proud of her 2001 "Vittorio de Sica Award," bestowed by the president of Italy. She died in Rome in April 2006, a few weeks before her eighty-fifth birthday, having appeared in more than 130 films, 60 television shows and more than 40 plays. "I had so much," she said a few months earlier. "Maybe I have had more than I gave—but I tried to give something."

Hitchcock's next picture was the first of only two films he directed during his business partnership with Sidney Bernstein. *Rope,* also his first color movie, is best categorized as an experimental movie, filmed almost completely in ten-minute takes.

Based on a play by Patrick Hamilton, the film concerns two young men (Farley Granger and John Dall)—who may or may not be lovers but certainly seem perversely gay. They strangle a friend for the sheer excitement of feeling superior over someone's life and death, and then they conceal the body in a piece of living-room furniture. That same evening they host a dinner party, at which their college professor (James Stewart) is present, along with other guests; the suspense derives from the gradual revelation of the macabre truth.

Ann Todd had noted Hitchcock's "schoolboy obsession with sex," and the playwright Arthur Laurents, who wrote the script for *Rope,* thoroughly agreed. "We never discussed the homosexual element of that script," Laurents recalled,

> but Hitchcock knew what he wanted to get away with. He was intrigued by the varieties of sexual life and conduct as he was by the varieties of movie-making methods—in fact, he was like a child who has just discovered sex and thinks it's all very naughty. He might have been indirect in dealing with sexual things, but he had a strong instinct for them. He thought everyone was doing something physical and nasty behind every closed door—except himself. He withdrew; he wouldn't be part of it.

Laurents added that Hitchcock

> lived in the land of kink. Initially, I thought he was a repressed homosexual. The actual word *homosexuality* was never said aloud in conferences on *Rope* or on the set, but he alluded to the subject so often—sly and naughtily, never nastily—that he seemed fixated if not obsessed . . . It tickled him that Farley [Granger] was playing a homosexual in a movie written by me, another homosexual; that we were lovers [in real life]; that we had a secret he knew; that I knew he knew . . . Sex was always on his mind; not ordinary sex, not plain homosexuality any more than plain heterosexuality. Perverse sex, kinky sex, that fascinated him. He himself didn't strike me as ever having much sex or even wanting sex.

The perverse and the kinky made their way into Hitchcock's social chatter, too, as in a new cocktail recipe he said he had devised for Laurents: "a new martini—gin and menstrual blood."

Hume Cronyn, on good terms with Hitchcock since *Shadow of a Doubt,* worked on the treatments for *Rope* and the film that followed. Cronyn recalled the director's tendency for risqué stories, which were "not very amusing, actually—the kind of jokes schoolboys tell, sniggering and childish."

Obsessed with perfecting every one of the twenty-five to thirty camera moves in *Rope's* every shot, Hitchcock lost touch with his cast: "The really important thing here is the camera, not the actors!" complained James Stewart, who asserted that he would never again work with this director. Years later, Hitchcock agreed that the ten-minute take "was quite nonsensical because I was breaking with my own theories on the importance of cutting and montage for the visual narration of a story . . . No doubt about it—films must be cut. As an experiment, *Rope* may be forgiven, but it was definitely a mistake when I insisted on applying the same techniques to *Under Capricorn*" a year later.

That picture—the final Transatlantic project—was equally ill fated, and after the film's eventual commercial failure, Hitchcock always insisted he had directed it only as a favor to Ingrid Bergman, who had loved the book. In fact, Hitchcock had known Helen Simpson, the author of the novel, who had also co-written the literary basis for his film *Murder!* in 1930. Selznick had bought the rights to *Under Capricorn* for Ingrid, and it had been on Hitchcock's list of potentials since 1944.

He directed the movie during the summer of 1948, in London; seen years later, the picture has much to recommend it that escaped reviewers in 1949. It has the luxuriantly morbid atmosphere of its setting, which is nineteenth-century Australia; glorious Technicolor; and Ingrid Bergman, in her third outing with Hitchcock. But the long, fluid takes once more made the cast miserable.

"He got such pleasure out of doing those camera tricks," Ingrid recalled,

> but of course the continuous shots and the moving cameras were very hard on everybody. We rehearsed for days, and then at last we put on makeup and had a try at a reel. We had perhaps six minutes just fine, and then suddenly something went wrong, and we had to begin the whole reel again. Hitch just insisted—he wanted those long uninterrupted takes. Then the prop men had the job of moving all the furniture while the camera was rolling forward and backward—and the walls were flying up into the rafters as we walked by, so that the huge Technicolor camera could follow us. It just drove us all crazy. A chair or a table for an actor appeared the moment before an actor needed it. The floor was marked with numbers, and everybody, and every piece of furniture, had to be on the cued number at the right moment. What a nightmare! It's the only time I broke down and cried on a movie set. I think Hitch did all this to prove to himself that he could. It was a challenge only to himself, to show the movie industry that he could accomplish something so difficult.

There was one glorious exception to her objections—Ingrid's nine-minute-long confession scene, when the camera never left her as she rose from a chair, walked around the room, leaned over a table and sat down again. After one rehearsal, Ingrid delivered the speech without a cut, and the effect is like a Richard Strauss aria. She begins the speech quietly, smiling as she recounts happy memories. Then she becomes resolute, recalling her marriage to a stableman against the wishes of her aristocratic family. From this, she rises to the climax, the dramatic description of her shooting of her brother. From there, she dips to a coda, the tearful expression of gratitude to her husband for his suffering on her behalf and his fidelity over the years.

Technically, getting the speech on film was a nightmare for Ingrid and the crew.

> We rehearsed a whole day, and the next day we put on the makeup and had a dress rehearsal, and then after lunch, we shot one take. We had six minutes and then something went wrong—the flyaway walls creaked, or someone's slippers squeaked. Then I had to time my words for the right moment for a man who was crawling with a table or chair on his back for you. If he was a little late—stop! So we stopped. Six minutes, five minutes, seven minutes filmed. Then something else would go wrong and we had to start over again, from the beginning. So much technique and so much for Hitch to show off, and that became very, very difficult. And the curious thing was that when it was finished, I asked Hitch if the speech was any good, and he said, "How do I know? I couldn't see you for the huge camera! I hope it was good, Ingrid—we rehearsed it!"

In a film not highly regarded even by most Hitchcock fans, Ingrid's uninterrupted speech has been studied for years by apprentice and accomplished film actors. In 1975, when she won her third Academy Award (for her supporting role in *Murder on the Orient Express*), Ingrid said, "Really, that was very nice, but I didn't think I deserved it. People were so impressed because I did a long dialogue [with Albert Finney] in a single take—but that was not nearly so long or demanding as my big nine-minute monologue for Hitch in *Under Capricorn*!" On the evening of the Oscar presentation, she was typically generous in accepting the award:

> Thank you very much indeed. It's always nice to get an Oscar, but in the past, he has shown he is very forgetful and has poor timing, because last year, when [Truffaut's film] *Day for Night* won, I couldn't believe that Valentina Cortese [one of the players in it] was not nominated, because she gave the most beautiful performance. And now, here I am—her rival, because she is nominated this year, and I don't like it at all. Where are you, Valentina? [She spotted her friend in the audience, and Cortese rose and blew Ingrid a kiss.] Ah, there you are! Please forgive me, Valentina, I didn't mean to win!

As in *Rope,* the problem with the long takes in *Under Capricorn* was a lack of subjective viewpoint, and the long takes are essentially anticinematic. Hume Cronyn put the matter succinctly: "I think this method led him astray. He became so fascinated by it that the line of the narrative got lost, and there was an awkwardness telling the story." Indeed, Hitchcock himself later summarized the basis of all good filmmaking when he said, "The best way to do it is with scissors."*

Ingrid had to agree. "He did this sort of thing in order to prove to himself that he could—it was a challenge to himself, and a challenge to show the movie industry what he could figure out. But the audience couldn't care less. If he had cut to a closeup or a medium shot and just told a good story and cut it as usual, the audience would be just as happy as if the camera

---

*This remark was the whole of his response to the applause at a gala in his honor, tendered by the Film Society of Lincoln Center, New York, on April 29, 1974. Moments before, the audience had seen the killing with scissors in *Dial "M" for Murder,* and, typically, Hitchcock's comment had a double meaning.

was rolling up- and downhill and keeping focus, going under tables and all that!"

In some ways, *Under Capricorn* continued themes in Ingrid's previous Hitchcock films, as she was the first to understand. From *Spellbound* came the motif of the secret and the transfer of guilt from childhood to a neurotic adulthood; from *Notorious,* there was the theme of a woman's alcoholic intemperance and the attempted poisoning of her. Most of all, however, *Under Capricorn* is the story of a face—Ingrid's. Her first appearance is indicated by a closeup of her bare feet at a dinner party, a neat marker of the film's dual themes of enslavement and lost manners. After that, the film is virtually a study of her tortured, confused, haunted but exquisite features—in mirrors, in medium shot, in close shot and from every angle. "Ah, yes," Hitchcock had Joan Chandler say in *Rope,* "Ingrid Bergman! She's the *Virgo* type—I think she's just lovely!"

As did he, and it may be that his obsession with technical matters for this film was his way of avoiding a new and unpleasant reality. On the weekend of her thirty-third birthday, which fell on Sunday, August 29, 1948, Ingrid went to Paris to discuss making a film with the Italian director Roberto Rossellini.

As the saying goes, the rest is history. Eventually, after returning to Los Angeles when *Under Capricorn* was complete, Ingrid Bergman left for Italy; made a movie with Rossellini on a volcanic island called Stromboli, which gave its name to the first of their five movies together; bore their son out of wedlock; and was vilified from the floor of the United States Senate as "a free-love cultist . . . an apostle of degradation" and "a force of moral evil." For years, her films were banned all over America, where she was threatened with arrest and imprisonment if she returned.

In a kind of mass hypocrisy, Americans felt betrayed by the woman who had recently played a nun in *The Bells of St. Mary's* and Joan of Arc on Broadway and in an epic movie—and who was thought to be only a simple housewife and devoted mother without any personal problems. "The devil himself is at work in her life," fumed the Boston *Pilot,* the official Catholic newspaper of that diocese. "Some people have tried to make romance out of a cheap, sordid, immoral affair [with Rossellini]. Miss Bergman has openly and brazenly flouted the laws of God, and decent, moral Americans should stay away from these practitioners of moral filth."

Similar sentiments were printed in Catholic periodicals all over the country, and were heard from far too many pulpits. Even beyond the Catholic realm, 5.5 million American social club women voted to boycott all of Ingrid Bergman's movies—*The Bells of St. Mary's* included. Alas, such condemnations (and they proliferated from Maine to California) were an egregious symptom of a gravely corrupt religious sensibility, not to say an outrageous social hypocrisy.

But it is worth adding that in Europe, Catholic clergymen and layfolk minded their own business; they had, after all, far more pressing postwar problems than condemning movie stars and directors, and they rightly considered the Bergman-Rossellini affair a private matter. In Rome, *Il Popolo,* the newspaper of the Catholic Party, considered the American condemnations "a pre-ordained plan of cannibalistic aggression against Miss Bergman." And the official Vatican newspaper printed no denunciation.

In the United States, the National Legion of Decency (sponsored by Catholic bishops to monitor films) wielded such power that it could ruin a film's financial success by condemning it. But—perhaps to everyone's astonishment—the Legion issued a remarkable statement: "It is our policy to judge the film itself, not the actors in it." And with those words—would wonders never cease?—they rated *Stromboli* an acceptable motion picture for public viewing. Perhaps the last citation on the matter should be the remark from an elderly Italian priest, who had no patience with merely human judgments: "Why do they talk about a scandal, when God has been so good and blessed their union with a child?"

"Nobody could have lived up to that unreal image people had of me during the 1940s," Ingrid said years later. In a way, that image began with Selznick: "I wanted to put Ingrid on a pedestal, and I insist upon keeping her on that pedestal." But she wanted nothing of the sort:

> When people saw that I did not perfectly fit that image, they felt betrayed and all hell broke loose. They decided that I had planned so much deception all along, and that when I left my husband and daughter I had no intentions of ever coming back—that I had wanted to go to Italy and be a star there, and to hell with everything else. But why would I have gone to Italy and to Rossellini if I wanted to be a big star? That would have been the worst possible place for that! In Hollywood, I was being offered the best scripts and the best directors in 1949—Hitchcock, Huston, Wyler, Mankiewicz, they all wanted to work with me. But I wanted something else. I wanted a different environment and a simpler kind of moviemaking. I wanted to expand my talents, and the Italians were making the kinds of movies that deeply impressed me.

When she returned to London to resume work on *Under Capricorn* after her first meeting with Rossellini, Hitchcock asked about her weekend. "I met a director from Italy, that's all," she replied.

"Hitch resented her going off with Rossellini," said Arthur Laurents, reflecting an impression common among those who knew Hitchcock well. "His resentment was not caused simply by the fact that he adored Bergman. It was also because she was leaving him for another director." Indeed, Hitchcock implied as much: "I am still," he said years later, "in mourning for the films I would have made with Ingrid Bergman, the films that never were. When she left for Italy and stayed there, it was a loss to me, to the world, and to her."

"I remember it very clearly," Ingrid said in May 1975. "Hitch looked down on me when I left Hollywood for Rossellini, to do neo-realistic films. He said, 'What for?' I told him that I wanted a change of movie styles—I wanted to do something different, something new. I was so fed up always to play the same people in the same background, with the same extras—it was always the same people, wearing different clothes. But Hitch couldn't accept that."

His relationship with Ingrid, as poignant and painful as it sometimes was, had been professionally beneficial for both of them, and it was eventually transformed into a lifelong friendship, thanks to her loyalty, goodwill and common sense. "But he never forgave Ingrid Bergman for having left him for Rossellini," according to François Truffaut.

Over the next five years, Alfred Hitchcock could not find the right leading lady for any of his films. To stir up the creative and emotional embers within him, he had to wait for a new alliance, another historic partnership like the one he had enjoyed with Ingrid. Finally, that happened, in the summer of 1953, with the entrance into his life of twenty-three-year-old Grace Kelly.

Chapter Ten

THE LURE

(1949-1950)

Marlene Dietrich, in *Stage Fright*

Pat Hitchcock had wanted to be an actress from her youth, and her talent and self-confidence (in addition to her father's name and connections) helped her to achieve early success. On January 27, 1942, she appeared on Broadway in John van Druten's play *Solitaire,* in the role of a precocious, well-to-do eleven-year-old girl who befriends a poor homeless man. In a long and demanding part, thirteen-year-old Pat acquitted herself "with childish innocence, sincerity and spontaneity," according to *The New York Times.*

Oddly, the producers put out the word that Pat was not thirteen but twelve years old, and this the press accepted. Perhaps the subterfuge was created because she seemed younger and smaller than her actual age; or perhaps it was thought that more praise would be forthcoming if a year were subtracted from her true age. Whatever the reason, this curious fiction persisted for the next several years, but without any positive impact on her early career. The attack on Pearl Harbor in December 1941, and America's sudden entry into World War II, altered everything in American life, Broadway fortunes included, and *Solitaire* closed after twenty-three performances. Those who recall it assert it was a good play, well written, staged and acted.

As the title character in *Violet,* Pat appeared on Broadway a second and final time almost three years later, beginning on October 24, 1944. Written and directed by Whitfield Cook and based on his magazine stories, the play and sixteen-year-old Pat (still billed as a year younger) were dismissed as "monotonous." *Violet* vacated the Belasco Theatre on November 11, after precisely the same number of performances as *Solitaire*. Alma was with her daughter in New York for both these early professional excursions, but Hitchcock was otherwise engaged: in early 1942, he was detained in California while directing the problem-ridden *Saboteur;* in autumn 1944, he was completing *Spellbound.*

After the final curtain of *Violet,* Pat returned to Los Angeles and graduated from the Marymount School in 1947, a few weeks before her nineteenth birthday. Still eager to be an actress, she won over her parents, who enrolled her at the Royal Academy of Dramatic Art, London. At the end of her studies two years later, Hitchcock offered his daughter a small role in *Stage Fright,* which he was directing in England during the summer of 1949. An inventive romantic-comic thriller, the picture concerns a drama student forced to play roles in real life in order to discover the identity of a killer.

The team of screenwriters for *Stage Fright* included Whitfield Cook, now a Hitchcock family friend—and perhaps more than that. Cook and Alma, according to biographer Patrick McGilligan, had a love affair, or a reasonable facsimile thereof. "It appears that, on October 1 [1948], after a cozy dinner at a restaurant, they began making love," McGilligan wrote. This is an extraordinary statement, and one wants to know precisely why "it appears" so. (As written, the assertion improbably suggests that a public dining room was the scene of a passionate encounter; surely this was not the case, even for the wife of a gourmand.) The only source for McGilligan's inexplicably coy report is (or was) *something* in the journal of Whitfield Cook, to which McGilligan claimed access but of which he cited only one phrase—about the lovemaking being "complicated by an over-

seas call." It is disappointing not to have anything clearer, by indi-
rect or direct citation, from Cook's journal; nor is there any ancillary statement from anyone about this astonishing inference.

If indeed this was a consummated love affair, Hitchcock's
reaction to it has never been recorded. In the event, he may
have been surprised, not least of all because Cook was (thus
McGilligan) "a bachelor with homosexual friends . . . [who]
spent as much time with men as with women." This is madden-
ingly vague writing: by "spent . . . time," McGilligan clearly
means "in bed." And does the phrase "a bachelor with homosexual friends" mean Cook was gay? Perhaps McGilligan was con-
strained by the fact that Cook was still alive when the
biography was written; but since he claims to have had access
to Cook's journals and to have conducted an on-the-record interview, why the double-talk?

It is unlikely that Hitchcock would have been unaware of
any romantic commotion between his wife and his screenwriter—if such was the case. He may have been complaisant,
or indifferent, or grateful that someone was offering Alma
what he could or would not; the possibilities are legion. "You
never knew quite what Hitchcock was thinking," said Frank
Launder, "because he always played his cards close to his chest."
Later, George Cukor concurred: "Hitch was so perverse! He'd
never tell you what he really thinks—never, never!" Whatever
did or did not occur, it seems that no one had the confidence of
either Mr. or Mrs. Hitchcock in this doubtful matter.

For the much-maligned *Stage Fright*, which (unjustly)
has never had a substantial fan base, Hitchcock had two very
different leading ladies, both of whom, he claimed, gave him
headaches.

Prior to filming, however, Hitchcock, Whit Cook and Alma

decided to include a unique element at the beginning of the picture—a flashback that tells the audience not the truth but a lie. Critics seized on this as a fatal flaw in *Stage Fright*: a flashback, it was proclaimed, must always tell the truth. But this objection can be made only by a careless viewer, for at the conclusion of the flashback, the narrator casts a sinister gaze at one of the leading ladies, grins malevolently and presses her hand down on a bloodstained dress, the incriminating evidence of the murder he has just described as committed by someone other than himself. Thus, Hitchcock clearly indicates that the flashback we have just seen is not to be trusted from the lips of this hostile character— who of course turns out to be the real killer. Nevertheless, the so-called "lying flashback" annoyed some injudicious critics, and Hitchcock found his own reasons—the actors—to discount the movie when it failed commercially.

On March 7, 1949, Warner Bros. had announced that their contract player Jane Wyman would appear in a new film, to be directed in London by Alfred Hitchcock, whom Jack Warner had signed for a four-picture deal. Two weeks later, Wyman won the Best Actress Oscar for her touching portrayal of an as- saulted deaf-mute in *Johnny Belinda*. In early May, she sailed for England, whence she received news of her final decree of di- vorce from the actor Ronald Reagan.

Jane had appeared in sixty-three films since 1931. An adapt- able and engaging talent, she was equally clever in comedies, mysteries, melodramas and musicals. With an irony Hitchcock may have appreciated, she had once been compelled to be a blonde in comedies, but she eventually reverted to her natural brunette color and to serious professional goals, of which she was entirely capable.

When *Stage Fright* failed to win critical or public approval, Hitchcock was sharply ungracious about Jane, despite her fine performance in a complex and difficult role. "I was stuck with her," he said.

> I had lots of problems with Jane Wyman. In her disguise as a lady's maid, she should have been rather unglamorous . . . But every time she saw the rushes and how she looked alongside Marlene Dietrich, she would burst into tears. She couldn't accept the idea of her face being in character, while Dietrich looked so glamorous, so she kept improving her appearance every day.

This was not quite the case, but the eventual commercial failure of the film forced Hitchcock to offer an explanation of what had gone wrong, and as usual, he preferred an actor to take the blame. It was certainly true that Jane resented the attention lavished on Dietrich. But when she "kept improving her appearance every day," she did so with the collaboration of the makeup and wardrobe crew, who were of course following instructions.

Jane's role as Eve Gill, a witty and resourceful drama student, required the character to become Marlene Dietrich's character's temporary housemaid. As Eve prepares her makeup and outfit to pass herself off as "Doris," a myopic Cockney frump, the scene is hilariously played, with Jane's thick eyeglasses, stringy hair, worn clothes, crude accent and dangling cigarette. But even Eve's mother (played by the great Dame Sybil Thorndike), sans spectacles, recognizes her daughter beneath this cover—and so Eve puts away the exaggerated homeliness. Charlotte Inwood (the Dietrich character) would, Eve rightly reasons, never accept so unkempt, graceless and homely a personal maid as the phoney Doris. The memorable Kay Walsh, who played the full-time maid Nellie Goode, was presented as plain and bespectacled, but not repellent. Hence, Eve's disguise had to be softened. All this is reflected in the production notes and files.

In fact, Hitchcock agreed to this improvement in Wyman's appearance, for the story requires Jane/Eve to play many subsequent scenes as the bogus maid, and neither the 1950 audience Hitchcock wanted to win over nor, more to the point, Jack Warner himself, back in Burbank, would have accepted Jane's unattractive appearance for the rest of the picture. As for the actress, she never responded to Hitchcock's charge, nor did she speak about him in any but the most admiring and grateful phrases.

Hitchcock's real difficulties occurred with Marlene Dietrich. "She adopted me," Jane said of Dietrich, years later. "She decided to take me under her wing that summer, and she told me what I should demand on the film and in my career." Famously called "the world's most glamorous grandmother" that year, when she was forty-seven, Dietrich insisted on a Dior wardrobe for herself, just as she required absolute control over how she was made up and photographed; indeed, she arrived at the studio early each morning to instruct cinematographer Wilkie Cooper on the proper lighting for herself. "Marlene was a professional star," Hitchcock said later. "She was also a professional cameraman, art director, editor, costume designer, hairdresser, makeup woman, composer, producer and director." It is not going too far to say that this was an Alfred Hitchcock movie except for Marlene's scenes, when it became a Dietrich movie—with Hitchcock uncharacteristically taking the line of least resistance.

The problems began prior to Dietrich's arrival in London, at the end of June. Before she agreed to the dates of production, she had to consult her American astrologer, Carroll Righter, for approval. She then paid Righter to draw up the astrological chart for co-star Richard Todd, who was signed to play the killer in *Stage Fright*. As he recalled, "When she heard that I was engaged to be married, she asked me for details of my birth date and also [his fiancée] Kitty's, saying she would send for a horoscope for us. It was just as well I did not share her obsession, because when the horoscope reached us, it was a terrible one, forecasting no good at all for Kitty and me." In fact, the Todds remained happily married for twenty-one years. "She wouldn't do anything on *Stage Fright* until she consulted her astrologer," Hitchcock said of Dietrich. "He should have received a credit!"

Hitchcock was also none too pleased when Dietrich took for her real-life lover the other leading man in the picture, Michael Wilding, who had been admirable with Ingrid Bergman in *Under Capricorn* and now played the detective in *Stage Fright*. Peggy Singer, the continuity assistant on *Under Capricorn* and *Stage Fright,* recalled that the Dietrich-Wilding affair was raucously carried on in the stars' dressing rooms and often delayed scheduled scenes.* Handsome, artistic and sophisticated, Wilding was married to actress Kay Young when he became Dietrich's new conquest—a list that already included the names of Josef von Sternberg, Douglas Fairbanks, Jr., John Wayne, Jean Gabin, Maurice Chevalier, Gary Cooper and James Stewart. (She rarely saw Rudolf Sieber, her husband since 1924, who managed a chicken ranch in Southern California.) Hitchcock knew of Dietrich's spicy reputation, but he had expected more professional behavior on his soundstage.

---

* Peggy Singer worked for other producers and directors after *Stage Fright*. In 1957, after marrying the film editor Douglas Robertson and moving from London to Hollywood, she rejoined Hitchcock as his assistant and eventually became his de facto associate producer, although he never accorded her that credit. Peggy Robertson worked for Hitchcock to the end of his career.

"We became inseparable," Wilding said of himself and Dietrich. "In fact, she would not move a step without me. She insisted that I accompany her everywhere, and she took as much interest in my appearance as she did in her own. But close as we became, there was an unfathomable quality about Marlene, a part of her that remained aloof. Sadly, our relationship came to an abrupt end." (When she learned of his marriage to Elizabeth Taylor in 1952, Dietrich was shocked.)

For this tangle of reasons, the mere memory of *Stage Fright* evoked an unusually angry animus in Alfred Hitchcock. Unable to establish a positive working relationship with Jane Wyman (who noted with annoyance that the cinematography favored Dietrich), and virtually powerless to correct Marlene Dietrich's control over everything related to her appearance, Hitchcock turned his venom on the entire British filmmaking system. Of good taste, he wrote to Jack Warner, "there is exactly none here whatsoever. Believe me, they have some pretty crude people. I don't want to bother you with the sordid details. They are my affair, really, and all I have to do is deliver you a picture. As soon as I'm finished shooting and I have the picture rough cut, I'm going to get the hell out of here." Rarely had he expressed himself in writing with such undiluted, irate misery.

"Hitchcock was a very distant man—cold and professional," recalled Richard Todd of his experience on this movie. "He was a strange man, and not a lot of help to his actors. He didn't rehearse, he just gave his first assistant a diagram of what he wanted and then went off to his office. Once we had rehearsed together and worked out our moves, he would come down to have a look, say if it was okay or not, and then shoot it." Hitchcock's cool aloofness and distance from the cast of *Stage Fright* was unusually apparent in 1949—doubtless because of his feeling of estrangement from England and the English, and perhaps because of tensions within the family. (Pat's small role was cut down to less than a minute.) A decade earlier, in the words of his later scenarist, Samuel Taylor, "He and Alma had shaken the dust of England from their shoes when they set sail for Selznick and Hollywood." They may have expected the return to be a triumphant or at least an amiable experience, but it was neither. When Hitchcock left London with his wife and daughter in autumn 1949, he had no immediate idea of the next project. He knew only that he needed to revive a career that, to some critics, seemed blocked.

Strangers on a Train did just that for him, and its success began what might be called a golden age of Alfred Hitchcock masterworks. From 1950 to 1964, he directed thirteen remarkably varied films and, with the inauguration of the decade-long Hitchcock television series in 1955, became a worldwide phenomenon.

Whit Cook wrote the treatment and Raymond Chandler the first drafts of the screenplay for *Strangers,* based on the novel by Patricia Highsmith; the final scenario came from the typewriters of Czenzi Ormonde (Ben Hecht's assistant) and Barbara Keon (Hitchcock's assistant), who worked closely with the director each day.

Produced during the last four months of 1950, the picture gave Robert Walker the role of a lifetime as the wealthy, epicene sociopath who meets tennis champ Farley Granger on a train and suggests that each commit a murder convenient for the other. More subtly than in the book but just as evident was the subtext of gay courtship in *Strangers on a Train,* and both the narrative and the accumulated scenes favor Walker and Granger. The leading lady was a Warner contract player, Ruth Roman, who was cast as Granger's fiancée, the daughter of a senator. She had appeared in more than twenty movies but was credited in only three, and was best known for her turn as Lothel in *Jungle Queen*. In 1949, she appeared in the gritty drama *Champion*, and Warner set her up for stardom. Their expectations were unmet, although Roman later had a long career in television.

Farley Granger recalled that Hitchcock drove himself, his crew and his actors with unusual zeal that autumn. But the director had a marked disinterest in Ruth Roman. "He was quite critical and harsh with her. Hitch was great fun, but in each film, he had to have one person he could harass." During the difficult filming of *Rope*, fifty-two-year-old Edith Evanson (as the housekeeper) had been the object of Hitchcock's curious, unaccountable disaffection; now, however improbably, it was an actress favored by the studio who received his verbal daggers—perhaps because she had not been his choice.

He offered his daughter Pat the role of Roman's outspoken sister, Barbara, and this turned out to be the most memorable of his daughter's three roles in her father's films. She dispatched it with a keen mix of cynicism, humor and terror and was especially effective during a terrifying scene in which her resemblance to the murdered woman almost causes the deranged killer to repeat his crime of murder by strangulation.

The image of strangulation (or attempted or implied strangulation) was dramatically rendered in *Strangers on a Train*, as in so many other Hitchcock films—among them *The Lodger, The Mountain Eagle, The 39 Steps, Secret Agent, Young and Innocent, The Lady Vanishes, Jamaica Inn, Shadow of a Doubt, Notorious, Rope, Stage Fright, Dial "M" for Murder, Rear Window, To Catch a Thief, Vertigo, Torn Curtain* and *Frenzy*. In social situations, Hitchcock frequently made a joke of such violence, delighting, for example, in showing friends "how to strangle a woman with just one hand." A famous photo sequence by Philippe Halsman shows Hitchcock doing various things to a bust of his daughter by Jacob Epstein. The final gesture: strangling her.

Chapter Eleven

ANNE, AND A
YEAR OF GRACE

(1951-1954)

Directing Grace Kelly, in *Dial "M" for Murder*

uring the four years after Ingrid Bergman appeared in her third and final film for Hitchcock, he had not found anyone like her, nor anyone remotely approaching his ideal of a leading lady. Nevertheless, by the summer of 1952, he had to proceed with his next picture for Jack Warner, *I Confess,* based on a French novel and play whose premise had intrigued Hitchcock for years. This was the story of a Catholic priest wrongly accused of murder who cannot exculpate himself because the killer confessed the crime to him in a formal act of sacramental confession. Further complications to the plot derive from the fact that the murdered man was blackmailing the priest's former (and now married) girlfriend.

Deeply talented, darkly handsome and exceedingly popular, thirty-two-year-old Montgomery Clift was cast as the taciturn, tortured cleric. Before he became a movie star, Clift had a successful stage career from the age of fourteen, with exceptional notices in Broadway plays by Robert E. Sherwood, Thornton Wilder, Lillian Hellman and Tennessee Williams. At twenty-eight, in 1948, he went to Hollywood and began working with first-rate directors—Fred Zinnemann *(The Search),* Howard Hawks *(Red River),* William Wyler *(The Heiress)* and, most recently, George Stevens, who cast him in *A Place in the Sun,* which marked the start of Clift's lifelong friendship with his co-star Elizabeth Taylor. With unfailing, discreet loyalty, Taylor listened to his obsessive guilt over his homosexuality, for which his remedies included a dangerous consumption of drugs washed down with copious amounts of alcohol.

"There are some actors I've felt uncomfortable with," Hitchcock said, "and working with Montgomery Clift was difficult because he was a method actor and a neurotic as well." Karl Malden, in the role of the detective inspector, had known Clift for years. "Monty was a friend, but he was already a sick man, in the grip of terrible addictions to drugs and drink. As a person, he was wonderful, a great talent, good enough to have been a protégé of the Lunts and Wilder—but he was an accident waiting to happen."

In the actress to play the married woman who is still in love with her former boyfriend (now a priest), Warner believed he had achieved a coup. The Swede Anita Björk had been highly praised for her performance in a film version of *Miss Julie,* and she was eager to meet Hitchcock and to appear in *I Confess.* But the actress arrived in Hollywood with a baby in her arms and a lover at her side. Warner, doubtless thinking of the American public's recent outrage over Ingrid Bergman, dismissed Björk forthwith.

Two weeks remained before the start of location shooting in Quebec that summer, and the picture still lacked a leading lady. Then Warner told Hitchcock that he had managed to sign the estimable Anne Baxter, a stage and screen actress since the age of thirteen. She had been a major contender to play Scarlett in *Gone With the Wind* and had appeared in more than thirty films; that year, she was twenty-nine, had won an Oscar for *The Razor's Edge* in 1946 and had co-starred in *All About Eve* in 1950. The granddaughter of Frank Lloyd Wright, Anne was a highly intelligent, greatly respected player who earned the affection and loyalty of her colleagues and fans. She had known the Hitchcocks from the time of *Lifeboat,* in which her husband,

John Hodiak, played the male lead, and so she anticipated a pleasant experience in *I Confess*.

In this, she miscalculated: Hitchcock let it be known that he was displeased with Warner's choice. "He gave me the impression that I wasn't attractive enough to be in his film," Anne recalled, "and so he ordered my hair to be dyed bright blond, and he merely had Anita Björk's costumes quickly altered to fit me. I didn't object to any of that, but there was a lot of Pygmalion in him—he was very proud of his practice of transforming actresses in order to fit them into his rather fixed ideal. There was also a terrific duality about him. He wanted to be thought of as calm and unflappable, but he could suddenly leap up with alarming speed—it was like lightning encased in the figure of Buddha. Moments like that usually occurred when he had ideas about the 'acting' of his camera; the work of the actors interested him much less" (an opinion shared by James Stewart during *Rope*).

As production commenced, Hitchcock was again fortunate to have the collaboration of Robert Burks, the cinematographer of twelve of his films, from *Strangers on a Train* through *Marnie*—every production except *Psycho*. "Bob Burks gave Hitch marvelous ideas, and he also had a very tense time with Hitch," said screenwriter John Michael Hayes, who wrote four Hitchcock scripts during the 1950s. "He worked long hours, and by the end of every picture was emotionally worn out. He was a painstaking craftsman and contributed greatly to every picture during those years."

Hitchcock's cool attitude toward Anne Baxter began an unending chain of difficulties for her. She had complex emotional scenes to perform with Clift, "but he was so ill and distraught that his eyes wouldn't focus. I needed something from him—some response—but there was nothing, just a blank and distant gaze. He was so disturbed and unhappy." In addition, there were physically challenging sequences.

> The storm scene in the long flashback was extremely diffi-cult—crew members hosed down Monty and me with blasts of cold water, and there were wind machines blow-ing the piped-in rainwater at the same time. We had to run across a field toward a house in this "storm"—more hoses, more wind—and Hitch called for repeated takes. He thought actors had it too easy and ought to be roughed up every so often. He was a genius, but he had a bit of the devil in him, no question of that!*

To make the enterprise even more frustrating for everyone, Clift would play no scene without the presence, approval and, effectively, the direction of his acting coach, a Russian immi-grant named Mira Rostova—a woman of no noticeable talent for either performance or teaching who had somehow at-tached herself to this insecure, unhappy actor. She had not ap-peared on stage or screen in America, but somehow Rostova had created the impression that she had a mystic insight into performance art. "She stood just off camera, nodding her en-dorsement of everything Monty did, or withholding it," Anne recalled, "and this of course enraged Hitchcock." Karl Malden agreed: "Monty was absolutely dependent on Rostova—no one could understand why—and this created constant tension

---

*The storm sequence and the actors' ordeal in *I Confess* recall similar moments in *The Skin Game*, *Jamaica Inn* and *Foreign Correspondent*—as well as anticipating the near-drowning of characters played by Kim Novak in *Vertigo*; Tippi Hedren in *Marnie*; and Julie Andrews, with Paul Newman, in *Torn Curtain*.

for everyone."* Two years later, Mira Rostova appeared with Clift in her only theatrical outing—an Off-Broadway production of *The Seagull*. "As Nina, she is handicapped by a florid style alien to the whole spirit of Chekhov," wrote the senior drama critic for *The New York Times*.

As Anne Baxter said, there was a "duality" in Hitchcock, who resented Clift's Method acting and reliance on Rostova but was simultaneously intrigued by the actor's evident self-laceration. Having dealt with gay actors and/or characters in *Rope* and *Strangers on a Train,* Hitchcock relished the gossip about Clift's private life and that of the German actor O. E. Hasse, who played the killer.

Then an unfortunate incident turned Hitchcock's behavior toward Anne from merely cool to downright gelid. One Sunday afternoon she invited Alma to join her for a drive out to the Canadian countryside. Alma accepted, reminding Anne that she would have to return to Quebec by dinnertime, for Hitchcock never dined without her. But unusually heavy traffic snarled the roadway on their return, and they arrived at the hotel over an hour late. "Alma ran through the lobby and into the dining room, where Hitch sat, a look of cold fury on his face. She tried to explain and to lighten the tone, but he would not be placated. I saw then how completely dependent he was on her, and I think she liked that dependence. He needed her to be with him at the dinner hour, and she hadn't been there. I apologized, but he never forgave me, and our relationship was permanently damaged."

---

* At precisely the same time, the vulnerable Marilyn Monroe was also under the useless tutelage of a Russian acting coach—Natasha Lytess. The 1950s was a period of dangerous cold war sentiment between the United States and Soviet Russia, but it was also notable for a curious idolatry about anyone who claimed even a remote connection to the traditions of the Moscow Art Theatre.

As she was to many actors and directors, Anne could have become a valued friend to the Hitchcocks, but this he would not permit. To François Truffaut, Hitchcock spoke with singular (and undeserving) asperity in 1963: "When you compare Anita Björk and Anne Baxter, wouldn't you say that was a pretty awkward substitution?"

The critics were chilly when *I Confess* was released in 1953, but their mostly negative reactions later seemed shallow and blinkered; more than a half century after the fact, this movie is more often rightly regarded by Hitchcock admirers as both important and rewarding.

As for Anne, she subsequently appeared in no fewer than seventy movies and television programs and enjoyed enormous success onstage in musicals, dramas and comedies. When she married a second time in 1960—to entrepreneur Randolph Galt—she acceded to his precipitous, eccentric desire to manage a cattle station in the Australian outback. To say that her life there was austere would be to glorify it: she lived in a tin house that had electricity for only two hours daily. She and Galt had two daughters, and Anne endured a miscarriage. Then one day, her husband simply walked out. The result of these formidable years was a remarkable book, *Intermission: A True Story*—"written with inner eyes and a dramatic sense," according to an astute reviewer in 1976. "She has balanced beautifully the internal and external 'plots' of her story. Had she transformed the material into fiction, someone would have compared Anne Baxter to Doris Lessing. Read this serious book and pray its author is at work on another." In February 1977, Anne married stockbroker David Klee, with whom she undertook the redesign and enlargement of a home in Connecticut—but Klee died suddenly eight months after their marriage.

In 1980, she was busy preparing several new roles. A woman of many interests and talents, of consummate charm and immediate warmth, she was disinterested in mere celebrity: "I just want to improve myself with every new project," she said. In early December 1985, she collapsed, suffering a massive stroke while walking along Madison Avenue in New York City; on the twelfth of that month, without regaining consciousness, she died. Anne Baxter was sixty-two.

"I have to consider whether my potential heroine is the kind of girl I can mold into the heroine of my imagination," Hitchcock had said earlier. "She must have real beauty and real youth." In late spring of 1953, seeking a leading lady for his film version of Frederick Knott's successful play *Dial "M" for Murder,* Hitchcock finally found the heroine of his imagination. Twenty-three-year-old Grace Kelly came from a wealthy Philadelphia family, had attended the American Academy of Dramatic Arts and had performed in a number of live television plays in New York and Hollywood. Her movie debut had been little more than a cameo in *Fourteen Hours,* and in Fred Zinnemann's *High Noon* she seemed awkward as the Quaker wife of Western lawman Gary Cooper, who was twenty-eight years her senior, looked every day of it and dominated the film. "When I saw the first cut of that picture," she said, "I raced back to New York from Hollywood and begged [the noted drama teacher] Sandy Meisner for acting lessons."

Although she was under contract to Metro-Goldwyn-Mayer, the studio executives seemed oddly lukewarm toward her, showed no interest in promoting her and blithely loaned her out for bargain prices. But when Hitchcock saw a preview of John Ford's still-unreleased African adventure *Mogambo,* in which Grace was a supporting player to Clark Gable and Ava Gardner, he saw the indefinable conjunction of elegance and sexuality that convinced him she could be transformed into a major star. Very few shared his intuition, but Jack Warner was eager to get on with *Dial "M"*, to be photographed in 3-D; besides, she came to his studio cheaply.

One of Hollywood's gimmicks, 3-D was a reaction to decreased movie attendance in the early 1950s, when television was invading the American home. The process, which required moviegoers to wear special disposable eyeglasses, did not interest Hitchcock at all, who saw it as fundamentally anticinematic, with its constant reminder to the audience that they were "out there" merely to be assaulted by visual tricks.

"Hitch felt frustrated and annoyed at having to use the cumbersome 3-D process," Grace said years later. "And poor Bob Burks had to tell him, 'Oh, no, Hitch—with this 3-D camera, you can't do this and you can't do that.' Almost the entire movie was filmed in a single set, and things would have proceeded much more easily in a traditional format, but we had endless rehearsals and were always doing an awkward dance around the enormous machine, which seemed to me the size of a room. Hitch was right when he said that most moviegoers would not see the picture in 3-D—the fad would soon be over, and most theaters screened it flat, which was no detriment to the film's effect at all."

Grace's co-stars were Ray Milland, Robert Cummings and (from the Broadway production) Anthony Dawson and John Williams. Filming began on July 30, 1953, and concluded on September 25; the release, however, had to be delayed until the conclusion of the New York run of the play, almost a year later. Despite the technical inconveniences, challenges and general nuisance, Hitchcock was in high spirits, thanks to Grace. He planned her hairstyles and wardrobe with her cooperation, and he accepted some of her important suggestions. As usual, he also tried to shock her with his crude jokes, sexual innuendoes and toilet humor. "I said I heard worse things when I was in convent school, and he loved that."

He also followed rumors of Grace's private life. At twenty-three, she was playful, athletic, popular and freewheeling. A devout Roman Catholic, Grace was nevertheless sufficiently independent to allow for love and its facsimiles without a burden of neurotic guilt. Her lovers (among them designer Oleg Cassini and actors Gene Lyons, Jean-Pierre Aumont and William Holden) made up an impressive platoon of men. She and her parents of course presumed she would eventually marry—preferably a Catholic, but certainly not a divorcé. Meantime, her youth, beauty, wit and talent were powerful attractions to just about every heterosexual man she met; she was, in other words, firmly in the Hitchcock tradition of Madeleine Carroll and Ingrid Bergman.

During the production of *Dial "M" for Murder,* Grace and Ray Milland (twenty-five years her senior) became ardent lovers, to the point that his two-decade-long marriage was seriously jeopardized. "Hitchcock the voyeur couldn't have been more delighted," wrote one biographer. Such a reaction was another example of what Anne Baxter called the duality in the director. He adored Grace; he was in love with her the way a schoolboy develops a hopeless crush on an unattainable object of desire; he was already planning a second and third feature for her, and he hoped for more after those.

Hitchcock marked his fifty-fourth birthday during production that summer. He seemed content with cosseting Grace, creating an image of apparently cool, chic sensuality whose inspiration was at least partly the woman herself and partly Hitchcock's intuition of what she might be or become under his tutelage. Decades later, her performances are remarkable for a quiet, cautious refinement and a warmth that forestalls remoteness. By projecting a credible hybrid of elegance and sex, Grace might forever belong professionally to Hitchcock, in roles created for her that were variations on herself. He even spoke to her of his long-cherished hope of one day making a film of J. M. Barrie's delicate, mystical romance *Mary Rose*.

Not only because of Grace's attractive suitors, such as Milland and others, Hitchcock clearly knew that any notion or attempt at frank sexual activity between them was more than unlikely; it would be disastrous. If she would only remain his willing and winsome Galatea—and she did—he might never lose her. But this was the height of improbability, the repetition of the Ingrid Bergman fantasy. Hitchcock was simultaneously a mature artist and something of an unseasoned, awkward and still socially insecure adolescent, resentful of the impulses that were paradoxically at the very source and center of his visual genius.

It is precisely this complex of elements that gives the life and character of Alfred Hitchcock such poignancy; that must evoke our compassion; and that in some marred, marvelous way for the better, still shares something of our common humanity. Were that not so, it would be impossible to explain his enduring worldwide popularity and his legacy of sleek entertainments that, remarkably often, are also high art.

The sexual revolution that exploded in the 1960s in America was being quietly but audaciously prepared by a few directors such as Hitchcock in the 1950s—the era of another Alfred who was preoccupied with sex: the notorious Dr. Kinsey, who had already published *Sexual Behavior in the Human Male*. Just when Hitchcock and Grace were at work on *Dial "M,"* Kinsey brought out a companion volume, *Sexual Behavior in the Human Female*—a topic that was all but taboo. At the same time, movies were pushing the boundaries of the permissible—like 3-D, a gradual new frankness in dialogue and dress was partly a response to the threat from television.

The often-lazy sprinkling of four-letter words and the easy exploitation of sex in movies were some years ahead, but things began to percolate when director Otto Preminger released his movie *The Moon Is Blue* in June 1953. Clark Gable had told Vivien Leigh that he didn't "give a damn" what happened to her at the end of *Gone With the Wind,* but fourteen years on, Preminger's characters used—for the first time in an American movie—the proscribed words *seduce, mistress* and, most offensive and therefore most publicized, *virgin,* a word that presumably could be uttered only with reference to one woman in religious history.

With that, the lid was off, and there were dire predictions about the imminent collapse of morality in America. Atomic and hydrogen bombs were being tested; there were signs of both dangerous and aggressive isolationism and imperialism; and the death penalty was routinely used as state-sanctioned murder. But the country's pulpits and classrooms thundered with imprecations against sex, particularly as it involved the feelings and needs of women. There was, therefore, a schizoid attitude in popular culture, a potent sign of which was the amalgam of affection and condescension with which Marilyn Monroe was regarded.

One of the oddest means taken to protect less frankly physical movie stars from any connection to sexual activity was by casting them opposite men old enough to be their fathers. Watching *Sabrina,* moviegoers somehow accepted that Audrey Hepburn would reject dashing William Holden in favor of Humphrey Bogart, who was thirty years older than she; that she would be romantically involved with Henry Fonda (twenty-four years older) in *War and Peace;* with Fred Astaire (Bogart's age) in *Funny Face;* and with Gary Cooper (twenty-eight years Hepburn's senior) in *Love in the Afternoon.* Watching her pictures decades later, we find that perhaps only Cary Grant was credible as her romantic leading man, and to hell with the twenty-five-year age difference between them in *Charade.*

Audrey Hepburn was lithe and lovely, entirely feminine but with a faintly boyish aspect, for she had no figure, much less curves; *gamine* and *elfin* were most commonly used to describe her—words that could never have applied to Marilyn Monroe. Audrey was also insistently European, and she evoked a some-what protective, romantic reaction from some in her audi-ences. But she was more of a fragile, stained-glass window figure than a sex symbol. This may be why her profoundest per-formance was in *The Nun's Story,* and her least credible was as a Manhattan call girl in *Breakfast at Tiffany's.*

Grace was exactly Audrey's age, and her leading men were usually also her elders: Gary Cooper, Clark Gable, Ray Mil-land, James Stewart, Cary Grant, Alec Guinness and (twice) Bing Crosby. Hence, the odd asymmetries in casting leading men opposite Grace and Audrey ought to be understood in light of radically shifting notions about sex in America, which was still in the stern grip of its Puritan roots.

As complicated as the 3-D process was for Hitchcock, his crew and cast, there was an even greater challenge during the week of rehearsals and multiple takes for the attempted stran-gulation of the heroine by the hired killer and her stabbing him with scissors. "This is nicely done," he said after one shot, "but there wasn't enough gleam to the scissors, and a murder with-out gleaming scissors is like asparagus without the hollandaise sauce—tasteless," which is a typical Hitchcock analogy, linking violence with food, a recurring motif absolutely central to his penultimate picture, *Frenzy*. The finished sequence, awkward and difficult even for the pliant, patient and cooperative Grace Kelly, remains one of the most explicitly disturbing in the Hitchcock catalogue. The attempted murder is a kind of sexual conflict, with inserted shots of Grace's legs—visible through her diaphanous negligee—pushing up against her attacker, and her gradually stifled whimpering recorded to resemble erotic moaning.

According to Grace, Hitchcock was able to sustain the demands of the picture because he was already preparing his next one, from a witty and suspenseful script by John Michael Hayes (which would be the first in Hitchcock's lucrative, multipicture deal with Paramount Studios). "He described all the details of the fabulous set for *Rear Window*—the apartments of the characters opposite Jimmy Stewart's, and their little stories. Hitch was thinking about it all the time, and when he had a moment to himself, he went off to confer with Mr. Hayes or the production designers." The result would be one of Hitchcock's indisputable masterworks and a perennial crowd-pleaser.

"The stamp of Hitchcock's genius is on every frame of the finished film," recalled Hayes, who wrote three more scripts for the director.

> But the impression he gave everyone—that he did every bit of it alone—is utter nonsense. Reading Hitchcock's interviews, it's possible to have the impression that *he* wrote the scripts, developed the characters and provided the motivations. I knew that he liked my script for *Rear Window* when he told me that *Alma* liked it—that was the only way he could offer a compliment. He also said that because I was receiving such a low salary, he thought I deserved a bonus. Then he said we ought to wait and see if *Rear Window* would look as good on film as it did on paper. And

when it did, he said the bonus would have to wait for the reactions of critics. By that time, it was clear that he kept putting me off because he wanted me to do his next picture at the same salary. When we disagreed on some points in the script for *To Catch a Thief,* Hitch told me, "Don't get me angry, or you won't get the bonus for *Rear Window,*" and I replied, "Hitch, don't ever mention that imaginary bonus again." He didn't, and I never got it.

But Hitchcock could also be surprisingly thoughtful toward Hayes: "When he learned that I'd never been to the south of France, he arranged for me and my wife to go, at studio expense, so that I could research the locales [for *To Catch a Thief*]. The trip was, of course, very welcome."

Despite his unpleasant recollections of working on *Rope,* James Stewart quickly signed on for *Rear Window* after reading the script and learning the identity of his co-star. He had new toupees created and called in expert cosmetologists, the better to deflect recognition that he was twenty-one years older than the leading lady.

Meanwhile, Hitchcock proceeded with his meticulous, deliberate construction of Grace's image. "She was rather mousy in *High Noon,*" he said, "but she blossomed out for me." Accordingly, the costume designer for *Rear Window* recalled that Hitchcock was virtually clinical in his precise ideas for Grace's wardrobe. "Every costume was detailed in the finished script," recalled Edith Head. "There was a reason for every color Grace wore, every style, and he was absolutely certain about everything. For one scene, he saw her in pale green, for another in white chiffon. He was really putting his dream together in the studio. Hitch wanted her to appear like a piece of Dresden china, something slightly untouchable."

For reasons more significant than costumes and the most

elaborate set in Hollywood history, *Rear Window* may properly be assessed as a film of unusual wit, surprising depth and appealing warmth. Both thriller and romance, it has not a moment to spare. "It was a satisfactory experience," Hitchcock said, "because it was the epitome of the subjective treatment. A man looks, he sees, he reacts—to a woman even more than to a situation. Thus, you construct a mental process. *Rear Window* is entirely a mental process, done visually." It is also, of course, the ultimate moviemaker's movie about moviemaking: the man who gazes is the chair-bound director who looks across at windows (like rectangular movie screens); gives people nicknames; makes up stories about them; and sends the blond "leading lady" into danger in an effort to resolve the mystery.

The cast list for *Rear Window* was considerably longer than that of *Dial "M."* Georgine Darcy, in the role of the curvaceous young dancer dubbed "Miss Torso," recalled "Grace was very sweet. Without makeup, you wouldn't know it was Grace Kelly. She wore glasses, and she was very unassuming, very much a lady, very quiet."

To Darcy's surprise, Hitchcock asked her what kind of pie she liked. Apple pie, she replied—and maybe cherry pie. "But I hate pumpkin pie, Mr. Hitchcock—ugh!" The next day, he shot the scene in which a neighbor's dog is found strangled. "I want you to look over there and throw up," Hitchcock said. "I didn't need to throw up, but that was the look he wanted from me. So he brought in a pumpkin pie, and he did the scene several times." Her filmed reaction closeup is more dismay than disgust—perhaps, as she remembered, because her director served the hated pumpkin pie with a dollop of crude Cockney jokes.

Hitchcock would have been delighted to begin *To Catch a Thief* immediately after the completion of *Rear Window* in January

1954, but Grace was still under contract to MGM. Executives there noted her increasing popularity and decided to loan her out for three films, to be made in less than four months—*The Bridges at Toko-Ri, The Country Girl* (for which she won the Best Actress Oscar) and *Green Fire,* in which she coped with the discomforts of the South American jungle. In May, exhausted after less than one day to herself, she joined Hitchcock, Cary Grant and the crew on the French Riviera for location work on *To Catch a Thief.*

The movie is magnificent to look at (and won for Robert Burks an Oscar for Best Color Cinematography); it also has a collection of unerringly right American and Continental actors with considerable charm, and some astonishingly risqué double entendres that escaped the censors' pencils. But despite all its prettiness, it is perhaps like a pleasant journey with handsome travel companions and a picnic lunch, and something of a disappointment after the brilliant combination of humor and suspense that characterized *Rear Window.*

The cat burglar sought by French police in *To Catch a Thief* was played by a winsome actress and acrobat named Brigitte Auber, then twenty-six and appearing in her first English-language film. Later, Hitchcock occasionally invited her to fine restaurants when he traveled abroad, on the apparent pretext that he had a starring role in mind for her. One evening, after dinner in Paris, they were seated in her car near the apartment she shared with her boyfriend. Auber was shocked when Hitchcock lurched toward her, attempting to kiss her "full on the mouth." She protested, and Hitchcock "appeared mortified by the incident. Over the years, he contacted her a few times, asking if they might patch up their friendship, but the bond was broken. The actress told Hitchcock she felt betrayed. 'One never imagines that someone like that has a crush on you,' she said. 'It was an enormous disappointment for me.'"

No such incident marred the friendship of Alfred Hitchcock and Grace Kelly.

Grace had completed eight films in less than three years, and for a year beginning in September 1954, she called a halt to this breakneck schedule to consider her future. She marked her twenty-fifth birthday that November, traveled and maneuvered various romantic entanglements. Her Academy Award for *The Country Girl,* presented in the spring of 1955, made it difficult for MGM to exact retribution for ignoring their increasing demands that she appear in whatever productions they lined up for her, no matter how frivolous, tedious or offensive. During this hiatus—on May 6, 1955, to be exact—she was shipped off to represent MGM at the Cannes Film Festival. As part of the extended activities, Grace agreed to meet Prince Rainier III for a photo session celebrating the principality of Monaco and the kingdom of Hollywood.

Grace Kelly made her last two movies between autumn 1955 and early spring 1956; that April, she married Rainier and became Her Serene Highness, Princess Grace of Monaco. She and Ingrid Bergman were the only women who had three leading roles for Hitchcock, and when she departed Hollywood for a new life at the age of twenty-six, he told the press he was pleased she had found the role of a lifetime. Privately, he was less cynical, as François Truffaut observed. "The former Cockney lad was rather awed by the title of 'princess' that the beautiful Philadelphia society girl acquired when she left Hollywood for the cliffs of Monaco."

Chapter Twelve

WOMEN WHO KNEW TOO MUCH

(1954-1957)

Directing Vera Miles in *The Wrong Man*

"From the days of the silent movies right up to the present time," Hitchcock said in the autumn of 1976, "I have never had any interest in motion pictures that I call 'photographs of people talking.' These have nothing to do with cinema whatsoever. When you just position a camera and photograph an actor or two or a group, and then do the closeups and the two-shots—well, I find that all very boring indeed. Of course, you've got to have dialogue—after all, in the silent pictures, no sound came from the mouths. But at least then the emphasis was on the pictorial and the visual."

His remarks provide an essential explanation of why his next movie, begun in October 1954, immediately after the completion of *To Catch a Thief,* may be regarded as an exercise in tedium. *The Trouble With Harry* is little more than ninety-nine minutes of actors talking (and talking some more), with only the repeated burying and unburying of a corpse for action. "The plot itself is too tenuous for a screen comedy," wrote a Paramount story editor. "Not recommended."

But Hitchcock could do as he pleased, and he went ahead. The result was a film entirely anomalous in his artistic catalogue: it is impossible to care much about anyone or anything, for the director seemed to put aside every one of his rules— nothing *happens.* The movie debut of twenty-year-old Shirley MacLaine (playing the mother of a six-year-old boy) was, in the fullness of time, considered auspicious, although in interviews

and books, MacLaine has but rarely and parenthetically mentioned Hitchcock's name.

Decades later, some academics have taken up the critical
sword on behalf of *The Trouble With Harry,* claiming to find in its
rambling and tortured dialogue all sorts of philosophical and
theological depths. "Well, jolly good luck to them," as Dr. Hartz
(Paul Lukas) says, watching a trainload of Britons escape his gun-
men in *The Lady Vanishes.* Anguished literary-philosophical excuses should be unnecessary in defending a Hitchcock picture;
his genius, after all, was to entertain a mass audience *and,* remarkably often, to deal with consequential matters. In this rare
case, he fell wide of the mark. (There was one happy outcome,
however: the movie was the first of eight historic collaborations
between Hitchcock and composer Bernard Herrmann.)

Then things happened quickly, and very much for the
better. For years, Hitchcock had tried to find a way of improving and remaking his 1934 British thriller *The Man Who Knew
Too Much.* At last, with the new year, 1955, he had his chance,
thanks to a dazzling, suspenseful and emotionally vivid script
by John Michael Hayes and a superlative cast headed by James
Stewart and Doris Day. Hitchcock admired Doris's emotional
range, and for years he had promised to find the right project
for her. Now he had it, in the story of a family on foreign holiday whose son is kidnapped to secure their silence when they
become unintentionally involved in a plot to assassinate a foreign dignitary. After the languid restiveness of *The Trouble With
Harry, The Man Who Knew Too Much* is Hitchcock back at the top
of his form, directing a picture remarkable for its frank depic-
tion of love lost and regained and a threatened family restored
to safety. It remains one of the most emotionally complex and
satisfying pictures of his career.

At thirty-two, Doris Day much anticipated working with Hitchcock, but she had never been outside the United States and had a lifelong terror of air travel—hence the requirement of location work in London and Marrakesh forced her to travel by train and ship. During her first meeting with Hitchcock in his offices at Paramount, he made it clear that he was (as she recalled) "very precise about exactly what he wanted for my wardrobe." But if his concern for her appearance repeated his approaches to Ingrid and Grace, nothing in his manner with Doris exceeded cool cordiality. She did not expect an immediate friendship, but she found him remote and uncaring about her performance—and this despite the fact that he had (he said) been eager to work with her for several years before this production.

From that day, "Hitch and Doris Day did not get on too well," according to the script supervisor, Constance Willis. Doris did not expect flattery, praise or social intimacy, but she was a serious professional who wanted to please her director, and throughout the filming, she had no indication that she was succeeding. For one thing, recalled cast member Bernard Miles, Hitchcock "always seemed more concerned with technical matters than with the actors. And he didn't like having anyone else on the set but himself to tell a joke—so he used to sulk or retire into himself if Jimmy Stewart or another player really made me laugh."

From April through July, when *The Man Who Knew Too Much* completed interior shooting back in Hollywood, his leading lady spent each day trying to determine just where she was miscalculating, just how she was disappointing the great master.

"He didn't direct. He didn't say a word. He just sat there, and all he did was start and stop the camera. Hitch never spoke to me before a scene to tell me how he wanted it played, and he never spoke to me afterward. 'Well, that's the way he is,' said

Jimmy Stewart.'" Throughout production, "not once did A. Hitchcock say a word to me that might have indicated he was a director and I was an actress." Her anxiety increased daily.

> I was convinced that I must have been the worst actress he'd ever had—he just never said anything to me about my work, and I had the impression that he felt saddled with an actress he didn't want. I felt I should try to get out of the picture long before we did most of the interiors back in California, and so finally I arranged a meeting with Mr. Hitchcock. I told him I knew I wasn't pleasing him, and that if he wanted to replace me with someone else, he could. He was astonished! He told me it was quite the reverse, that he thought I was doing everything right—and that if I hadn't been doing everything right, he would have told me.

The finished film may be the finest of Doris Day's fifty movie and television performances, but this was not a collaboration she wanted to repeat. "Hitchcock never gave actors any real direction," according to Reggie Nalder, who played the hired assassin in the Albert Hall sequence. "You really didn't know where you stood with him. He told very crude and dirty stories like a schoolboy, and he stared right at my crotch whenever he talked to me, never once looking me in the eye."

Days before Hitchcock departed Hollywood for the foreign work on *The Man Who Knew Too Much* in April 1955, he saw an actress on television's *Pepsi-Cola Playhouse*. She was twenty-five-year-old Vera Miles, and he immediately summoned her to a meeting, announcing big plans to turn her into the next Grace Kelly. This was evidently irresistible, for within days, Vera signed a five-year, three-picture deal with Alfred J. Hitchcock Productions. Her contract specified that she was never to appear in advertisements for swimsuits or lingerie and that Edith Head would design her wardrobe not only for films and television but also for general wear in private life—"so she wouldn't go around in slacks looking like a Van Nuys house-wife," he said.

Hitchcock was about to launch his own TV series, and he promised Vera the starring role in the premiere episode, which turned out to be "Revenge," a kind of curtain-raiser for her first Hitchcock feature, *The Wrong Man.* Her somewhat severe beauty and slightly neurasthenic gaze were perfect for the part of an emotionally disturbed woman. In "Revenge," her husband re-turns from work and she tells him she has been attacked by an intruder. As they drive in their car, she sees a man and cries, "That's him! That's the one who did it!" The enraged husband follows the stranger and kills him. He then returns to his wife, and they resume their journey—until she points to another man and cries out, "There he is! That's the man!"

"I feel the same way directing Vera that I did with Grace," Hitchcock told a reporter. "She has a style, an intelligence and a quality of understatement." He seemed to disregard—or felt he could soften—the absence in Vera's photos of the single most important quality that gave Grace Kelly's image so much nuance and appeal: warmth. His plans for Vera moved along at a rapid gallop: more clothes and makeup tests, more discus-sions about projects, more talk about her personal wardrobe and more considerations about where and with whom she must and must not be seen publicly. "Vera Miles is the girl who is going to replace Grace Kelly," Hitchcock told the editor of *Cosmopolitan* magazine.

He also chose to discount the fact that Vera had a full life, with two young children by her first husband and a recently contracted second marriage. But she was to be completely made over—as if turned into a new creation without a past—and to this enterprise he gave himself with obsessive fascination. "Hitch had an obsession with her, sure," according to his associate producer Herbert Coleman. "But it never went beyond imagining."

"He has never complimented me," the actress said while they were filming *The Wrong Man* in New York during the late winter and spring of 1956, "or even told me why he signed me." If he had hoped his attitude would keep her alert and docile, he'd miscalculated. To begin with, as costume designer Rita Riggs observed, "Vera was a lovely girl, too independent to be anyone's Trilby [to Hitchcock's Svengali]."

She worked carefully and effectively with Hitchcock and Henry Fonda on *The Wrong Man,* a disturbing black-and-white movie based on a true story of a man falsely accused of armed robbery. As the victim's wife, Vera gave a haunting performance of a sensitive woman's descent from depression into madness, her expression becoming gradually more distant and affectless, as she loses faith in everything—the judicial system, her husband and herself.

After delays due to script problems and illness, Hitchcock was finally ready to begin production on *Vertigo.* "Vera's wardrobe, hair and makeup tests had been completed," Hitchcock said, recalling the events of autumn 1956. "Everything had been very carefully planned and prepared, and Jimmy [Stewart] was ready and waiting. Then she got pregnant, and in the spring, she withdrew—and this was going to be the part that would make Vera a major star, a real actress." Hitchcock considered her departure a defection from their mutual best interests.

"Over the span of years," Vera Miles reflected later, "he's had one type of woman in his films—Madeleine Carroll, Ingrid Bergman, Grace Kelly. I tried to please him, but I couldn't. I was stubborn, and he wanted someone who could be molded." As for *Vertigo:* "He got his picture—and I got a son."

She remained under contract to Hitchcock, appearing in a few of his television programs, and was later assigned a supporting role in *Psycho.* "I lost all interest in her, and I couldn't get the rhythm with her going again," he said. When Hitchcock and I discussed *Vertigo* at some length in the autumn of 1976, I suggested that Vera might have given him the performance he wanted, but that her replacement, Kim Novak, was born for the role of a Kansas girl (like Vera) twice refashioned by exploitative men into the image of another. "Vera walks on the ground" was my analogy during our conversation, "while Kim seems to float—she's the ghostly figure you wanted for *Vertigo.*" His quiet response: "Perhaps. At least I got to throw the new girl into the water."

And so Hitchcock had to force the actress finally cast in *Vertigo* to be a surrogate—to substitute for the one he had initially chosen for the role. This, of course, is the major theme of the picture.

Just twenty-four, Columbia Studios' Kim Novak had dispatched a few uneven screen appearances, but *Picnic* had established her as a major new star—physically opulent, frankly carnal and rumored to be difficult. She was also splendidly photogenic in Technicolor, and she had a breathless quality suggesting that she was simultaneously available and remote. But she required what is sometimes called special handling.

Kim Novak was no last-minute compromise for Hitchcock; indeed, she was the only other serious candidate for the challenging role in *Vertigo.* She was also an established commodity, had appeared on the cover of *Time* magazine, was one of Hollywood's two or three bankable stars and justified the presence of James Stewart in a way that the uncertain and still widely unknown Vera Miles never could have. Hitchcock, however, could never let go of his resentment that his plans for Vera had been stymied. "The majority of actors are stupid children," he said more than once, particularly in the context of *Vertigo*. "Think of Kim Novak. In the second part of *Vertigo*, when she's dark-haired and looks less like Kim Novak, I even managed to get her to act. But the only reason I took her was because Vera Miles was pregnant."

Connie Willis, the script supervisor for the Northern California location filming of *Vertigo* before Peggy Robertson assumed those duties permanently in Hollywood, was forever grateful to Alfred Hitchcock for all she learned from him during their work on *The Man Who Knew Too Much* and *Vertigo*. "But I did see in Hitch that suppression of natural, instinctive feelings which the Victorian era demanded," she told me, "and that meant that all sorts of fantasies would emerge—not to mention fetishes, and with Hitch, it was black high heels and blondes."

In fact, the shoes provided the first sticking point. "Kim said she couldn't possibly wear them," Edith Head recalled, "because they would exaggerate what she thought were her rather fleshy calves." Virtually the entire wardrobe Hitchcock and Edith Head had prepared for her became points of conflict for Kim Novak, much like the earlier disagreements with Nita Naldi.

Many years later, Novak acknowledged, "Before shooting started, [Hitchcock] sent me over to Edith Head, who showed me a set of drawings. When I saw them, the very first thing I said was, 'I'm sorry—I don't wear black shoes.' She said, 'Alfred Hitchcock wants you to wear these shoes,' and I said, 'I'm sure he doesn't mind.' I didn't think it would matter to him what kind of shoes I wore. I had never had a director who was particular about the costumes, the way they were designed, the specific colors. The two things he wanted the most were those shoes and that gray suit. When Edith Head showed me that gray suit, I said, 'Oh, my God, that looks like it would be very hard to act in—it's very confining.' Then we had the first fitting of the black dress, and that was even worse, and I said, 'This is so restrictive.' And she said, 'Well, maybe you'd better talk to Alfred Hitchcock about all this!' "

"Miss Novak arrived with all sorts of preconceived notions that I couldn't possibly go along with," Hitchcock said. "I don't like to argue with a performer—there's no reason to bring the electricians in on our troubles. So I went to her dressing room and told her about the dresses and hairdos that I had been planning for several months."

She was not easily convinced. "I'll wear anything," Kim Novak said, hastening back to Edith Head's office for refuge, "so long as it isn't a suit—and any color, so long as it isn't gray." Edith then showed her the relevant pages of the script: "This girl must look as if she's just drifted out of the San Francisco fog"—hence her pale coloring, the formally swept blond wig, the gray suit, the white gloves. "She walks and drives a car in San Francisco," Edith explained to her, "where everyone wears suits—and the script specifically calls for a *gray tailored suit.*"

"If it has to be a suit," continued Kim, "I like *purple* suits or white suits."

"Handle it, Edith," Hitchcock said when he heard of this ongoing contretemps. "I don't care what she wears—as long as it's a gray suit."

In *Vertigo,* Kim Novak wears a gray suit, black shoes, a black evening dress, a capacious white coat and everything else mandated by the director—and when she saw the finished film, she may have realized that he had been right all along, that few actresses have ever been more gloriously dressed and photographed. Very much to the point, her outfits seem undated fifty years later. Like the film itself, her wardrobe is timeless.

From preproduction through filming, tensions mounted. "I never sat down with him for dinner or tea or anything," Kim recalled—"except one cast dinner, and I was late to that. It wasn't my fault, but I think he thought I had delayed in order to make a star entrance, and he held that against me. During the shooting, he never really told me what he was thinking." Like many of her predecessors (most recently, Doris Day and Vera Miles), Kim was never sure "if Hitchcock ever liked me."

For many years, Kim Novak's few documented remarks about Hitchcock were cool. With time and the establishment of *Vertigo* as one of the great motion pictures of all time, she was more sanguine: the role and the movie were "so much of what I was going through already at Columbia. We'd be told, 'You're special, you're different, we want you,' and then someone would say, 'We want you, but we want you to look like somebody else.'" Which, of course, was precisely the case with both the actress and her role in *Vertigo*—as she later acknowledged. "It was almost as if Hitchcock was Elster, the man [in the film] who was telling me to play a role—here's what I had to do and wear . . ." James Stewart agreed: "I could tell it was a very personal film even while he was making it." So did Samuel Taylor, who wrote the final screenplay for the picture: "Anyone who saw him during the making of it could see, as I did, that this was a story he felt very deeply indeed."

Vertigo was the high mark of Kim Novak's career, and she was never again offered anything remotely as significant. Retir-

ing from film and television at the age of fifty-seven, she withdrew from Hollywood to manage a livestock farm with her
second husband, a veterinarian.

Vertigo is a testament to Alfred Hitchcock's lifelong fascination for making over actresses according to his dream ideal of
blond perfection. He supervised everything about their presen-
tations onscreen, from hairstyles to wardrobes, from makeup to
shoes, from camera angles to the final cut.

"He made you over, didn't he?" Stewart shouts at Novak at
the finale, referring to the man who "created" Madeleine from
Judy. "He made you over just like I made you over—only better. Not only the clothes and the hair, but the looks and the
manner and the words. And then what did he do? Did he train
you? Did he rehearse you? Did he tell you exactly what to do
and what to say? You were a very apt pupil, weren't you? You
were a very apt pupil!" So much could be (and was) said of the
director and his leading ladies. But this close template between
the artist and the art is neither rare nor surprising, for the
artist, after all, has no other raw material with which to work
than his own inner life, however much it is to be treated and
transmuted.

To call *Vertigo* a masterpiece of moviemaking is no longer
considered a peculiar judgment. It has something of the myth of
Pygmalion and Galatea, and something of Tristan and Isolde—
and everything of a greatly inspired, greatly troubled and terribly lonely fantasist. Throughout his life and career, Hitchcock
strove to realize his dream ever more fully, but that involved a
conflict between repression and refinement, between reality
and art. "I made the film in order to present a man's dreamlike
nature," he said; the man was Hitchcock himself. Like Stewart
in *Vertigo,* Hitchcock chose fantasy over reality, and for this, the

medium of film was perfect, for the carefully designed and art-fully presented beauty of an actress is itself very much illusion. (As Ingrid Bergman said, "The hair is fake, the teeth are fake, the clothes . . . and lighting performs miracles . . .") But from that art and artifice derive deeper realities that have nothing fake about them.

And what of Hitchcock and men? He cultivated actors like Cary Grant, Joseph Cotten, James Stewart and Henry Fonda for what they could provide him in his films—precisely the reasons they cultivated him. But there were never solid friend-ships. "He was never deeply friendly with any of his famous [male] stars," according to Hitchcock's authorized biographer, "even if, as with Cary Grant and James Stewart, he liked them and worked with them as often as possible"—four times each, in fact. But Hitchcock made no attempt to conceal his discom-fort and even his resentment of men such as John Gielgud, Michael Redgrave, Laurence Olivier, Gregory Peck, Rod Tay-lor, Sean Connery and Paul Newman—most of all, perhaps, because they had the confidence that comes from good looks and the adulation of fans.

It is true to say of Alfred Hitchcock what biographer Leon Edel wrote of Henry James: a "spiritual transvestism" (which fascinated Hitchcock in both its literal and figurative senses) paradoxically protected a sense of masculine integrity, and all his life he harbored "within the house of the [artist's] inner world the spirit of a young adult female, worldly-wise and cu-rious, possessing a treasure of unassailable virginity and inno-cence. For this was the androgynous nature of the creator and the drama of his [art]: innocence and worldliness."

This goes a long way toward a compassionate understanding of perhaps the greatest conflict and pain in the life of Alfred

Hitchcock: that he recoiled from what he most desired, that he knew the deepest meaning of romantic vertigo, the simultaneous desire to fall, and the fear of falling, in love. In *Vertigo,* we learn about Alfred Hitchcock as much from the complex dualities of Kim Novak's character as from the tormented, doomed lover portrayed by Stewart, for Kim is both victim and victimizer. She appears cool, remote and aloof, but she yearns to express a raging passion. "It was actually his heroines that he identified with," continued Hitchcock's authorized biographer.

In this regard, Hitchcock's mature films poignantly explore the nature of absence and of loss. In *The Man Who Knew Too Much,* it is the loss of family security abroad; in *The Wrong Man,* the loss of innocence and family unity at home; in the trilogy *Vertigo—North by Northwest—Psycho,* the loss of identity itself, for there is no living person at the center of these three great works. Madeleine Elster, George Kaplan and Mrs. Bates are the ultimate MacGuffins.

The emotional landscape of *Vertigo* is both heartbreakingly personal and disturbingly universal—Hitchcock's ultimate statement on the romantic fallacy. He much resembled his countryman Ernest Dowson (1867–1900), whose one loving relationship, with a London waitress, was almost certainly an invention of his fervent imagination. Never convinced that he could find real love, Dowson wanted to kill off all its possibilities in advance and lament the loss forever after. All the stories in his collection *Dilemmas* (1895) tell of frustrated love, of a man's melancholy retreat into the solitude of the disturbed romantic.

In Dowson's most famous poem, "Cynara," the impassioned lover cries out for madder music and stronger wine, even as he grieves in the shadow of his lost love. *Vertigo* begins with a tight closeup of an anonymous woman's face, from whose right eye the credits spiral outward. From there to the uncompromisingly tragic ending of *Vertigo*, Hitchcock (like Dowson, in *A Comedy of*

Masks) was gripped by the contrast of mask versus face—a common currency in Victorian allegories. As Samuel Taylor recalled, "Hitch knew exactly what he wanted to do in this film, exactly what he wanted to say, and how it should be seen and heard. It was his story from first frame to last—and every moment of it revealed him."

Chapter Thirteen

NO ONE AT THE CENTER

(1958-1960)

Directing Janet Leigh, in *Psycho*

"Hitch's main purpose in life," according to Ernest Lehman, who wrote the screenplay for *North by Northwest,* "was not the one that might seem obvious—namely, the making of movies. He had to make them, of course, to keep the franchise on his reputation, his fortune and his lifestyle. But making movies was hard work and produced considerable anxiety in him. His greatest pleasure was just to feel comfortable, to sit and spin tales with a writer, and to play with ideas—to be at ease, eating and drinking, without stress."

The production of the great comic thriller *North by Northwest,* made from mid-summer to late autumn 1958, took the company from New York to Mount Rushmore, South Dakota, and from the scrub brush flatlands of central California to the MGM studios in Culver City. No Hitchcock movie up to this time had required so much travel since the remake of *The Man Who Knew Too Much.* A fast-paced comic thriller about an innocent man trying to clear his name of murder, about political depravity and sexual blackmail, *North by Northwest* differs sharply in tone and style from the several films preceding and following it, but it shared some of the same sober concerns: great comedy is not frivolous, after all. But after the obsessive and unwittingly self-revelatory romanticism of *Vertigo,* Hitchcock evidently wanted breathing space. Just when some critics were complaining that he had lost his comic sense after *To Catch a Thief,* Ernie Lehman provided him with means for a response.

With *Vertigo* and *North by Northwest,* Hitchcock concluded two quartets of films—four each with Cary Grant and James Stewart. From *Rope* through *Vertigo,* Stewart had become a kind of surrogate representative of Hitchcock; only Sean Connery would come that close, in *Marnie.* Admired and celebrated as one of America's exponents of the ordinary man as hero, Stewart became in a way what Hitchcock considered *himself* to be: a theorist of murder (*Rope*); a chair-bound voyeur drawn to and fearful of love (*Rear Window*); a protective but manipulative husband and father (*The Man Who Knew Too Much*); and the passionately haunted pursuer of an impossible, duplicitous ideal (*Vertigo*).

These four roles provided the actor with the most substantial opportunities of his career and Hitchcock with an alter ego acceptable enough to engage the audience's sympathies. Of course, none of this was deliberate on Hitchcock's part—the works would not have their own energetic lives and inner logic if they were schematic movie memoirs. But seen after the fact, the allusive autobiographical elements provide another window through which their richness may be appreciated; and as always, the artist could not leave himself outside the studio doors. The images and stories came from him or were at every turn shaped or approved by him. Given his control and approval, his rejection of this suggestion or his acceptance of that one; given his attention to every detail of music and sound effect, wardrobe and camera placement, the pictures *were* him, and they could be no other.

Cary Grant, on the other hand, may have represented not what Hitchcock considered himself to be but what he would *like to have been:* the suave, irresponsible playboy (in *Suspicion*); the ultimate Prince Charming to a blonde he nearly destroys (in *Notorious*); the innocent hero who wins the glamorous Grace Kelly (in *To Catch a Thief*); and (in *North by Northwest*) the theater-going advertising executive whose frantic, perilous journey ends with the blonde lifted up from espionage and into bed.

For his leading lady opposite fifty-four-year-old Cary Grant, Hitchcock chose thirty-four-year-old Eva Marie Saint, a happily married wife and mother in her private life. After a prolific career on television, she had won a Best Supporting Actress Oscar for her movie debut in *On the Waterfront* and had completed three more films before Hitchcock signed her to play the role of the deadliest blonde in his long catalogue. Delighted to be working with him, she presented no problems, and their collaboration succeeded without tension.

"I acted just like a rich man keeping a woman," Hitchcock said of his preproduction work with the actress—

> just as Stewart did with Novak in *Vertigo*. I watched every hair on her head. I had two wardrobes made for her, and then I saw that for half of it she was being dressed as a waif, as in *On the Waterfront*. So I took her along to Bergdorf Goodman's [in Manhattan] and I sat with her as the mannequins paraded by. I chose the dresses and suits for her— a basic black suit, a heavy black silk cocktail dress with wine-red flowers; a charcoal-brown, full-skirted jersey and burnt orange burlap for action scenes. I took a lot of trouble with Eva Marie Saint, grooming her and making her appear sleek and sophisticated. Next thing you know, she's in a picture called *Exodus*, looking dissipated!

Toward this straightforward and cooperative actress, Hitchcock had no romantic inclination—there was nothing like the knotty relationship with Vera Miles, nor was there any of the Kim Novak dustup. Eva Marie Saint was only docile and cooperative.

Of Alfred Hitchcock's fifty-three motion pictures, the most famous is certainly *Psycho,* a landmark in American movie history and the film that quickly made him a man of great wealth and power (not to say influence). Based on a slim novel by Robert Bloch that was itself inspired by a grisly series of killings, the screenplay was certainly the best of Joseph Stefano's work.

Janet Leigh was the thirty-two-year-old wife of actor Tony Curtis, mother of two girls and a seasoned performer—but she still lacked an enduring or memorable credit on her long résumé. "My camera is absolute," Hitchcock told Janet when they met. "I tell the story through that lens, so I need you to move when my camera moves, stop when my camera stops. I'm confident you'll be able to find your motivation to justify the motion. I'll be happy to work with you, but I will not change the timing of my camera." And that was the extent of their first preproduction meeting in the autumn of 1959. To costume supervisor Helen Colvig, Hitchcock said of his small *Psycho* cast—perhaps thinking of Novak—"Either they wear the clothes and do the part the way I want, or they're not going to be in it."

Janet worked fewer than twenty days on *Psycho,* but for the rest of her life she was identified with this film in a way that perhaps no other actress has ever been immediately linked with a movie. Indeed, her international fame derived from six damp days of work that December, when she stood in a shower for long hours, with Alfred Hitchcock never far away.

"It was challenging for everyone," she recalled years later, speaking of that week.

> I had to repeat the same gestures and actions over and over, taken from different angles. Then there were delays due to

the moleskin coverings I wore, so as not to be completely nude on the set. And there were the usual problems with cameras and lenses—and my skin was puckering like a prune from all the shower water, so we had to stop for makeup retouches. The finished scene is brilliant, but we had no idea of that while we were doing it. Hitch thought of this as a little thriller he was making with his TV crew, and for a while he even thought of trying to release it on television—but of course as he planned it, the shower murder couldn't have gone out on TV in those days.

Janet always insisted that Hitchcock never asked her to perform the shower sequence in the nude, but that was not the recollection of his staff, the crew and the studio executives. Makeup supervisor Jack Barron, for example, recalled Hitchcock saying he was working on Janet to do the sequence naked, but she adamantly refused. Later, Hitchcock asked if she would yield to him for a few shots intended for the European release version of *Psycho,* but she was not to be moved.

Experimenting with various forms of the desiccated skull to be used for the corpse of the late Mrs. Bates, Hitchcock tested them out on his star. "Some hair-raising screams emanated from behind my door when I walked in on these hideous, shriveled monstrosities sitting in my makeup chair. Looking back [in 1995], I puzzle over whether this was just a gag or an effort to keep me a bit on edge, thus in [her character's] jittery state of mind. Knowing Mr. Hitchcock, it could have been." Hitchcock wanted to keep the tone on the *Psycho* set from becoming somber or depressed ("We were dealing with unusual material"), but he also needed to sustain a sense of disquiet and unpredictability.

Hence he supplemented his usual jokes, limericks and sight gags with extraordinarily detailed direction of Janet Leigh, which certainly gave an air of gravity to the proceedings. No aspect of her performance was left unplanned or unsupervised, as Hitchcock provided detailed on-the-spot drama coaching for her, which was extremely rare for him to do. "Before every shot, he went to her very quietly and really gave her direction," recalled script supervisor Marshall Schlom.

A different tone accompanied the huddled whispers before they filmed the movie's first scene, for which Hitchcock was not getting the desired sexual sparks in the lunchtime hotel-room tryst between Janet Leigh (wearing only a bra and half-slip) and John Gavin (bare-chested) as her lover. Hitchcock took Janet aside and instructed her to be bold: she ought to fondle Gavin (whom she had met for the first time only ten minutes earlier) as if the couple were involved in real sexual foreplay—"See what you can do about it, Janet." She agreed, and Hitchcock said that he would give Gavin a similar direction. A moment later, just millimeters away from the actors, Hitchcock beckoned to a young crewman, murmuring in his ear, "Mr. Gavin has an ee-reck-shun." Later, Janet learned that Hitchcock had given Gavin no warning: "I was the one Hitch had used," she said. "I adored him, but he did have that mischievous mind."

Anthony Perkins was forever after associated with *Psycho,* too. Twenty-seven, tall, attractively odd and edgy, he had performed terrifying scenes of emotional breakdown in a picture called *Fear Strikes Out.* This achievement had convinced Hitchcock that the young actor—agitated, somewhat delicate and hypersensitive—would be perfect as the monstrous but somehow boyishly sympathetic Norman Bates, who (Perkins felt) was not just a monster but also a tortured soul. For much of his life, so was Tony, mostly because he was never able to accept and integrate his homosexuality. His lovers (Tab Hunter and dancer Grover Dale, among others) brought him little serenity, and, like Montgomery Clift, he ineffectually sought to become heterosexual through psychotherapy.

Working with Hitchcock, Janet was anxious to please, and Tony was pleased to be anxious. Until her death in 2004 at the age of seventy-seven, she never again enjoyed anything like the success or notoriety of *Psycho*, with which she is forever linked—just as he was forever imprisoned by the persona of Norman Bates, until he died at sixty in 1992. They may have sometimes quietly resented the ironclad associations, but the movie guaranteed them immortality.

Vera Miles was the only participant not to benefit from this historic motion picture. Summoned to play Janet's sister in fulfillment of her contract, she was given an unflattering wardrobe and fitted with a cheap and obviously artificial blond wig, her head having been completely shaved for a recent picture. "Vera was very angry throughout the filming of *Psycho*," according to Rita Riggs. "Mr. Hitchcock made her look like a dowdy, old-maid schoolteacher . . . [and] for most of the film, we saw a lot of the back of her head. But it was Mr. Hitchcock's choice. He was very disappointed with Vera, in whom he invested a lot of time, thought and emotion in preparing *Vertigo*. Now, with *Psycho*, this was some of his perversity coming through."

Rightly studied for its technical virtuosity and rich thematic imagery, *Psycho* is a grimly brilliant study in perversity. It also marked the sharpest stylistic and thematic break in the history of the Hitchcock catalogue. "He truly thought that he never got angry," Ernest Lehman said. "In fact, he said he didn't believe in anger, that it was a foolish and wasteful emotion. But there were times when he was seething with anger—all of it carefully repressed."

That *Psycho* followed the wounded romanticism of *Vertigo* and the genial cynicism of *North by Northwest* is not so surprising. All three films have as their emotional focus a desperate, duplicitous blonde; all three films have at the center a person who is unknown, nonexistent or dead. However different their tones and styles, these films were a triptych of pain created amid Hitchcock's loneliness, illness and fear of death. *Vertigo* was, as all his associates knew, a very personal film. The cool and witty adroitness of *North by Northwest* could not disguise the fact that it was a bittersweet farewell to the era of glamour and romance. And with *Psycho,* the content, style and tone of Alfred Hitchcock's films changed forever.

Chapter Fourteen

OBSESSION

(1961-1962)

Tippi Hedren, during the final ordeal of *The Birds*

"I prefer a woman who does not display all her sex at once," Alfred Hitchcock said in 1962. "I like women who are also ladies, who hold enough of themselves in reserve to keep a man intrigued. On the screen, for example, if an actress wants to convey a sexy quality, she ought to maintain a slightly mysterious air." At the time, he was editing *The Birds*—an apocalyptic thriller (very loosely based on a du Maurier story to which he owned the rights) in which those creatures attack humans, for reasons deliberately never explained.

"I seem to have developed a reputation for preferring blonde leading ladies in my films," Hitchcock continued, naming Madeleine Carroll, Joan Fontaine, Grace Kelly and Eva Marie Saint (but not, unaccountably, Ingrid Bergman). "And now, in *The Birds,* I am introducing another young lady who happens to be blonde—Miss Tippi Hedren. A woman of elegance will never cease to surprise you."

During the early autumn of 1961, Hitchcock and Alma were sipping morning coffee in their kitchen, watching the *Today* news program, when a black-and-white commercial for a liquid diet supplement was broadcast. This product did not interest him, but the lady of the brief narrative did—a blond model with a good figure, sensual but not brassy, and obviously so successful on her Sego regime that men and boys alike whistled as she strolled along. Before leaving home for his office,

Hitchcock was on the phone to his agents at the MCA agency, instructing them to find "that girl" and bring her in.

Tippi Hedren had been a successful model for over a dozen years and was then living in Los Angeles. Apart from a blinkingly brief appearance (also as a nameless model) in a 1949 movie, and a quick walk-on in a 1951 television comedy (uncredited), she completely lacked both training and experience as an actress. There was no doubt, however, that she was enormously photogenic, with bright eyes, an unaffected smile and remarkable poise in front of a camera.

On instructions from the studio executive who reached her, she brought her portfolio and some commercial reels to a meeting at Universal Studios on Friday, October 13. They pored over her photos, chatted briefly with her and then asked, to her astonishment, if she would like to sign a seven-year-contract, beginning at $500 weekly. They would not identify the producer. Thirty-one, divorced, with a four-year-old daughter—and aware that the modeling business quickly loses interest in women her age—she felt that this was "a wonderful opportunity, a life-saving gift to have a guaranteed income for myself and my daughter." Without knowing anything more, but presuming that she would be employed on television or in studio commercials, she signed the contract after a quick consultation with her agent, Noel Marshall.

"Would you like to know who this person is?" asked the agent when the ink was dry.

"Oh, that would be very nice."

"Alfred Hitchcock."

The following Tuesday, October 17, Tippi was asked to return to Universal. She was shown into Hitchcock's private office, where he sat with folded arms, looking content and pleased with himself: after all, the terms she had accepted had been a great bargain for him. They chatted for much of the afternoon—about things such as travel, food and wine, but there was not a single reference to anything about movies or TV. At the end of the day she was convinced that Hitchcock simply wanted talent available for his television series but that he had nothing special in mind for her. "I had been a model, and I had no thought of becoming an actress—much less a star." Subsequently, they were joined by Edith Head, Robert Boyle, Peggy Robertson and others on the director's team, and things began to happen quickly. As Boyle recalled, it was clear that Hitchcock was once again undertaking "the Svengali approach to his leading lady. It was love at first sight."

Nathalie Hedren was born on January 19, 1930, at a hospital in tiny New Ulm, Minnesota, near the family home in the hamlet of Lafayette. Dorothea and Bernard Hedren already had a four-year-old daughter named Patty; the girls' mother was a dedicated rural schoolteacher, and their father operated a modest general store. In infancy, Nathalie was nicknamed "Tupsa" by her father—a Swedish adjective referring to a "cute" or "adorable" little girl; soon the child was called Tippi, and so everyone addressed her for the rest of her life.

As everywhere, the Great Depression affected the Hedrens harshly. Bernard lost his store, and Tippi's beloved dog died for the family's lack of money to pay for distemper injections. "From that time on," recalled Patty, "Tippi wanted to raise dogs and cats." But times were so harsh that pets were out of the question, and Tippi recalled one Christmas when she gratefully received a single present—a coveted bar of soap.

By the time she was in secondary school during World War II, the shy child had blossomed into a cheerful, vivacious teenager, industrious at school and attentive to her family. One day, as she got off a streetcar in downtown Minneapolis, a woman handed her a business card: "Tell your mother to bring you down to Donaldson's Department Store, young lady—I think you could model teenage fashions for us on Saturday mornings." So began a modeling career, and by 1947, Tippi was in postwar New York working hard but happily for Eileen and Jerry Ford at Ford Models. Among many glossy magazines, she appeared on the covers of *Glamour, Seventeen* and *McCall's,* and her photo was all over New York when she was a finalist in the popular Miss Rheingold beer contest—a distinction she lost (as did her contemporary, a model named Grace Kelly).

Soon she was appearing regularly in television commercials, "and that's where I first met photographers and cameramen who really delighted in embarrassing, insulting and rude behavior." She learned to cope, ignoring what she could and walking away from what she could not. During a fleeting appearance on the TV comedy *The Aldrich Family* in 1951, one of her co-players was a good-looking eighteen-year-old named Peter Griffith. They married the following year, and in August 1957 their daughter, Melanie, was born. By this time, Peter was producing commercials, and eventually turned to property management. "But our marriage broke up. I think Peter [three years her junior] should have done a lot more dating before we got married." The Griffiths were divorced in 1961, and Tippi, hoping for work in West Coast commercials, took Melanie and headed for Los Angeles. She rented a home in the neighborhood known as Westwood, and there, in October, she took the telephone call from the agents for an unnamed Hollywood producer.

With his trainee firmly under contract, Hitchcock set about directing her in three days of elaborate and expensive screen tests. Wardrobes and hairstyles were prepared for her, and Hitchcock and Alma coached her in scenes from *Rebecca,* *Notorious* and *To Catch a Thief.* Speaking of Tippi's trial run, actor Martin Balsam (the detective in *Psycho,* brought back to play opposite her in the tests) said, "It was evident that she was very nervous and unsure of herself, but she had studied every line and every move that was asked of her, and she tried to do everything just right, everything Hitch asked of her."

"I signed her to a contract because she is a classic beauty," Hitchcock told a reporter that season. "Movies don't have them anymore. Grace Kelly was the last." At the same time, Hitchcock asked Edith Head to design clothes for Tippi's private life, and as a subtle but proprietary step toward changing her identity, he required that her first name always be printed in single quotation marks (a gesture he left unexplained). By the time of the end-of-year holidays, Hitchcock was tutoring Tippi on the fine points of wine and food.

She had heard that Hitchcock was working with writer Evan Hunter on the screenplay for *The Birds,* but that project was never mentioned in connection with plans for her. "Every actress in town wanted that part, and I really never thought of myself as a candidate." After four months of daily private tutorials on a wide variety of polite topics, Tippi was told to arrive at Chasen's restaurant one Thursday in February 1962, where Lew Wasserman also joined the Hitchcocks. At her place was a small gift box from Gump's, the prestigious shop in San Francisco; inside was a gold-and-seed-pearl pin with three birds in flight. "We would like you to play Melanie Daniels in *The Birds,*" Hitchcock announced solemnly.

Wasserman said little, for he had led the campaign to deter Hitchcock from what he considered the foolish notion of casting a novice in a leading role that would include unprecedented physical demands. "The studio did not back me," Tippi recalled, "because I had no experience. The men at Universal asked him,

'Hitch, what are you doing? Are you *crazy?*' But he told them that he had complete confidence in me, that he would enable me to do it. From that evening, I felt terrific responsibility, terrible pressure, and my focus in life was trying to do everything I could to justify his faith in me. If he thought I wasn't doing exactly what he wanted, every day during preparation for *The Birds,* he would sulk or pout or seem hurt or disappointed."

From that evening, she was instructed to attend every meeting Hitchcock had with the screenwriter, cinematographer, wardrobe supervisor, production designer and sound technicians—she was receiving, she felt, "years of technical education in a few months." Unusually for him, Hitchcock discussed the script with her, her character's motivations and those of the others, and the relevance of each scene to the whole. For her every appearance in the picture (which meant almost every moment), he had points to make. "At this stage, he was fantastic to work with as my director, mentor and drama coach. I could never have had this kind of preparation from anyone else, anywhere." As Peggy Robertson, Evan Hunter, Bob Boyle, Edith Head and others confirmed, Tippi was a remarkably quick study and a willing, affable colleague. "Well, she has nothing to unlearn," Hitchcock said.

Slowly but deliberately, the makeover of Tippi Hedren began and continued each day. Hitchcock thought the string of pearls she wore to their first meeting was "too large for the afternoon color" of her clothes, and so the proper length was purchased for her. He then supervised the precise color for the wigs and the style of her own hair, and for each subtle element of her makeup. He altered the line and cut of the green suit she wears in the picture (six of them would be required for the five months of production); he took weeks to select accessories and jewelry appropriate for a spoiled, wealthy but resourceful San Francisco socialite; and he labored over the choice of the char-

acter's mink coat. (At the end of production, with a great gesture of generosity, he presented her with the coat as a gift from
him; she later learned that in fact the cost had been charged to
the picture.)

"Once we began filming," Tippi recalled, "he rarely directed me or anyone else." But the fact is that he had little interest in the other players and left their questions or problems
to his assistant director, James Brown. To the cast were added
the honored stage actress Jessica Tandy; leading man Rod Taylor; thirteen-year-old Veronica Cartwright, already a seasoned
player with impressive credits; Suzanne Pleshette, who had
performed in thirty movies, television dramas and Broadway
plays; and a complement of skilled character actors. Production began in late March 1962 in the towns of Bodega and
Bodega Bay (about sixty miles north of San Francisco), and
filming of the interior sequences, back at Universal Studios,
was completed in early July.

"Tippi Hedren is really remarkable," Hitchcock told Associated Press reporter Bob Thomas, who had known him for years
and was surprised to hear such lavish praise (or any at all) from
the master about an actor. "Get a look at that girl—she's going
to be good. I gave her the leading role, a big part. Svengali
Hitch rides again!" To a team from *Look,* a popular national
weekly magazine, Hitchcock went further: "Tippi has a faster
tempo, city glibness, more humor [than Grace]. For her
scenes, she displayed jaunty assuredness when I asked for
that—a pertness, an attractive throw of her head. And she
memorizes and reads lines extraordinarily well and is sharper
in expression [than Grace]."

As usual, Hitchcock relished all the specialized practical
challenges and complexities inherent in realizing *The Birds.*

"Technically, this was the most difficult film I ever made," he told me years later. "We [i.e., Ray Berwick, an experienced bird wrangler] trained birds for closeups, and we got them to fly here and there on command. But we also had to super-impose images of thousands of other birds, artificially stripped in on separate pieces of film, for many scenes." The budget for *The Birds* quickly climbed over $3 million.

But things began to change.

"Hitch was becoming very domineering and covetous of Tippi," according to Rod Taylor,

and it was very difficult for her, because this was her first movie, and she had no basis for comparison with any other director or production. She was like a precious piece of jewelry he owned, and little by little, no one was permitted to come physically close to her during the production. "Don't touch the girl after I call 'Cut!'" he said to me repeatedly, which was difficult because we had so many scenes together. As he became more and more possessive, he wouldn't let me or anyone else ride in the studio cars with her, which we often shared for the sake of convenience during location work up north. He was very firm about that—oh, no, I must not ride with her, as if that would taint his goddess. He was putting a wall around her, trying to isolate her from everyone so that all her time would be spent only with him.

As Tippi recalled, "He was developing this obsession for me, and I began to feel very uncomfortable because I had no control over him. I had to be very careful, very watchful." Hitchcock started to observe and study her constantly, to stare at her on the set, to listen in when she spoke to others or made a phone call. Flowers, wine, gifts and handwritten notes characterized by schoolboy sentiment arrived at her home and in her dressing room. "He tried to control everything—what I wore and ate and drank."

He then had his assistants occasionally pilfer samples of her handwriting, which he sent to a graphologist for analysis. Most alarmingly: "I was stalked. First, he wanted to know which friends I was seeing during my own private time away from work—and where I was going. He never thought anyone was good enough for me; he simply disapproved of everyone in my life. Then I realized that sometimes I was being followed to events, to restaurants or social occasions—and I *was* being followed, and some of his staff and studio executives *were* receiving reports and relaying them back to Hitch, all about my ordinary comings and goings." At the same time, her young daughter, Melanie, realized that "Hitch was taking her away from me, and suddenly I wasn't allowed even to visit my mom at the studio."

Tippi began to feel that she had to do her best to avoid him, "but that was almost impossible. Everyone—from [Hitchcock's assistant] Peggy [Robertson] to [studio chief] Lew Wasserman and the men in the front office—was covering for him. I told them I was becoming very unhappy with all this, but he was Alfred Hitchcock, the great and famous director, and I was Tippi Hedren, an inexperienced actress who had no clout." This was emerging as a tale of raw, unchecked power in the days before charges of harassment could be considered; this was nothing less than an episode in which an abusive employer exploited his dependent employee, ignoring her feelings and leaving her without recourse. "I couldn't just resign or quit my contract—there would have been a major lawsuit, and I was a single mom with a little girl to support. I would have been blacklisted all over town—would have been unable to find work anywhere. So I tried to cope."

Further resentment arose over Hitchcock's frequently indelicate conversation. "He told me dirty jokes and filthy limericks, especially after he learned that I really didn't like that sort of thing. I guess he thought it kept me off-guard, uneasy."

The history of music, painting, sculpture, theater and movies is filled with the names of creative artists who are entirely dedicated to molding a career, shaping their presentation of a subject, controlling a performance. Many good directors have done this. But now, after decades of sublimation and suppression, Alfred Hitchcock was overstepping a line. Not content with setting forth his dream or ideal, he was acting like the owner of another's life. But Tippi was under contract, and for the present she felt she had no recourse but to finesse an increasingly awkward environment. "It isn't always like this," Suzanne Pleshette told her by way of reassurance. "There's more to Hollywood than this . . . experience you're having." But this was cold comfort in 1962.

As tensions increased, Alma came to visit Tippi at the end of one week. " 'Oh, Tippi, dear,' she said to me with real concern in her voice, 'I am so sorry you have to go through all this—I am *so* sorry.' "

This is a remarkably difficult statement to comprehend. The fact is that the actress was *forced* to endure it, as if it were little more than an alteration to her wardrobe or additional time in a makeup chair or on a publicity tour. "Alma was like Hitch's mom," Tippi said. "She looked out for him, protected him." Everyone knew about Alma's influence over her husband, and Alma knew very well that circumstances were becoming more and more problematic. Why didn't this little powerhouse of a woman tell her husband to desist, to stop this sort of destructive behavior, to cease humiliating himself? There may never be satisfactory answers—or the only answer may be that she tried and could achieve nothing. Whatever transpired between the Hitchcocks on the matter of Tippi Hedren, Alma's effective lack of control resulted in a kind of unwitting collusion, however uncalculated, heedless or ill considered.

Late one afternoon that spring, as Tippi recalled, "Hitch and I were in the back of a limousine returning from Bodega Bay to the motel where the cast and crew were staying for several nights. When we drove into the parking lot, some of our co-workers were there waiting for us. And when he saw that *they* saw us, he reached over and violently embraced me in the back of the car, to make everyone think that we were in a romantic clinch! I pushed him away and got out of the car, and I thought I would give him the benefit of the doubt—maybe he was just trying to make me nervous, to keep his control, to show me off."

As Robert Boyle said years later, "In all the films I had anything to do with"—over a quarter century, as art director for *Saboteur* and *Shadow of a Doubt* and production designer for *North by Northwest, The Birds* and *Marnie*—"he was always pressing the problems. I suspect he had a certain fear of elegant blondes. His behavior was almost compulsive. He once said to me, 'I have all the feelings of everyone encased in an armor of fat.' He felt that he was not attractive physically, but at the same time he recognized that he had all those same yearnings [as others had], and he was frustrated by what he perceived as a difficulty, if not an impossibility, which was to experience requited love."

When principal photography was complete, the technical challenges could begin, consuming even longer time than filming with actors. There would be the complex process of Technicolor correction; the invention and placement of electronic sounds, for Hitchcock proscribed the use of a musical sound track; and the editing of a picture composed variously of live action, animation, trick shots, mechanical birds (for the scenes involving children) and thousands of live trained birds of several varieties (gulls, crows, ravens, blackbirds, finches, pigeons). Two-hour Hollywood features routinely contain between 400 and 700 separate shots; *The Birds* has more than 1,500.

But before the finished film could be put together, there was a final, harrowing time for Tippi Hedren. Perhaps because he knew how dangerous the event would be, Alfred Hitchcock kept until the last week of shooting the appalling finale of the story, in which Melanie Daniels climbs alone to a room in the house, enters and is viciously attacked by hundreds of birds. "Hitch," she asked him when they were in story conferences, "why doesn't she summon Mitch [the Taylor character]? Why does she do this? Hitchcock's reply: 'Because I tell you to do it.' "

When the time came, she was at first shocked and then felt betrayed—even before the ordeal began and the cameras rolled for a week, recording a sequence that surpasses even the stylized shower murder of *Psycho,* which seems restrained by comparison.

Since work on the picture began early in the year, Hitchcock, his bird trainer, the production designer and the assistant director had all told Tippi that of course mechanical birds would be used for this final sequence, and that she would certainly not be subjected to the risks of a live bird attack. But when she arrived on the set early that Monday morning, it was clear that Hitchcock and company had always had a different intention.

"I walked on to the set, and there was a chain-link fence all around and on top. Jim Brown [the assistant director] seemed embarrassed, he looked everywhere around the set except at me, and then he finally said, 'We can't use mechanical birds after all—we have to use live birds.' With that, he left, and there I was. Now what? Soon after, in came bird handlers with their long gloves and gauntlets, carrying huge boxes of squawking birds—gulls, crows, pigeons, all kinds."

Very soon, she had her answer. "The men stood Tippi in the corner of the room and just began throwing birds at her," recalled Rod Taylor, "one after another, again and again, take after take." The agitated birds darted and swooped about, and by noon on the first day of that week, the set and the actress were (in the words of Jessica Tandy) "just covered in bird shit." Often the set had to be cleared for cleaning and scrubbing. Hitchcock, meanwhile, remained in his trailer dressing room, emerging only to call "Action!" and "Cut!" It was as if he were both embarrassed and frightened by what he was asking his star to endure.

"All of this had been prepared well in advance," she later learned. "Nothing could have been done with such speed—the arrival of the birds and the handlers, the careful placing of the wire fence and everything on the set—they knew from the first day what they needed, that they had to use live birds, but they had lied to me. You can't just do this thing spontaneously—it had all taken complicated planning. And they had to leave it all to the end."

One day of filming this ordeal was insufficient for the final effect, and work continued on Tuesday. Cary Grant visited the set and told Tippi that he admired her courage. But the fact is that an experienced actress would have objected loudly to this treatment. Moviemaking often pitches actors, stuntmen and crew into uncomfortable situations, and difficult scenes, often unforeseen, frequently go with the professional territory. But there is no precedent for Tippi Hedren's ordeal; years later, of course, the sequence would have been easily and safely achieved by computer.

Monday and Tuesday left Tippi exhausted and unnerved,

but she was told it would all be over by Wednesday morning. But the torture continued all day Wednesday and Thursday. "It was frightening and exhausting for me, and it seemed to go on forever."

Hollywood has a long history of imposing painful tasks on actors and stuntmen. Lillian Gish and Richard Barthelmess endured freezing temperatures and real ice floes for climactic scenes of Griffith's *Way Down East*. Harold Lloyd lost a thumb and finger for the sake of a movie and never used doubles for his most dangerous stunts. Buster Keaton took enormous risks, and Lon Chaney caused himself acute pain for the makeup and distortions that made him famous; thousands more have fallen from horses, leapt from buildings and dashed through flames while the cameras rolled. A single actor, however—especially a woman—is rarely subjected to the sort of violence asked of Tippi Hedren in making *The Birds*.

Finally, on Friday, Hitchcock and his crew prepared for the last moments of the scene, when the battered female lead cowers in agony and shock on the floor of the room. For the first four days, birds had swept around Tippi, pecking and nipping. Pauses were called; her costume was torn a bit more; makeup artists created facial gashes, lacerations and the impression of terrible wounds; stage blood was dripped—and then filming resumed.

There was one last technique to be applied. "The wardrobe team placed bands around sections of my body before I put the costume on, and then thin, almost invisible elastic wires were pulled through holes in the clothes. They pulled the strings through—and then they loosely tied one leg of the birds to the strings, so that the birds would pounce all over me, unable to fly away."

The torment continued throughout the day.

Late on Friday, after five full days, the occasion reached a critical mass. "One bird that was tied to me jumped from my shoulder onto my face and landed just near my eye, scratching my lower eyelid."

She collapsed, sobbing hysterically and shouting that she could do no more—that the birds had to be taken off her, that this had to stop at once. Everyone withdrew, embarrassed and apologetic.

Carried to her dressing room—dazed, shaking and almost in clinical shock—she was told to rest before going home for the weekend. But when crewmen came to rouse her, she was unresponsive, and for an unnervingly long time, she did not respond. Physicians ordered her to remain at home for ten days of complete rest. "But we can't do without her!" Hitchcock protested. "We need her on Monday for the last few shots."

"Are you crazy?" a doctor asked the director. "Are you trying to kill her?"

Chapter Fifteen

THE END
OF ART

(1963-1964)

Preparing Tippi Hedren for a scene in *Marnie*

Tippi's contract required her to travel for the promotion of her Hitchcock films, and so, on release of *The Birds* in the spring of 1963, she joined him (and frequently a handful of studio executives and assistants) for a publicity tour. The picture was screened at the Cannes Film Festival, and everywhere there were odd gimmicks: in some cinema foyers, for example, birds labeled "Alfie" and "Tippi" were suspended in cages.

That autumn, Tippi was assigned the leading role in Hitchcock's next picture, *Marnie*—the story of a frigid compulsive thief (Marnie Edgar) trapped and blackmailed by an equally troubled man named Mark Rutland (Sean Connery).* This role she undertook as if by default, for Hitchcock had hoped in vain to lure Grace Kelly back to work as the film's star. Joseph Stefano had first worked on the treatment, and then Evan Hunter came aboard, but he was dismissed when he failed to write the honeymoon rape scene.

"I told him," Hunter recalled,

that audiences would lose all sympathy for the male lead if he rapes his own wife on their honeymoon. I told him that

---

* Tippi Hedren received $500 weekly as salary for *The Birds* and $600 for *Marnie*, which Hitchcock thought was royal compensation. She accepted these sums—much less than her modeling career had paid—in the belief that it was wiser to have a regular weekly income, guaranteed for seven years, than to depend on the shifting monies of modeling for a woman who had reached the dangerous age of thirty-one.

the man would be comforting, that the couple would work things out. But Hitchcock lifted his hands and sketched a rectangle in the air, framing an imaginary camera image. Then he moved his hands toward my face, as if moving in for a close shot. "Evan," he said, "when he sticks it in her, I want that camera right on her *face*!"

Insisting that he would not write the scene, Hunter was fired at once and replaced by Jay Presson Allen, then in her maiden voyage on the seas of Hollywood scriptwriting.*

Like *Vertigo, Marnie* is certainly one of Alfred Hitchcock's most direct creative acts of self-revelation. "He was always trying to put his own personal feelings up on the screen," said Robert Boyle, "and I think that was one of the things he was doing with *Marnie*. He was doing it through Tippi and through his filmmaking, and exploring some of his own feelings and his compulsive behavior."

Boyle was on the mark. In its finished form, the movie became a haunted and haunting tale of a man's desire to control completely a woman who rejects him—only blackmail forces her to comply by marrying him. "You don't love me!" Marnie cries out to Mark. "I'm just something you've caught. You think I'm some kind of animal you've trapped!"

"That's right—you are! And I've caught something really wild this time, haven't I? I've tracked you and caught you and by God I'm going to keep you!" As Truffaut asked, "Can there be any doubt that Sean Connery . . . is expressing Hitchcock's

---

* In 1979, Peggy Robertson recalled that Jay Allen was often in tears at the end of her daily script sessions with Hitchcock—not because of any inappropriate conduct on his part, but because Jay quickly realized she was out of her depth on a subject she couldn't write (like the honeymoon rape). Years later, she often spoke on the record about her apprenticeship with Hitchcock, admitting her inability to resolve some of *Marnie*'s thornier script problems.

own feelings as a frustrated Pygmalion?" This, of course, precisely expressed the nature of the deteriorating relationship, due to destructive demands made by the director on his star.

Jay Allen saw Hitchcock's treatment of Tippi, but she, too, was new to Hollywood and said nothing. "He was mad for her, just as he had been obsessed with a series of cold blond actresses before. He was very Edwardian, and he put lids on himself. To work out his repressions, he created a framework—his art. It was his way of legitimizing everything, of transforming his feelings." Oddly, she came to Tippi one day: "Can't you just love Hitch a little bit?" Tippi asked what she meant, but Jay could not elaborate, and the conversation ended. "The problem was that Tippi wanted her own life," Jay said years later, "and so she couldn't help making him unhappy."

As Tippi Hedren's predicament deepened during the filming of her second picture, she was not alone in facing unforeseen problems. Hitchcock extended his efforts to train other actresses during preproduction. Young Mariette Hartley had a smaller role, but Hitchcock took time to explain to her how he used storyboards. She recalled that the director often made jokes and kept the crew at ease. "I was in the presence of a genius," she said later, "but his sense of control left little room for improvisation. Still, he taught me a tremendous amount in the short time I worked with him." Then Hitchcock refused to speak to her, and thereafter he retained a mysterious silence to the end of production. "I went up to him and asked if in some way I had offended him," she recalled years later. "His reply was, 'Miss Hartley, I think you have problems with men.'" This may be a classic example of projection, for it was, of course, Hitchcock who had problems with people in general.

Engaged to play the significant supporting role of Sean

Connery's jealous sister-in-law, Diane Baker was offered the role without being permitted to read the script; but because this was to be an Alfred Hitchcock picture, she accepted. Diane had already appeared in more than twenty features and television films since launching her career in 1959 with *The Diary of Anne Frank,* and she had recently concluded a term contract with Twentieth Century-Fox.

"I was invited to the Hitchcocks' home," she recalled, "and I sat in their kitchen while Alma prepared lunch for us. She told me how much I resembled Grace Kelly, and she said that I could *become* another Grace Kelly—which astonished me. Then she brought out photos of Grace to make her point, while Hitch sat there watching me. I felt I was in another kind of world. I didn't want to be made over into the image of another woman Hitch was still looking for, and I didn't want to sign a contract with him or any producer. My contract at Fox had expired and I wanted to freelance." The Hitchcocks were not pleased.

Hitchcock's increasingly obsessive behavior alarmed his seasoned associates, the major Universal Studios executives and the entire company of *Marnie.* Considering the exigencies of this complex and demanding picture, Hitchcock was alert, creative and quick to meet its technical challenges—in other words, he had lost none of his ingenuity, nor had he become uncertain of his ability to provide artisans and actors with the precise counsel required. Diane Baker recalled that, at the outset, "Hitch taught me so many wonderful things about camera angles and gestures and acting subtleties. He was a magnificent teacher."

But after the first scenes were filmed at the end of November, things turned even more sour and tense. When Diane Baker arrived for work on her assigned days, she was astounded and bewildered.

I was on the set constantly, even when I had no scenes to do, and I never saw Tippi enjoying herself with the rest of the cast and crew. She was never allowed to gather around with the rest of us, and he demanded that every conversation between her and Hitch be held in private. None of us ever saw her having a warm, friendly professional relationship with him. Throughout December, nothing could have been more horrible for me than to arrive on that movie set and to see her being treated the way she was. I had never seen that, I didn't expect it, and I didn't understand any of it.

Hitchcock then attempted a divide-and-conquer strategy. "The most uncomfortable part of it all for me," Diane added, "occurred when he maneuvered me for a conversation outside Tippi's dressing room trailer. There was a high window built into it, and he stood me there and spoke very loudly—saying negative things about her, to make her angry or jealous, or to cause some reaction. Which just showed how little he really knew her. After I'd had enough of this, I asked him one day, 'What do you say about *me* behind my back?' He said oh, no, that I was just fine, and that he would never say anything bad about me." But Hitchcock's tactics to create a wedge of enmity among his co-stars failed, even with Connery, who was told, "Don't touch the girl."

There were unfriendly, alienating strategies to secure good performances, too, as Diane added. "He often did strange and upsetting things. He turned his back on you just before a take—and then he whispered to someone like [MCA agent] Edd Henry or Lew Wasserman, who were frequent visitors to the set. He made you feel as if he was saying something derogatory about you."

"Nobody knew what to do about all this," according to Tippi. "Everyone—I mean *everyone*—knew he was obsessed

with me. He always wanted to have a glass of wine or champagne, with me alone, at the end of the day—'to talk about the
next day's work,' he said. But he was really isolating me from
everyone. I wasn't flattered by all this special attention—he
was alienating me from everyone else, and that added another
level of discomfort. To make things even worse, by this time he
was drinking heavily at lunch. By late afternoon, I just wanted
to go home to my daughter, study the next day's [script] pages
and try to relax."

That became more and more difficult—especially during
the shooting of a scene in which Marnie has been found out by
Mark and is packing her things at the riding lodge. "Hitch came
over to me just before we shot the scene and whispered to me,
'Touch me.' He made sure no one else could hear, and his tone
and glance made it clear exactly what he meant. It was disgust-
ing, and I was furious. I was made to feel humiliated. He had absolutely no consideration for my feelings." Shaken, Tippi went to
see Peggy Robertson at the end of the day. "Peggy told him how
unhappy I was, but it didn't matter to him. He thought no one
had any feelings to hurt, and the word *respect* wasn't in his vo-
cabulary. It was very strange, because Peggy came back to me
and reported that Hitch said only that he was so sad because I
had never invited him alone to my home for dinner! I became
almost sick thinking of being alone with him at home.

"There were so many insulting and offensive things, all during production. This was a side of life I had never seen and
knew nothing about. At the same time, I had the huge responsibility of this difficult and demanding role."

From that time, she was essentially not permitted to leave the
studio at the end of the day's work until Hitchcock gave the sign.
As she recalled years later, "It reached the point that I just
couldn't stand to see or be with him. Every day, there was a rea-

son for me to be unhappy, every day he planned some private meeting with wine or champagne, and every day I thought, 'How can I get out of this one?' I remember driving from my home to the studio every day, asking myself, 'How can I get out of this job?' But of course I couldn't. They would have sued me for a great deal of money—that threat was implied more than once."

Hitchcock also began to give unwelcome signs to Diane Baker. At first, she tried to cope with the private lunches for two, but he drank wine, got red in the face and often dropped off to sleep while working during the afternoon. "Once at lunch he told me that actresses should never be married, which at first I thought was amusing and then very strange." Jim Brown, the assistant director, often had to poke Hitchcock awake, to ask if a shot was okay to print. Diane politely refused further midday meals.

"Then came his strange topics of conversation," she added. "He wanted to talk to me about sex. He said he had no intimate relationship with Alma for decades—well, that's a difficult remark to respond to! And then he loved to talk about toilet matters, too. He told me, for example, about a French king who invited honored guests to observe him defecating. I had never heard such stuff, and I didn't know what to do or say." Since the 1930s, Hitchcock had scarcely altered the shock tactics employed with some vulnerable young women.

One curious interlude involved another actress who found favor in Hitchcock's eyes. Cast in a small role of one of his teleplays was Claire Griswold, wife of the actor and director Sydney Pollack. "You and I are going to do business," he told her—and then he signed her to a seven-year-contract. A personal wardrobe was again designed ("Bring me your body, and I will dress it"), and three lavish screen tests were prepared— longest of all, a scene from *To Catch a Thief*. Claire recognized at once what was happening and decided she did not like it. "I was very touched by his evident need to re-create Grace Kelly—or whoever it was he wanted to re-create—but I didn't really want to go along with that sort of thing."

Invited to dine at the Hitchcock home, the Pollacks were surprised that Hitchcock barely addressed Claire's husband or took any interest in his career. Hitchcock was creating an odd kind of rivalry: on the one hand, Tippi Hedren was being openly held before Griswold as a competitor for Hitchcock's full attention; on the other hand, Claire was placed in the center of a struggle between two directors.

When Hitchcock finally settled on Tippi for *Marnie,* Claire felt that she would be free for the next year. She discussed this at lunch with Peggy Robertson and explained that she and her husband planned to expand their family during this time. Peggy advised Claire that there would be no appropriate time for that within the next seven years: Claire was expected always to be available, for any role, under any circumstances. Not long after, Hitchcock's office was informed that Mr. and Mrs. Sydney Pollack were awaiting the birth of their second child. The following year, by mutual consent, the Griswold-Hitchcock contract was terminated, and Claire settled very happily into the private life she always preferred.

Things became more tortured as the filming of *Marnie* progressed. "One day, he came into my dressing room," recalled Diane Baker. "He closed the door behind him—he didn't say anything—walked across to me, put his arms around me and planted a kiss, hard, right on my mouth. It wasn't a friendly or fatherly kiss, and I was shocked. I didn't say anything. I grabbed a tissue, wiped my lips and then wiped my makeup off his lips. I went to the door and opened it, and, still without a word, he left.

"I had never been sick during a production or because of a job," Diane said years later, "but before Christmas, I was so ill from the tension of making *Marnie* that a doctor was sent to my home. The whole thing was taking quite a toll on me, and of course it was even worse for Tippi." From Hitchcock, Diane received a pink clock radio as a holiday gift, with a note: " 'I want you to think of me every single night before you go to sleep.' That caused me a little panic—how would I deal with this when I saw him after the holidays?"

Years later, the situation would have at once produced charges of sexual harassment. But it was virtually unknown for employees of movie studios to mention such things at the time. A platoon of powerful producers routinely acted like Hitchcock, and it was up to young actresses to find a way to cope, to submit (the better to advance their careers) or to complain in private. "In 1963," Diane added, "no one thought in terms of legal recourse or sexual harassment—and we would have been completely ignored if we spoke out. In fact, we *were* completely ignored.

"I did complain to Monique James [casting agent for Universal]," Diane continued. "I also spoke to Peggy Robertson. But nothing happened. I liked Peggy, but her loyalty was to Hitchcock, and she just wanted some information from me that she could report back to him—how upset I was, for example, and if I was going to talk to anyone about all this. I felt there was a terrible collusion going on, and I was right. Everything got back to him, and when he learned that I was unhappy and complaining, his attitude toward me changed completely. I was glad not to be under contract to him, the way Tippi was— I could finish the job and get away."

In the new year, 1964, things became even uglier still. "Lew Wasserman and his wife, Edie, started in on me," Diane added. "Messages were left at the Universal gate for me that they wanted me to come to their home for dinner. I knew what was happening, and so did everyone else."

Indeed, Wasserman attempted to exert damage control. He sent one of the executive team to Tippi's dressing room one day. "We all know about your private life," the man said nervously. When she asked just what he meant, he had to remain silent. He had no idea what he was talking about; he had hoped for some voluntary, scandalous self-revelation from her. Meanwhile, Hitchcock and Lew were still bringing the major Universal executives onto the set, to see what Hitchcock said was his proudest accomplishment, the creation of a major new star for whom he still planned a big future. "You'll be making five hundred thousand dollars a year," Hitchcock told her expansively—a great deal of money in the 1960s. "It was a carrot he thought I'd go for, but I remember thinking I'd give it all up for peace and freedom."

The Hitchcock-Wasserman relationship had flourished for many years because of a long-term business arrangement. "Lew had become a second father figure [to Hitchcock] with all the attendant mingling of love and guilt, gratitude and resentment," wrote John Houseman. "Fear of displeasing him by failure to deliver his new film on time and the dread of being punished by the withdrawal of favors such as his prestigious bungalow suite at Universal Studios loomed no less 'dark' [for Hitchcock] toward the end than the anxieties of sexual frustration, and had an equally destructive effect on Hitchcock's work." In fact, the long Wasserman-Hitchcock relationship ended badly, and in 1977, tears rolled down Hitchcock's cheeks when he told a visitor, "Lew never comes to see me anymore," he said, almost in a whisper.

Hitchcock really believed that Tippi would be his, that he could somehow leave Alma and have a new life: this was perhaps the extreme point of his delusion. "He told me," Tippi recalled, "that he had a fantasy—that he and I were standing in his living room, and the rays of the moon were coming in and enveloping us." The moment was certainly like a beautiful cinematic fantasy, a totem of his expectation of a new life with Tippi. But it was also astonishingly presumptuous, not least of all because she had never given him any indication that she shared his feelings. "He was so sure that I was in love with him. That whole time was really very sad, very difficult." That year, Tippi was making a life with her agent, Noel Marshall, whom she eventually married; Hitchcock made no secret of his displeasure at the news. "For him," according to Tippi, "there was no one else in my life—*could never be anyone else* in my life except him." One can reasonably add that *Marnie* is a triumph of one woman's performance over unimaginable circumstances.

On St. Valentine's Day, February 14, 1964, Hitchcock sent Tippi a long, impassioned telegram. After recounting the legend of the two ancient Christian martyrs named Valentine, he wrote that they were probably two legends about one man—himself. He then referred to his emotional martyrdom and signed the message "Alfredus." About the same time, unwilling to let her out of his sight, Hitchcock refused permission for Tippi to make a quick journey to New York to receive the "Star of Tomorrow" citation from *Photoplay* magazine. If an accolade did not originate with him, it had neither meaning nor relevance.

The matter reached its breaking point in March 1964, near the end of production on the day Tippi was drenched with water for the closeups in the scene in which Connery saves her from an attempted suicide by drowning, in a pool aboard a cruise ship. Her memories are acute and indelible.

"We were ready for the scene when Hitch called me into his office on the set. He stared at me and simply said, as if it was the most normal thing in the world, that from this time on, he expected me to make myself sexually available and accessible to him—however and whenever and wherever he wanted. That was the moment, after three years of trying to cope, when I finally had enough—that was the limit, that was the end."

With that, she jumped up. "I can't go on with this," she shouted at him. "I can't put up with another day—I want to get out of this contract. I don't want to be around you anymore."

Hitchcock's next step was to propose what can only be called prostitution. "He said, 'Well, you can't get out, can you? What will happen to your child, and to your parents?' I replied that no one who loves me would ever want me to be in a situation in which I was so miserable. But he didn't stop, and then the threats began. 'I'll ruin your career,' he said. 'You'll never work again anywhere. I'll destroy you.'"

It was precisely as Connery says in *Marnie*: "I've tracked you and caught you, and by God I'm going to keep you!" *Marnie* is, even at face value, a film about Hitchcock. "There must be something wrong with the girl if she doesn't want me"—that is the point of Mark's exploitation of Marnie, and of Hitchcock's conduct toward his star.

After more than forty years, Hitchcock had hoped at last to star Tippi in a film of J. M. Barrie's delicate, sentimental fantasy *Mary Rose;* Jay Allen had written a first draft of the screenplay.

Now Hitchcock threatened to cancel what he called the role of a lifetime. She was intransigent.

This episode in the life of Alfred Hitchcock cannot be ignored, for it is a frank case of extreme sexual harassment that may not be dismissed or minimized. Nor was the successful completion of *Marnie* any justification for Hitchcock's conduct. The events comprise a stern cautionary tale; they also document the unfortunate decline of a great genius, who lost all control over himself, and this marked the end of his art.

There has been a consensus that one can say or write anything about Alfred Hitchcock—except the fact of his frailty, his faults, his suffering or the suffering he caused others. His status as an icon has made many people, even some surviving colleagues, blind to this appalling time. Consequently, the pain for which he was responsible, the deep unhappiness he visited on himself, has been ignored or minimized; in the bargain, some people effectively approve or at least discount the sexual harassment.

Did the long, dishonorable history of powerful Hollywood men and the so-called casting couch convince Hitchcock that his actions were acceptable? To assert that this is merely the way things are done, that this is typical of this or any industry, means to dismiss it as merely a quotidian reality and therefore to assent to it: "Well, these things happen." Do Hitchcock's most zealous admirers minimize or even dismiss this sad episode because they think such treatment of actresses is merely boyish high jinks? Was Hitchcock so respected that his associates—and later some of his partisans—thought it of little consequence how he treated Tippi Hedren and Diane Baker? Hitchcock may have felt he could get away with anything. Alas, in this case he was right.

"He was never in love with me," Tippi insisted years later. "He was obsessed with me, and that's very different. When you love someone, you don't frighten them, disgust them or want to hurt them. You want them to come to you, not feel repelled." Indeed, had he behaved differently, Hitchcock might have gained the lifelong friendship of Tippi and Diane; as with others, he could have been a mentor and father figure. But he lost all discretion. "He could not or would not control himself," Tippi added, "and he made no attempt to. It wasn't just selfish conduct—frankly, it was sick conduct." She was hurt and surprised that Alma did not intervene more forcefully on her behalf: "Alma was the mom—she watched over him, but by this time, she couldn't control him." The fact that Tippi never did anything to provoke Hitchcock made his sexual obsession "his problem, really, not mine. I had no control over him, and that realization kept me sane during those three years."

Hitchcock followed through on his promise to ruin Tippi Hedren's career, keeping her under contract, inactive and unemployed, for several years after the release of *Marnie*. An impressive list of directors contacted him, eager to borrow her. The response was invariable: "She isn't available." Tippi was especially disappointed to learn later from François Truffaut that he had wanted her for a film but that Hitchcock had turned him down. "It was really a shame," Truffaut told me. "He was never the same Hitchcock after this time." Eventually, Hitchcock acceded to a request from Charles Chaplin, who brought Tippi to London for a picture; soon after, Hitchcock agreed to cancel her contract.

"Some people have claimed that I had some cordial meetings with Hitch in his office later, to patch things up and establish a friendship. I have no recollection of anything like that. I did agree to meet him and Alma at Claridge's when I was working for Chaplin. I had sent Hitch and Alma some roses as a welcome to London, but when I was summoned to the Hitchcock suite, the flowers were next to a steaming wall heater, so they had died very quickly. The meeting was very awkward." British representatives for Chaplin and Hitchcock suggested that the two directors, with Alma and Tippi, be photographed together. Hitchcock refused: "Why would I want to do that?"

Virtually every element of the truth about this time eluded him. "Nothing ever came of her," he said of Tippi in 1972, "because she didn't want to do television." That was not so: what she did not want was to be directed by him.

Diane had additional scenes in *Marnie,* but Alma convinced her husband they were unnecessary, and they were cut.

Hitch knew that I was due in Israel for preproduction on my next picture. I had just one more shot for him—a process shot that was delayed and delayed, and finally completely postponed. I kept asking when I could do this bit of work and leave. No answer came from anyone. I missed the rehearsals in Israel and arrived late. I really believe it was a kind of punishment for me.

Diane's memories of *Marnie* were so painful that for years she said nothing. "I wanted to forget the whole experience, and I never went to any of the tributes to Hitchcock during his lifetime or afterward." Happily, Diane's career flourished, not only as a film and television actress worldwide, but also as a director, producer and acting teacher.

Notwithstanding her mentor's stated goal—to ruin Tippi's life and career—no such thing occurred. Certainly, he made it impossible for her to accept work offers over the next two years, and by the late 1960s, as so often happens in Hollywood, the momentum created for her by *The Birds* and *Marnie* fell victim to changing movie fashions and the myopically lukewarm critical response to those pictures. Over the next decades, she often returned to work in film and television, but these projects decidedly took second place to a much deeper commitment.

In 1969 she went to Africa to appear in a picture. "While I was there, I became deeply concerned about the dangers to the survival of wild animals because of sport hunting, poaching and encroaching civilization." She and Noel Marshall, then her husband, decided to rescue some of the most endangered animals in Africa and America, and then to make the film *Roar,* which showed that wild animals are not appropriate as house pets. By the mid-1970s, she had taken in dozens of abused or abandoned lions, tigers, leopards, cheetahs, cougars and elephants on a tract of land an hour's drive from Los Angeles.

Tippi did not establish a zoo or animal park in 1972. Instead, her nonprofit Shambala Preserve (the name is from the Sanskrit, meaning a place of harmony for all living beings) is like an animal orphanage, where she has continued to rescue big cats from illegal owners, from abuse by low-life circuses, private zoos and unscrupulous people who charge fees for the sport of shooting animals. She and a dedicated staff provide veterinary care, proper nutrition and safe ground.

With great tenacity, Tippi successfully sponsored a congressional bill making it illegal to breed exotic animals privately and as pets in the United States. Shambala remains her life's work, a refuge for battered and rejected animals, and a place where educational programs continue to change for the better people's attitudes toward wild creatures. The honors and awards she has received for this tireless work have been equaled by her citations for important humanitarian work—especially in relief programs for the victims of floods, earthquakes, famine and war. In many of these efforts, she has been joined by her daughter, the popular and talented actress Melanie Griffith.

For Tippi Hedren, time and a purposeful life healed the pain of the Hitchcock years, and in 2007, she could say compassionately, "This poor man was desperate for something he never had in his lifetime."

A week after his death in April 1980, an international convention in Rome celebrated his remarkable career—a three-day program of lectures, discussions and interviews that had been scheduled months earlier. Among the American contingent were Tippi Hedren, Farley Granger, Ernest Lehman, Peggy Robertson and the author of this book. On the morning of May 6, en route from the Hotel de Ville to the press events at the Hotel Parco dei Principi, Peggy Robertson turned to Tippi and said, "You know, he never got over you."

Afterword

THE LEADEN
ECHO AND
THE GOLDEN
ECHO
(1964-1980)

"I am convinced," wrote François Truffaut, "that Hitchcock was never the same after *Marnie,* and that its failure cost him a considerable amount of self-confidence. This was due not so much to the financial failure of the film (he had had others), but rather to the failure of his professional and personal relationship with Tippi Hedren." Truffaut was on the mark. After *Marnie,* no subsequent Hitchcock picture has any emotional statement to make.

Psycho had brought him the greatest wealth of his career. But with that picture—so different from anything he had ever done—something was shifting in his personality. That movie has a pervasive sense of doom: it proclaims the triumph of the kingdom of death—and it gazes calmly at monstrous, murderous lunacy and at the annihilation of personality in a way unlike any other Hitchcock film. Even its perverse humor cannot mask the sense that the director is describing not only the world of nightmare but also something mad and malevolent in the chilling world of everyday, recognizable situations. Therein lies its ultimate horror.

But with *Psycho,* even as he tried desperately to push back the frontiers of what was permissible in American movies, something hardened in Alfred Hitchcock—something forever closed over his always fragile capacity for warmth. There would never again be films with the warmth of *Rear Window, To Catch a Thief* or *The Man Who Knew Too Much,* nor the mature indictment of romantic self-abnegation that characterized the genius of *Vertigo.* Poisonous politics would never be treated again with the blithe, wise humor of *North by Northwest.*

The causes for this decline cannot be reduced to a single physical or psychological ailment. On the one hand, it is unfair to expect any artist to repeat or to exceed recent successes—especially when the forms of popular entertainment shift as violently as they did in the 1960s and after. Hitchcock was dependent on studio approval and public endorsement, and he was very much of his time—how could he not be? It would have been absurd for him to imitate a maverick young moviemaker.

It is tenable, however, that after 1964 he had somehow lost the resources to cope with the shifting fortunes of fame, popularity and cinematic fashion; that he could not counter his increasing terror of illness, incapacity and age; that his sense of detachment, of isolation, made him merely angry instead of pitching him into creative solitude. Always an indulgent tippler, he drank in perilous quantities after 1965, and writers working with him were often at a loss to understand how they ought to proceed. Perhaps most poignant of all was his egregious lack of friends. He might have become mentor, friend, éminence grise to a generation of filmmakers, actors and students, but he knew not how to offer himself, nor did he seem much to care.

After *Marnie,* indeed, something died in him. There was nothing more for him to say in art or life, and his bewilderment at finding himself an antique in a strange new Hollywood was enormous. Thenceforth, Wasserman and his colleagues at Universal made commercial demands on Hitchcock to which he was forced to yield: to cast major stars in the next picture, for example, and to dismiss the great Bernard Herrmann as composer in order to secure a more contemporary "pop" sound track from others.

In addition, the Hitchcock style was dead in the 1960s. During the course of many interviews between 1964 and 1980, he was often asked to name his great pleasures in life, and making pictures was no longer among them: "The things that make me happiest in the world are eating, drinking and sleeping. I drink like a fish—have you seen what a red face I have? And I could die eating." He was certainly frank, but there is something humorless and pathetic in his words.

As for collegial endorsement: Hitchcock had been nominated five times for an Oscar, for his direction of *Rebecca, Lifeboat, Spellbound, Rear Window* and *Psycho*. But he had never won. "Always a bridesmaid, never a bride," he muttered to a few people in private; in public, he shrugged and asked, "Who needs another doorstop?" But he deeply resented the industry's continuing snub.

At the Academy Awards ceremony on April 10, 1968, he received the honorary Irving G. Thalberg Award, presented to "creative producers whose bodies of work reflect a consistently high quality of motion picture production." When Hitchcock stepped to the microphone that evening, everyone expected a witty, ironic little discourse—the kind familiar from his television programs. "Thank you," he said without expression, and with those two words, he left the stage. Some thought his brevity betokened lightly veiled contempt, and they were probably correct.

Tippi Hedren, among others, saw that Hitchcock was "a very, very unhappy man. His only friends were his businessmen." He increasingly isolated himself after 1964, refusing most invitations unless he was the main attraction. He made excuses for his absence, and eventually the offers dried up. "He really had nothing else in this world except food, wine and fooling around with movies," said Marshall Schlom, once his assistant director.

Hitchcock was not a man to sit back, kick off his shoes and confide in people—except, it seems, in Alma. Sidney Bernstein, whom he knew for most of his life, was fundamentally a business partner; privately, they were little more than the professional equivalent of golf buddies. Hitchcock's agent and later his boss, Lew Wasserman, made Hitchcock rich—and Hitchcock made Lew rich—but that relationship later came to a shameful conclusion when Wasserman virtually abandoned him, refusing even to visit the director's bungalow or trailer during the last days. The unpleasant fact is that Wasserman found Hitchcock an embarrassment.

His fiftieth film, *Torn Curtain*, released in 1966, was troubled long before production began. First, Hitchcock objected to the stars forced on him—Julie Andrews and Paul Newman. To Hitchcock's fury, their combined salaries made up a quarter of the $6 million budget. Second, he and novelist Brian Moore, who later tried unsuccessfully to have his name removed from the credits, could not make the dated cold war antics of Hitchcock's original story outline compelling or the characters anything but wooden. Filming was awkward for everyone: Newman did not get on at all with Hitch, who was in turn openly contemptuous of Andrews: "I tried to dispense with her services on the strength that she was a singer and not a serious actress [but] the studio considered her a sure box-office draw."

To assert that Julie Andrews was not a serious actress demonstrated just how ungraciously out of touch Hitchcock was: her recent performance in *The Americanization of Emily* counters this negative judgment, for Andrews was an actress of both range and stature on stage and screen. Had Hitchcock not been eager to have the singing actress Doris Day in *The Man*

Who Knew Too Much? (Privately, Julie was so upset by the experience that she urged her friends not to see *Torn Curtain*.)

"Hitch just went through the motions on that movie," Samuel Taylor said. "He knew it was a loser, and he became very depressed and lost all interest in it." Lila Kedrova, in a small but colorful role, said that Hitchcock seemed not to want to direct her or anyone else. Instead, according to uncredited writer Keith Waterhouse, Hitchcock loudly berated and even tormented minor players in *Torn Curtain* for not jumping off a bus in the proper manner.

His almost constant anger was now both evident and alienating. Hitchcock never had the gift of friendship, but he could always attract acquaintances to be entertained. In the last decade of his life, as his old colleague Hume Cronyn sadly recalled,

> There was something tragic about Hitchcock—an element of snob in him that became really tragic in its consequences. Because he never took people close to heart, in the latter years he became a sad and rather isolated figure. I visited him often and found him weeping. He said not only that the work was not proceeding well, but that he never went out, never saw anyone, was never invited anywhere. But all of that was Hitch's own fault. He had encouraged that kind of distance with people, and so they left him alone—which is what he'd wanted. And so he was lonely, and it was all very sad.

Nor could Samuel Taylor's nearly round-the-clock efforts salvage Hitchcock's next picture, a production Universal chose for the director after the disappointment of *Torn Curtain*. "The trouble with *Topaz*," Hitchcock said in 1975, "is that there are too many foreigners—Frenchmen, Cubans, Russians and the rest—all of them speaking English. It's a letdown, really." But there were problems far more acute than language dissociation: for one thing, Hitchcock, Taylor and Universal could not decide on an ending for the movie. Several were shot, none of them satisfactory, and for all the film's travelogue color and a few inventive set pieces, *Topaz* is generally regarded (except by the most defensive Hitchcock aficionados) as cold and remote, an almost embarrassingly bad movie. Audiences, as Samuel Goldwyn said in another context, stayed away in droves.

There were other, more embarrassing problems on *Topaz*. During a publicity photo session, cast members Karin Dor and John Vernon were in costume, and Hitchcock decided to pose them for the photographer. Glancing first at Vernon's cigar, Hitchcock called aloud to Karin Dor, "Karin, put it in your mouth. Come on, Karin—you know you've had it in your mouth before." This was not amusing to the actress, and everyone present felt awkward and embarrassed. Hitchcock angrily stopped the photo session and departed.

Frenzy, produced in London in 1971 and released the following year, restored Hitchcock's critical acclaim, but the explicitly violent story of a serial killer alienated many. Structurally, the movie is icily brilliant, but there is nowhere for the audience to apply its sympathies, no one with whom to identify, root for or support.

Hitchcock's final picture—*Family Plot,* released in 1976—was a quiet coda. He was no longer an alert and spry director but a man who had become ill, somnolent, uncaring and alcoholic. He looked terrible, moved with obvious pain and found every day a trial; his staff was alternately sympathetic, frustrated and resentful. He fired and replaced the leading man after filming had begun, and the atmosphere of the production was anxious throughout.

Still, the director could surprise a young actress. Karen Black was one of two leading ladies in the picture, and when he kissed her one day before work, she was astonished that he thrust his tongue into her mouth. "I think he was probably born an exuberant spirit," she said coolly, "and that's why he French-kissed me. He just felt like it."

"Hitchcock was a neurotic," Truffaut wrote, "and it could not have been easy for him to impose his neurosis upon the whole world."

The fantasies Hitchcock spun, to which his writers gave form and structure and which his actors enlivened, depended on the emergence of mysterious images from deep within him—images that were often terrifying and violent, some-times tender. From his own secret longings and vivid imagina-tion came small gems of stories. But the plots and characters would always be subordinate to the images—just as in dreams, the narrative is never quite logical or clear and is always subor-dinate to the images.

His tortured and lonely life—and particularly his complex, unresolved feelings about women—enabled him (indeed, forced him) to draw deeply from a common human reservoir of imagery and dream, fear and longing. Had his films been simple representations of his own fantasies and dreams, with no wider reference, he would perhaps have won a small group of like-minded admirers. But he expressed those images, de-sires and half-remembered dreams in terms that moved, as-tounded, delighted, frightened and aroused awe from millions around the world, in widely disparate cultures.

That is the secret of the unassailable genius of Alfred Hitch-cock. In *The Lodger,* for example, a woman shrieks in terror when her fiancé, a detective, playfully snaps handcuffs on her as he refers to marriage bonds. In *Vertigo,* a beautiful, remote blonde, clutching a nosegay, stands dazed before an old tombstone in a cemetery garden. In *The Birds,* the failure of human relationships is marked by the sudden, inexplicable revolt of nature itself.

If there is anything that can confidently be said about dreams and longings, it is that they are intensely private. Even when they are articulated, it is hard to transmute into words the oddness of an image, the comic-grotesque distortions of inner time and space, the weird amalgams of feeling that leave us less certain of the comforting artifice with which we so often present ourselves to the world. In giving form to his fantasies, Hitchcock explored and exposed things not only in himself but also in others—realities more or less actual, more or less potential. He showed us not what *all* of life is like but what *some* of life is like, all the time, everywhere, and what all of life is in constant danger of becoming.

Beginning in 1971, Alma Reville Hitchcock suffered the first of several strokes, and by the end of the decade, she was mostly confined at home. She had been a creative contributor to some of her husband's films, she was always the dependable in-house critic, and she remained Hitchcock's co-conspirator in his dealings with producers, writers and studio executives. Indeed, he never wavered in his high regard for her judgments and even her casual opinions. "She was the only person he was really afraid of," according to Charles Bennett. Production designer Robert Boyle, who knew the Hitchcocks from 1942, agreed: "He relied on Alma—well, it was partly reliance, partly fear."

On the morning of April 29, 1980, Alfred Hitchcock died quietly in bed. Over the next two years—until her death on

July 6, 1982—Alma became more frail and disconnected from reality. Photographs of her late husband bewildered and sometimes upset her, as if they were images of someone she had once known, very long ago, in a dim and half-remembered past. Finally, she ignored the pictures altogether, and then she seemed more at peace with herself, and much calmer.

Notes

For brevity, details of interviews are supplied only at the first citation; unless otherwise stated, subsequent quotations from the same source derive from the identical interview with that source.

FOREWORD

page xv   "Actors are cattle": The remark was made countless times—e.g., in David Clayton, "Hitchcock Hates Actors," *Filmindia,* July 1947; and to Oriana Fallaci, reprinted in Gottlieb, *Alfred Hitchcock Interviews,* p. 64.

AH often elaborated on the possible origin of his remark about actors as cattle: "A few years prior to my arrival in Hollywood, I had been quoted as saying that all actors are cattle. I'm not quite sure in what context I might have made such a statement. It may have been made in the early days of the talkies in England, when we used actors who were simultaneously performing in stage plays. When they had a matinée, they'd leave the set, I felt, much too early for a matinée, and I suspected they were allowing themselves plenty of time for a very leisurely lunch. And this meant that we had to shoot our scenes at breakneck speed so that the actors could get out on time. I couldn't help feeling that if they'd been really conscientious, they'd have swallowed their sandwich in the cab, on the way to the theater . . . I had no use for that kind of actor" (Truffaut, p. 140).

As for "actors should be treated like cattle," AH said this, e.g., in an after-dinner speech at the Screen Producers Guild dinner on March 7, 1965, when he received the

Milestone Award. The last time he made public remarks on the topic of actors as cattle occurred at the American Film Institute's Life Achievement Award, on March 7, 1979, at the Beverly Hilton Hotel, Beverly Hills, California; the program was later televised.

page xv   "Actors! I hate the sight of them!": See Spoto, *The Dark Side of Genius,* p. 301.

page xvi   "Some of us actors . . .": Ingrid Bergman, at the AFI Life Achievement Award, March 7, 1979. It was broadcast on national television the following Monday, March 12, and subsequently released in home video format.

page xvi   "sometimes he merely . . .": Princess Grace of Monaco, in her foreword to Spoto, *The Art of Alfred Hitchcock,* p. xiii.

page xvii   ". . . nice understatement": Truffaut, p. 111.

page xvii   "was very good": *Ibid.,* p. 227.

page xvii   "As far as Hitchcock . . .": Quoted in Sullivan, p. 258.

page xvii   "Hitch was an enigma . . .": John Michael Hayes, in the extra material on the Universal DVD release of *The Trouble With Harry* (2005).

CHAPTER ONE

page 3   "All my early training . . .": To Peter Bogdanovich, in 1963.

page 3   "general factotum": Quoted in "Close Your Eyes and Visualize!" *Stage* (July 1936): 52–53.

page 4   "I was quite dogmatic": *Ibid.*

page 4   "I had no intention . . .": See, e.g., Truffaut, p. 31.

page 4   "wanted to be a director, . . .": Balcon, p. 19.

page 5   "I was in a cold sweat": AH, with John J. Newnham, "My Screen Memories," *Film Weekly,* May 2, 1936.

page 6   "Fear? It has influenced . . .": Marcel Lalott, "Murder by a Babbling Brook," *Hollywood Studio,* Oct. 1973.

page 6   "Valli was big stuff . . .": London *New Chronicle,* dated March 1, 1937.

page 10   "sappy": *Variety,* Nov. 3, 1926.

page 10   "a Wiener schnitzel": *Photoplay,* Jan. 1927.

page 11   "It was a very *gemütlich* . . .": To Truffaut, p. 39.

page 12   "a very bad movie": Truffaut, p. 39.

page 12   "She arrived . . .": Bob Thomas, "Alfred Hitchcock: The German Years," *Action* (Jan.–Feb. 1973): 23–25; Truffaut, p. 41; and the London *News Chronicle,* dated March 2, 1937.

page 12   "we allowed people . . .": AH, "Life Among the Stars," in the *News Chronicle,* March 1–5, 1937; reprinted in Gottlieb, *Hitchcock on Hitchcock,* pp. 37–38.

page 13   "Nita turned out . . .": *Ibid.,* pp. 36–37.

page 14   "fostered the impression . . .": Barr, *English Hitchcock,* pp. 9–10.

page 14   "It hadn't taken the landlady . . .": Lowndes, p. 46.

page 15   "had sheltered him . . .": *Ibid.,* p. 256.

page 16   "They wouldn't let . . .": Spoto, *The Dark Side of Genius,* p. 85.

page 17   "Before a camera, . . .": From the British Film Institute's online notes for the career of Ivor Novello (1893–1951).

page 17   "Some people . . .": Elsie Randolph to DS, Jan. 23, 1981.

page 17   "It was just too tempting": Ackland, p. 35.

page 18   "Hitch had very strong feelings . . .": Cotten, p. 66.

page 19   "spoke in a curious . . .": June, p. 156.

page 20   "Psychologically, of course": Truffaut, p. 47.

page 20   "a murderous fascination . . .": British Film Institute's "Screen Online" notes for *The Lodger.*

page 20   "Like Hitchcock himself, . . .": Philip Kemp, "The Icy Blondes," in Mogg, pp. 126–27.

CHAPTER TWO

page 25   *"The Lodger* was really . . .": To Truffaut, Bogdanovich and DS.

page 28   "Hitch was ungrudgingly . . .": Ivor Montagu, "Working with Hitchcock," *Sight and Sound* (Summer 1980): 189–90.

page 28   "Among the additions . . .": AH to DS, during our first extended interview in his on-set trailer, July 22, 1975.

page 29   "It is possible . . .": *The Bioscope,* Sept. 16, 1926.

page 30   "because she asked me to": Fallaci interview in Gottlieb, *Alfred Hitchcock Interviews,* p. 59.

page 30   "I could have been . . .": John Russell Taylor, "The truth about Hitch and those cool blondes," *The Times* (London) April 5, 2005. AH confided this remark to playwright Rodney Ackland, who told it to Taylor.

page 30   "Hitch and Alma . . .": Samuel Taylor to DS, Dec. 2, 1980.

page 30   "Alma was his co-writer, . . .": Elsie Randolph to DS, Jan. 23, 1981.

page 31   "celibate . . .": Ken Mogg's contributions to Hitchcockian scholarship include management of an important website, from which this is excerpted: www.sensesofcinema.com/contents/directors/05/hitchcock.html.

page 31   "My grandmother . . .": Mary Stone, in the extra material, "The Hitchcocks on Hitch," on the Warner Bros DVD of *Strangers on a Train* (2004).

page 32   "Lilian was a good . . .": AH to DS, Nov. 21, 1976.

page 34   "His women must kill . . .": McGilligan, p. 122.

page 34   "He never stopped playing . . .": *TV Times* (London), Oct. 29, 1964.

page 35   "It was initially set up . . .": Barr, *English Hitchcock,* p. 81.

page 35   "We made the film silent": Ronald Neame, interviewed by Matthew Sweet at the National Film Theatre (London), Oct. 19, 2003.

page 39   "Hitchcock has been so faithful . . .": *The Times* (London), Jan. 1, 1930.

page 39   "Under Mr. Hitchcock's guidance, . . .": *The Times* (London), June 24, 1929.

page 39   "Hitchcock's films resemble . . .": *The Times* (London), May 25, 1936.

page 39   "creative artist . . .": *The Times* (London), Sept. 23, 1930.

page 39   "I asked him later . . .": Norah Baring, "The Man Who Made *The 39 Steps:* Pen Portrait of Alfred Hitchcock," *Film Pictorial,* Nov. 23, 1935, pp. 14–15; reprinted in Gottlieb, *Alfred Hitchcock Interviews,* pp. 12–13.

page 40   "He was a darling": Elsie Randolph to DS, Jan. 23, 1981.

page 40   "was engrossed . . .": Ackland and Grant, p. 33.

page 40   "the conversation . . .": Kendall, p. 116.

page 40   "He sent me up . . .": Thornton, pp. 108–109.

page 41   "continually on the *qui vive* . . .": *Ibid.*

page 43   "had to be handled . . .": AH, "Nova Grows Up," *FilmWeekly*, Feb. 5, 1938.

CHAPTER THREE

page 48   "I am no longer concerned . . .": "Meet London's Mr. Hitchcock," *The NewYork Times,* April 7, 1935.

page 48   "I had wanted . . .": AH, "My Screen Memories," *Film Weekly,* May 23, 1936.

page 49   "You owe everything to me": From Charles Bennett's unpublished memoirs, cited on Ken Mogg's scholarly website; also Bennett to DS, Nov. 1981.

page 50   "had a monstrous ego . . .": Mogg, p. 20.

page 51   "He is blazingly ambitious": Quoted in Sullivan, p. 258.

page 52   "She is both beautiful . . .": The review excerpts are from *The New York Times,* Jan. 15, 1934; Aug. 24, 1930; and July 26, 1940.

page 53   "There has been . . .": AH, in "My Screen Memories," *Film Weekly,* May 30, 1936.

page 53   "Hitch, without . . .": McGilligan, p. 4, mentions that Hitchcock much liked to use this introduction, doubtless to see people's reaction.

page 54   "There they were": "Life Among the Stars," *News Chronicle,* March 5, 1937; reprinted in Gottlieb, *Hitchcock on Hitchcock,* p. 45.

page 54   "Madeleine and I shared . . .": Barrow, p. 75–76.

page 54   "a gleeful delight . . .": Taylor, pp. 108–109.

page 55   "What interests me": *Sight and Sound* 25, no. 3 (Winter 1955–56): 158.

page 55   "bring out all kinds . . .": Quoted (but without attribution) in McGilligan, p. 173.

page 55   "There was no better . . .": Jack Whitehead to DS, Nov. 7, 1981.

page 55   "It had long been . . .": Montagu, p. 90.

page 55   "I sometimes wonder . . .": Frank S. Nugent, "Mr. Hitchcock Discovers Love," *The NewYork Times Magazine,* Nov. 3, 1946.

page 55   "she entered into the spirit . . .": AH, "My Screen Memo-ries," a five-part series "written in collaboration with John K. Newnham," *Film Weekly* (May 2, 9, 16, 23 and 30, 1936); the citation is reprinted in Gottlieb, *Hitchcock on Hitchcock,* p. 22.

page 55   "Bring on the Birmingham tart!": Barrow, p. 75.

page 55   "dead set . . .": McGilligan, p. 174.

page 56   "I just gave him a look . . .": Emerson Batdorf, "Let's Hear It for Hitchcock," *Cleveland Plain Dealer,* Sunday magazine, Feb. 1, 1970.

page 56   "We deliberately wrote the script . . .": Montagu, "Work-ing with Hitchcock," *Sight and Sound* (Summer 1980): 193.

page 56   "We'll do it one more time": The incident was told by Madeleine Carroll's friend Googie Withers to the Aus-tralian film historian Brian McFarlane. It is also recorded in Sweet, p. 169.

page 56   "Nothing pleases me . . .": "Alfred Hitchcock Tells a Woman that Women Are a Nuisance," *Film Weekly,* Sept. 20, 1935.

page 56   "I don't exactly hate . . .": *Ibid.*

page 57   "was sexually impotent": McGilligan, p. 177.

page 57   "I know that Hitch . . .": *Ibid.*

page 57   "I did it with . . .": Quoted by Joseph Stefano to DS, Feb. 26, 1982. Hitchcock made the identical assertion to me during our luncheon on Nov. 23, 1976.

page 58   "Lorre was . . .": John Gielgud, in McFarlane, *An Autobiog-raphy of the British Cinema,* p. 216.

page 59   "Madeleine Carroll was charming . . .": *Ibid.*

page 61   "I knew that . . .": Quoted in *The New York Times,* July 12, 1940.

page 61   "Who knows if any of us . . .": *Ibid.*

page 62   "the most glamorous woman . . .": Heiskell, p. 45.

page 63   "I knew a young Englishwoman . . .": Her speech was reprinted in *The New York Times,* Nov. 18, 1940. Madeleine Carroll's sister Marguerite died in London on Oct. 7, 1940.

page 64   "In my French home . . .": *The New York Times,* March 4, 1945.

page 65   "Don't be silly. . . .": *The New York Times,* Dec. 19, 1948.

CHAPTER FOUR

page 69   "I discovered . . .": Michael Balcon, "My Hollywood Star Captures," *Film Weekly,* Jan. 18, 1936.

page 71   "On the set . . .": C. A. Lejeune, "Hitchcock, The Man Korda Cannot Sign," *World Film News,* no. 2 (May 1936).

page 71   "Paramount paid me . . .": Sylvia Sidney to DS, Oct. 23, 1984. Subsequent quotations from Sidney derive from the same conversation with DS.

page 72   "Hitch had called and courted her . . .": Charles Bennett to DS, May 18, 1981.

page 72   "she had nice understatement": Truffaut, p. 111.

page 73   "really wicked wit": Nova Pilbeam to Brian McFarlane (in June 1990), *An Autobiography of the British Cinema,* p. 453.

page 73   "and he finds . . .": *The New York Times,* Feb. 5, 1938.

page 74   "She imparts sincerity . . .": *Kinematograph Weekly,* Nov. 25, 1937; *Variety,* Dec. 8, 1937.

page 74   "Her name, . . .": McFarlane, *An Autobiography of the British Cinema,* p. 453.

page 75   "It's what people did . . . I never go back . . .": Suzie Mackenzie, "Pat Hitchcock: The woman who knew too much," *The Guardian,* Aug. 28, 1999.

page 75   "There was a strange . . .": Elsie Randolph to DS, Nov. 23, 1981.

pages 75–76   "I don't think . . . a perfectly normal life . . .": Helena de Bertodano, "Even scarier than *Psycho:* his 'great production,' " *The Times* (London), April 5, 2005.

page 76   "When my own girls . . .": Patricia Hitchcock O'Connell to DS, Nov. 25, 1976.

page 77   "I suppose . . .": Margaret Lockwood to DS, Jan. 16, 1981.

page 77   "He wasn't really . . .": Michael Redgrave to DS, Sept. 3, 1980.

page 78   "He felt that he was not really . . .": Samuel Taylor to DS, Nov. 2, 1982.

page 78   "The art of filmmaking . . .": Truffaut, p. 124.

page 79   "sloppy, stiff, . . .": Callow, p. 129.

pages 79–80   The quotations from Maureen O'Hara and Emlyn

Williams are cited in Chandler, pp. 117 and 199; more accurate are O'Hara's extended recollections in O'Hara and Nicoletti, p. 25.

CHAPTER FIVE

page 83   *"Rebecca* was a very pleasant . . .": Patricia Hitchcock O'Connell, on the DVD of that film, released in 2001 by the Criterion Collection DVD.

page 84   "When moving pictures . . .": AH, "Films We Could Make," *London Evening News,* Nov. 16, 1927.

page 84   "a coherent body . . .": *un oeuvre coherent* was the phrase Truffaut used in conversations with DS in December 1976.

page 85   "We try to . . .": AH to DS, Nov. 18, 1976.

page 85   "what critics consider . . .": Krohn, p. 16.

page 85   "He thought movies": *Ibid.*

page 87   "analysis that . . . was . . .": Thomson, p. 306.

page 88   "It's not a Hitchcock . . .": Truffaut, p. 127.

page 89   "made all the important decisions . . .": O'Connell and Bouzereau, p. 2.

page 89   "Alma's participation was constant": *Ibid.,* p. 4.

page 90   "she was widely assumed . . .": John Russell Taylor, "The truth about Hitch and those cool blondes," *The Times* (London), April 5, 2005.

page 90   "I would put my hand . . .": *Ibid.*

page 90   "She puts up . . .": AH, "The Woman Who Knows Too Much," *McCall's* 83 (March 1956): 14.

page 91   "too coy and simpering . . .": Haver, p. 319.

page 91   "much in love with Joan Fontaine . . .": Thomson, p. 305.

page 92   "knew ways . . .": *Ibid.,* p. 331.

page 92   "We liked each other . . .": Fontaine, pp. 106–107.

page 93   "Joan is young, pretty, gay . . .": Aherne, p. 286.

page 93   "The British brigade . . .": Fontaine, p. 108.

page 94   "He seemed to want . . .": Joan Fontaine to DS, July 23, 1974.

page 94   "But he didn't give me . . .": Chandler, p. 130.

page 94   "My grandmother . . .": Leff, p. 74, retold by Chandler, p. 125.

pages 94–95 "She was not a good . . .": Quoted in Leff, p. 74.

page 95   "I am aware . . .": Selznick, in an unsent letter to AH dated Sept. 19, 1939: see Behlmer, p. 307.

page 95   "I think Joan has been handled . . .": Behlmer, pp. 312–13.

page 95   "She was practically . . .": Quoted in Leff, p. 63.

page 95   "A well-trained . . .": *Ibid.,* p. 64.

page 95   "dozens of isolated lines": *Ibid.,* pp. 79–80.

page 96   "Although Hitchcock is . . .": Geoffrey T. Hellman, "Alfred Hitchcock: England's Best and Biggest Director, Goes to Hollywood," *Life,* Nov. 20, 1939.

page 96   "Many of the actors . . .": Leff, p. 52.

page 96   "There were very unpleasant things . . .": Judith Anderson to Leonard Leff, in a 1986 telephone interview included on the Criterion Collection DVD release of *Rebecca* (2001).

page 97   "the dirtiest joke . . .": Leff, p. 44.

page 97   "Well, Miss Bates . . .": *Ibid.,* p. 72.

page 97   "You're supposed to be . . .": Haver, p. 322.

page 98   "His pauses . . .": Behlmer, p. 313.

page 98   "Joan Fontaine at moments . . .": *The Times* (London), June 27, 1940.

page 100   "Hitchcock had a habit . . .": Quoted in *Focus in Film,* no. 30 (June 1978).

page 100   "Hitch was always playing . . .": Laraine Day, on the Warner Bros. Home Video DVD release of *Foreign Correspondent* (2004).

page 102   "I liked [Carole] . . .": Chandler, p. 133.

page 102   "Oh, you've looked . . .": Quoted in Leff, p. 92.

CHAPTER SIX

page 108   "He brings his wife . . .": *Dialogue on Film,* no. 5: American Film Institute, Center for Advanced Film Studies (1972); reprinted in Gottlieb, *Alfred Hitchcock Interviews,* p. 92.

page 110   "If I came on the set . . .": Quoted in Leff, p. 267.

page 111 "Hitchcock's material . . .": Samson Raphaelson to DS, Dec. 21, 1980.

page 112 "No, not necessarily. . . .": Truffaut, p. 44.

page 112 "The whole subject of the film . . .": *Ibid.*

page 113 "I have a raving . . .": Harry E. Edington to J. J. Nolan, Feb. 5, 1941; RKO production files for *Suspicion.*

page 113 "Hitchcock does not appear . . .": S. Rogell to Edington, April 1, 1941.

page 113 "The scenario": Fontaine, pp. 124–25.

page 114 "habit of saying . . .": Brian McFarlane, "Joan Fontaine," *Cinema Papers* (Australia) (June 1982): 234; cited in Leff, p. 91.

page 114 "stepping in . . .": Fontaine to DS, July 24, 1974.

page 114 "did not feel the rapport . . .": Nelson, p. 123.

page 114 "I thought the original . . .": Nelson, p. 124.

page 114 "But I'm sure I didn't . . .": Chandler, p. 138.

page 115 "far finer than *Rebecca* . . .": Howard Barnes, in the New York *Herald Tribune,* Nov. 21, 1941.

page 115 "The ending is not up to . . .": Bosley Crowther, in *The New York Times,* Nov. 21, 1941.

page 115 "least satisfying": Nelson, p. 123.

page 116 "I had heard . . .": Houseman, *Run-Through,* pp. 479–480.

page 116 "But I had to take . . .": AH to DS, Nov. 24, 1977; see also Truffaut, pp. 145–46.

page 117 On the Wilder-Hitchcock collaboration, see the essay by Max Alvarez, "Wilder and Hitchcock: Writing and Re-writing *Shadow of a Doubt,* in *The Thornton Wilder Society Newsletter* 2, no. 2 (2007): 2, 5.

page 117 "I was seventeen . . .": Teresa Wright spoke with DS about her early life and career very many times during her thirty-one-year friendship with DS (1974 to her death in 2005). This and the quotations following in this chapter draw from our conversations over the years.

page 118 uncommon charm: Brooks Atkinson, in *The New York Times,* Nov. 19, 1939.

page 119 "the best actress . . .": Harold Heffernan, Aug. 26, 1941.

page 120 "I got on very well . . .": AH to DS, July 22, 1975.

page 122 "She had a genius . . .": Stephan Talty, "A Genius for Decency," *Film Comment* (Oct. 1990): 18–19.

page 123 "It has been chilly": Teresa Wright telephoned me the night before she died.

CHAPTER SEVEN

page 127 "We were always . . .": Hume Cronyn to DS, June 4, 1974.

page 127 "black and blue . . .": Bankhead, p. 229.

page 128 "She had no inhibitions . . .": Brian, p. 138.

page 130 "I was under contract . . .": Ingrid Bergman spoke with DS many times from 1975 to 1982; she spoke particularly about Selznick on May 8, 1975. All subsequent quotations from Ingrid in this and the next chapters are from our conversations during those years.

page 131 "Lindstrom was terribly . . .": W. H. Dietrich to DS, Oct. 23, 1995.

page 131 "almost desperately anxious . . .": Selznick to Margaret McDonell, July 10, 1943.

page 132 "beaming amid . . .": Hecht, p. 396.

page 132 "I won't do . . .": Bergman to DS; see also Hecht, p. 481.

page 134 "Selznick believed in treating . . .": Gregory Peck to DS, April 14, 1981.

page 137 "Although Hitchcock meticulously . . .": Leff, p. 135.

page 138 "I have to consider": AH, "How I Choose My Heroines," in Reed and Spiers, p. xxiii; reprinted in Gottlieb, *Hitchcock on Hitchcock*, p. 75.

page 144 "because [Selznick said] I think he is entitled . . .": Behlmer, p. 392.

CHAPTER EIGHT

page 150 "Miss Bergman just can't help . . .": Frank S. Nugent, "That Phenomenon Named Bergman," *The New York Times Magazine*, Dec. 16, 1945.

page 152 "You have become an industry": Bergman, p. 156.

page 152 "I fell in love . . .": Larry Adler to DS, June 9, 1996.

page 153   "By the time . . .": Bergman, p. 102.

page 153   "like a cat . . .": Quoted in Harmetz, p. 146.

page 154   "dominating . . . You think . . .": The incident involving Carol Stevens and Cary Grant is described in Leff, p. 266.

page 154   "I don't get . . .": Nugent, "Mr. Hitchcock Discovers Love."

page 154   "the great privilege . . .": AH to DS, July 25, 1975; almost identically, AH to Truffaut, pp. 261–62, and to Bogdanovich, p. 26.

page 158   "I almost frightened myself": Edmond J. Bartnett, "Not Born to Evil," *The New York Times,* Sept. 1, 1946.

CHAPTER NINE

page 165   "Whatever Miss Valli thought . . .": Howard Taubman, "Fact vs. Fiction in the Discovery of a Star," *The New York Times,* Jan. 11, 1948.

page 167   "On the train . . .": Alida Valli to DS, May 12, 1989. Subsequent quotations from her to DS derive from conversations that month.

page 168   "This, of course . . .": This and later quotations from Gregory Peck to DS are from conversations on April 24, 1983, and April 30, 1985.

page 169   "Hitchcock [had a] lifelong . . .": Houseman, p. 158.

page 169   "he drove us crazy": Cited in Leff, p. 222.

page 169   "he was not a director . . .": Alida Valli, in *Il Brivido del Genio,* a three-part television documentary for RAI (1985).

pages 169–170   "In the right part, . . .": *Daily Mail,* March 10, 1930.

page 170   "He took the trouble . . .": Ann Todd to DS, Jan. 19, 1981, and in interviews thereafter through 1992. See also her book, p. 75.

page 170   "a very complex man . . .": Ann Todd, in *Il Brivido del Genio.*

page 174   "We never discussed . . .": Arthur Laurents to DS, Oct. 19, 1981.

page 174   "lived in the land . . .": Laurents, pp. 124–30, *passim.*

page 175   "not very amusing, . . .": Hume Cronyn to DS, June 21, 1974.

page 175 "The really important thing . . .": James Stewart to DS, Feb. 26, 1982.

page 181 "I wanted to put . . .": Selznick to Petter Lindstrom, April 15, 1944.

page 182 "I am still . . . in mourning . . .": Chandler, p. 289; similarly, to DS, Aug. 1978.

page 182 "But he never forgave . . .": Truffaut, p. 325.

CHAPTER TEN

page 185 "with childish innocence . . .": Brooks Atkinson, in *The New York Times,* Jan. 28, 1942, and Feb. 8, 1942.

page 186 "monotonous": Lewis Nichols, in *The New York Times,* Oct. 25, 1944.

page 186 "It appears that, . . .": McGilligan, p. 428.

page 187 "a bachelor . . .": *Ibid.,* pp. 427–28.

page 187 "You never knew . . .": Brown, p. 89.

page 187 "Hitch was so perverse! . . .": Lambert, p. 128.

page 189 "I was stuck with her": AH to Peter Bogdanovich (1963).

page 189 "I had lots . . .": Truffaut, pp. 190–91.

page 191 "When she heard . . .": Richard Todd, p. 240.

page 191 "She wouldn't do anything . . .": Chandler, *It's Only a Movie,* p. 13.

page 192 "We became inseparable": Wilding, pp. 60–76.

page 192 "there is exactly none . . .": Quoted in Sullivan, p. 155.

page 192 "Hitchcock was a very distant man . . .": Richard Todd, in the Italian TV documentary *Il Brivido del Genio,* RAI, 1985.

page 192 "He was a strange man, . . .": Richard Todd, interviewed in McFarlane, *An Autobiography of the British Cinema,* p. 564.

CHAPTER ELEVEN

page 198 "There are some actors . . .": Arthur Knight, "Conversation with Hitchcock," *Oui* magazine, Feb. 1973, p. 116.

page 198 "Monty was a friend, . . .": Karl Malden to DS, Nov. 10, 2007; see also his book *When Do I Start?,* pp. 229–33; and his Oral History, pp. 17 and 163.

page 199   "He gave me the impression . . .": Anne Baxter to DS, Sept. 15, 1980; see also her comments on the RAI production *Il Brivido del Genio.*

page 199   "Bob Burks gave Hitch . . .": John Michael Hayes to DS, Feb. 27, 1982.

page 201   "As Nina, . . .": Brooks Atkinson, in *The New York Times,* May 12, 1954.

page 202   "When you compare . . .": AH to Truffaut, p. 202.

page 202   "written with inner eyes . . .": Louise Bernikow, in *The New York Times,* Sept. 19, 1976.

page 203   "I have to consider . . .": AH in Reed and Spiers, p. xxiii; see also Gottlieb, *Hitchcock on Hitchcock,* p. 75.

page 203   "When I saw the first cut . . .": Princess Grace (Kelly) of Monaco to DS, Sept. 22, 1975.

page 205   "Hitchcock the voyeur . . .": McGilligan, p. 471.

page 210   "She was rather mousy . . .": Quoted in Fawell, p. 142.

page 210   "Every costume . . .": Edith Head to DS, July 22, 1975; see also Head and Ardmore, pp. 153–54.

page 211   "Grace was very sweet. . . .": Quoted in Chandler, *It's Only a Movie,* p. 217.

page 212   "full on the mouth": The incident is recorded in McGilligan, pp. 550–51.

page 213   "The former Cockney lad . . .": Truffaut, p. 325.

CHAPTER TWELVE

page 219   "very precise . . .": Doris Day to DS, Dec. 12, 1981.

page 219   "Hitch and Doris Day . . .": Constance Willis to DS, May 17, 1983.

page 219   "always seemed more concerned . . .": Bernard Miles to DS, Jan. 20, 1981.

page 219   "He didn't direct. . . .": Hotchner, p. 152.

page 220   "Hitchcock never gave . . .": Reggie Nalder to DS, April 11, 1981; see also *Kinoeye: New Perspectives on European Film* 3, no. 2, and www.kinoeye.org/03/02/delvalle02.php.

page 221   "so she wouldn't . . .": AH to Hedda Hopper, March 7, 1961.

page 221   "I feel the same way . . .": Robert Marks, "Vera Miles—Hitchcock's New Star," *McCall's,* May 1957.

page 221   "Vera Miles is the girl . . .": *Cosmopolitan,* Oct. 1956, p. 67; see also *Mademoiselle,* Dec. 1959.

page 222   "Hitch had an obsession . . .": McGilligan, pp. 537–38.

page 222   "He has never complimented me": Marks, "Vera Miles."

page 222   "Vera was a lovely girl, . . .": Quoted in Rebello, p. 63.

page 222   "Vera's wardrobe, . . .": AH to DS, July 24, 1975; similarly, see Fallaci, p. 256.

page 223   "Over the span . . .": Quoted in Rebello, p. 64.

page 223   "I lost all interest . . .": Truffaut, p. 247.

page 224   "The majority of actors . . .": Fallaci, p. 255.

page 224   "But I did see in Hitch . . .": To DS, May 17, 1983.

page 224   "Kim said she couldn't . . .": Edith Head to DS, July 22, 1975.

page 224   "Before shooting started, . . .": Kim Novak, interviewed by Stephen Rebello in 2003; see www.labyrinth.net.au/~muffin/kim_novak_c.html.

page 225   "Miss Novak arrived . . .": AH to Truffaut, pp. 247–48.

page 225   "I'll wear anything": Head and Ardmore, p. 15.

page 225   "Handle it, Edith": Head and Calistro, p. 116.

page 226   "I never sat down . . .": Quoted in McGilligan, p. 555.

page 226   "so much of what . . .": Kim Novak, interviewed by Anwar Brett for *The Dark Side* magazine (UK), no. 73 (June/July 1998): 21; see also his essay in *Film Review,* May 1997, p. 25.

page 226   "I could tell . . .": James Stewart to DS, Feb. 26, 1982.

page 226   "Anyone who saw him . . .": Samuel Taylor to DS, interviews from 1974 through 1980.

page 228   "He was never deeply friendly . . .": John Russell Taylor, "The truth about Hitch and those cool blondes," *The Times* (London) April 5, 2005.

page 228   "spiritual transvestism": Edel, p. 259.

CHAPTER THIRTEEN

page 233   "Hitch's main purpose . . .": Ernest Lehman to DS, April 12, 1975, and additional conversations from 1976 to 2000.

page 235   "I acted just like a rich man . . .": AH to Hedda Hopper, March 7, 1962; see also Arthur Knight, "Conversation with Alfred Hitchcock," *Oui,* Feb. 1973; Rui Nogueira and Nicoletta Zalaffi, "Entretien avec Alfred Hitchcock," *Ecran,* no. 7 (July–Aug. 1972), trans. DS; and Jon Whitcomb, "Master of Mayhem," *Cosmopolitan,* Oct. 1959.

page 236   "My camera . . .": Leigh with Nickens, p. 43.

page 236   "Either they wear . . .": Rebello, p. 74.

page 236   "It was challenging . . .": Janet Leigh to DS, March 23, 1982, and afterward.

page 237   "Some hair-raising screams . . .": Leigh with Nickens, pp. 46–47.

page 238   "Before every shot . . .": Rebello, p. 90.

page 239   "Vera was very angry . . .": *Ibid.,* pp. 73–74.

CHAPTER FOURTEEN

page 243   "I prefer a woman . . .": AH, in *The Hollywood Reporter,* vol. 172, no. 39, Nov. 20, 1962.

page 244   "a wonderful opportunity . . .": In this, in the following chapter, and in the afterword, the citations attributed to Tippi Hedren derive from my conversations with her during November 2007. We first discussed her work on *The Birds* and *Marnie* in June 1974, and my discussions with her continued over more than thirty years.

page 245   "the Svengali approach . . .": From the Robert F. Boyle Oral History at the Academy of Motion Picture Arts and Sciences (1992); interviewed by George Turner.

page 247   "It was evident . . .": Martin Balsam to DS, March 1, 1982.

page 247   "I signed her . . .": Thomas McDonald, "Watching 'Birds,'" *The New York Times,* April 1, 1962.

page 248   "Well, she has nothing to unlearn": "On Style," *Cinema* 1, no. 5 (Aug.–Sept. 1963): 34.

page 249   "Tippi Hedren is really remarkable": This and the following citation are drawn from "Tippi Hedren—Hitchcock's New Grace Kelly," *Look,* Dec. 4, 1962, pp. 55–58.

page 250   "Hitch was becoming . . .": Rod Taylor to DS, March–April

1982; also, cf. *Lifetime: Intimate Portrait of Tippi Hedren,* a Feury/Grant Production for TV (2001) and *Magnificent Obsession: Tippi Hedren,* Prometheus/Van Ness for TV (2003).

page 251 "Hitch was taking her away . . .": *Lifetime.*

page 255 "just covered in bird shit": Jessica Tandy to DS, June 3, 1974.

CHAPTER FIFTEEN

page 261 "I told him": Evan Hunter to DS, Dec. 3, 1981. His remarks are virtually identical on the transcriptions of taped story conferences for *Marnie* throughout late 1962; see also Hunter, pp. 75–76.

page 262 "Can there be any doubt . . .": Truffaut, p. 346.

page 263 "He was mad for her, . . .": Jay Presson Allen to DS, Nov. 12, 1980.

page 263 "I was in the presence . . .": Quoted in Moral, p. 110.

page 264 "I was invited . . .": Diane Baker to DS, Nov. 3, 2007.

page 267 "You and I . . .": Claire Griswold Pollack to DS, March 1, 1982.

page 267 "Bring me your body, . . .": *Ibid.*

page 270 "Lew had become . . .": Houseman, *Entertainers and the Entertained,* p. 159.

page 271 "Lew never comes to see me . . .": AH to DS, Nov. 27, 1977.

page 275 I discussed Hitchcock's treatment of Tippi Hedren with François Truffaut in December 1976, when I spent several days with him during production of his film *L'Homme qui aimait les femmes,* in Montpellier, France.

page 275 "Nothing ever came . . .": Janet Maslin, "Alfred Hitchcock," *Boston After Dark* 3, no. 24 (June 12–20, 1972).

page 277 "You know, he never . . .": The events in Rome were coordinated by DS, who gave the keynote address and was present when Peggy Robertson spoke to Tippi Hedren.

AFTERWORD

page 281 "I am convinced": Truffaut, p. 327.

page 283   "The things that make . . .": Rui Nogueira and Nicoletta
           Zalaffi, "Hitch, Hitch, Hitch, Hurrah!" in *Écran* 7 (July–
           Aug. 1972), reprinted in Gottlieb, *Alfred Hitchcock Interviews,*
           p. 122.
page 283   "He really had nothing . . .": Rebello, p. 97.
page 284   "I tried to dispense . . .": *Ibid.*
page 285   "There was something tragic . . .": Hume Cronyn, in *Il
           Brivido del Genio,* RAI, 1985.
page 285   "The trouble with *Topaz*": AH to DS, July 22, 1975.
pages 286–287   The incidents with Karin Dor and Karen Black are
           reported by McGilligan, pp. 690–91 and 726.
page 287   "Hitchcock was a neurotic": Truffaut, p. 346.
page 288   "He relied on Alma . . .": Quoted in Moral, p. 131.

Bibliography

Ackland, Rodney, with Elspeth Grant. *The Celluloid Mistress.* London: Allan Wingate, 1954.

Aherne, Brian. *A Proper Job.* Boston: Houghton Mifflin, 1969.

Auiler, Dan. *Hitchcock's Notebooks.* New York: HarperCollins, 1999.

———. *Vertigo: The Making of a Hitchcock Classic.* New York: St. Martin's Griffin, 1998.

Balcon, Michael. *Michael Balcon Presents . . . A Lifetime of Films.* London: Hutchinson, 1969.

Bankhead, Tallulah. *Tallulah: My Autobiography.* London: Victor Gollancz, 1952.

Barr, Charles. *English Hitchcock.* Moffat (Scotland): Cameron and Hollis, 1999.

———. *Vertigo.* London: British Film Institute, 2002.

Barrow, Kenneth. *Mr. Chips: The Life of Robert Donat.* London: Methuen, 1985.

Behlmer, Rudy, ed. *Memo from David O. Selznick* (rev. ed.). New York: The Modern Library, 2000.

Belton, John, ed. *Alfred Hitchcock's Rear Window.* Cambridge: The University Press, 2000.

Bergman, Ingrid, and Alan Burgess. *Ingrid Bergman: My Story.* New York: Delacorte Press, 1980.

Bogdanovich, Peter. *The Cinema of Alfred Hitchcock.* Garden City, N.Y.: Doubleday, 1963.

Brian, Denis. *Tallulah, Darling.* London: Sidgwick and Jackson, 1972.

Brown, Geoff. *Launder and Gilliat.* London: British Film Institute, 1977.

Brown, Peter Harry. *Kim Novak, Reluctant Goddess.* New York: St. Martin's, 1986.

Callow, Simon. *Charles Laughton: A Difficult Actor*. London: Methuen, 1987.

Chandler, Charlotte. *Ingrid: A Personal Biography*. London: Simon & Schuster, 2007.

———. *It's Only a Movie—Alfred Hitchcock: A Personal Biography*. New York: Applause Theatre and Cinema Books, 2005.

Cotten, Joseph. *Vanity Will Get You Somewhere*. San Francisco: Mercury House, 1987.

Edel, Leon. *Henry James, 1895–1901: The Treacherous Years*. Philadelphia: J. B. Lippincott, 1969.

Falk, Quentin. *Mr Hitchcock*. London: Haus Publishing, 2007.

Fallaci, Oriana (trans. Pamela Swinglehurst). *The Egotists: Sixteen Surprising Interviews*. Chicago: Henry Regnery, 1963.

Fawell, John. *Hitchcock's Rear Window: The Well-Made Film*. Carbondale and Edwardsville: Southern Illinois University Press, 2001.

Fontaine, Joan. *No Bed of Roses: An Autobiography*. New York: William Morrow, 1978.

Forster, Margaret. *Daphne du Maurier*. London: Arrow, 2007.

Gielgud, John. *An Actor and His Time*. New York: Clarkson N. Potter, 1980.

Glancy, Mark. *The 39 Steps: A British Film Guide*. London: I.B. Tauris, 2003.

Gottlieb, Sidney (ed.). *Alfred Hitchcock Interviews*. Jackson: University Press of Mississippi, 2003.

———. *Hitchcock on Hitchcock*. Berkeley: University of California Press, 1995.

Harmetz, Aljean. *The Making of the Wizard of Oz*. New York: Knopf, 1977.

Haver, Ronald. *David O. Selznick's Hollywood*. New York: Knopf, 1980.

Head, Edith, and Jane Kesner Ardmore. *The Dress Doctor*. Boston: Little, Brown, 1959.

Head, Edith, and Paddy Calistro. *Edith Head's Hollywood*. New York: Dutton, 1983.

Hecht, Ben. *A Child of the Century*. New York: Simon & Schuster, 1954.

Heiskell, Andrew, with Ralph Graves. *Outsider, Insider: An Unlikely Success*

Story—The Memoirs of Andrew Heiskell. New York: Marian-Darien Press, 1998.

Hotchner, A. E. *Doris Day: Her Own Story.* New York: Morrow, 1976.

Houseman, John. *Entertainers and the Entertained.* New York: Simon & Schuster, 1986.

————. *Run-Through.* New York: Simon & Schuster, 1972.

Hunter, Evan. *Me and Hitch.* London: Faber and Faber, 1997.

June. *The Glass Ceiling.* London: Heinemann, 1960.

Kendall, Henry. *I Remember Romano's.* London: Macdonald, 1960.

Krohn, Bill. *Hitchcock at Work.* London: Phaidon, 2003.

Lambert, Gavin. *On Cukor.* New York: Putnam's, 1972.

Laurents, Arthur. *Original Story By: A Memoir of Broadway and Hollywood.* New York: Knopf, 2000.

Lawrence, Gertrude. *A Star Danced.* Garden City, N.Y.: Doubleday Doran, 1945.

Leff, Leonard. *Hitchcock and Selznick.* Berkeley: University of California Press, 1987.

Leigh, Janet, with Christopher Nickens. *Psycho: Behind the Scenes of the Classic Thriller.* London: Pavilion, 1995.

Leitch, Thomas. *The Encyclopedia of Alfred Hitchcock.* New York: Checkmark/Facts on File, 2002.

Lowndes, Marie Adelaide Belloc. *The Lodger.* Doylestown, Penn.: Wildside Press, n.d. (reprint of the 1913 British and 1914 American publications).

McFarlane, Brian. *An Autobiography of the British Cinema.* London: Methuen, 1997.

————, ed. *The Encyclopedia of British Film.* London: Methuen, 2005.

McGilligan, Patrick. *Alfred Hitchcock: A Life in Darkness and Light.* New York: Regan Books, 2003.

Malden, Karl. *An Oral History with Karl Malden* (Douglas Bell, interviewer). Academy of Motion Picture Arts and Sciences Oral History Program/Margaret Herrick Library. Beverly Hills: Academy Foundation, 2007.

Malden, Karl, with Carla Malden. *When Do I Start?—A Memoir.* New York: Simon & Schuster, 1997.

Massey, Anna. *Telling Some Tales.* London: Arrow, 2007.

Mogg, Ken. *The Alfred Hitchcock Story.* London: Titan, 1999.

Montagu, Ivor. *With Eisenstein in Hollywood.* Berlin: Seven Seas, 1968.

Moral, Tony Lee. *Hitchcock and the Making of Marnie.* Lanham, Md.: Scarecrow Press, 2002.

Nelson, Nancy. *Evenings with Cary Grant.* New York: Citadel/Kensington, 2002.

O'Connell, Pat Hitchcock and Laurent Bouzereau. *Alma Hitchcock: The Woman Behind the Man.* New York: Berkley Books, 2003.

O'Hara, Maureen, with John Nicoletti. *'Tis Herself: A Memoir.* New York: Simon & Schuster, 2004.

Powell, Michael. *A Life in Movies.* New York: Faber & Faber, 2001.

Rebello, Stephen. *Alfred Hitchcock and the Making of Psycho.* New York: HarperPerennial, 1990.

Reed, Langford, and Hetty Spiers. *Who's Who in Filmland.* London: Chapman and Hall, 1931.

Ryall, Tom. *Alfred Hitchcock and the British Cinema.* London: Athlone, 1996.

Spoto, Donald. *The Art of Alfred Hitchcock.* New York: Hopkinson and Blake, 1976; New York: Doubleday Dolphin, 1999 (centennial edition).

———. *Blue Angel: The Life of Marlene Dietrich.* New York: Doubleday, 1992.

———. *The Dark Side of Genius: The Life of Alfred Hitchcock.* Boston: Little, Brown, 1983; New York: Da Capo, 1999 (centennial edition).

———. *Laurence Olivier: A Biography.* New York: HarperCollins, 1991.

———. *Notorious: The Life of Ingrid Bergman.* New York: HarperCollins, 1997.

Sullivan, Jack. *Hitchcock's Music.* New Haven and London: Yale University Press, 2006.

Sweet, Matthew. *Shepperton Babylon.* London: Faber & Faber, 2005.

Tavistock, Marchioness of, and Angela Levin. *A Chance to Live.* London: Headline, 1991.

Taylor, John Russell. *Hitch: The Life and Times of Alfred Hitchcock.* New York: Pantheon, 1978.

Thomson, David. *Showman: The Life of David O. Selznick.* New York: Knopf, 1992.

Thornton, Michael. *Jessie Matthews: A Biography.* London: Hart Davis, 1974.

Todd, Ann. *The Eighth Veil.* London: William Kimber, 1980.

Todd, Richard. *Caught in the Act.* London: Hutchinson, 1986.

Truffaut, François. *Hitchcock* (rev. ed.). New York: Simon & Schuster, 1983.

Walker, Michael. *Hitchcock's Motifs.* Amsterdam: Amsterdam University Press, 2005.

Wilding, Michael. *The Wilding Way.* New York: St. Martin's Press, 1982.

Wood, Robin. *Hitchcock's Films Revisited* (rev. ed.). New York: Columbia University Press, 2002.

Index